PUFFIN B

So Much to Tell

Valerie Grove writes for *The Times*. She has written acclaimed biographies of the author Laurie Lee and Rumpole creator John Mortimer. Her biography of the writer Dodie Smith, entitled *Dear Dodie* (Chatto, 1996), was listed as one of twelve finalists for the NCR Award. She is married to the journalist Trevor Grove and lives in London.

Praise for *So Much to Tell*

'Enchanting and fast-flowing . . . Kaye Webb's story is inspirational – and entertaining' *Literary Review*

'Webb's charismatic personality is brought vividly to life' *Daily Express*

'Grove's lively book is a must-read for those of us whose childhood was shaped by Webb's Puffin books . . . it offers a seductive recreation of a now almost lost world of wartime and 1950s London' *Financial Times*

'Webb remains a fascinating and heartbreaking character, and Grove's account of her life is sensitive, lively, insightful and utterly unsentimental' *Irish Times*

'Not only is there the great joy of remembering the writers you loved as a child. It is also powerfully cheering to read about a woman who took such pleasure in her career' *Observer*

'Grove tells her story with care, liveliness and clarity' *Sunday Times*

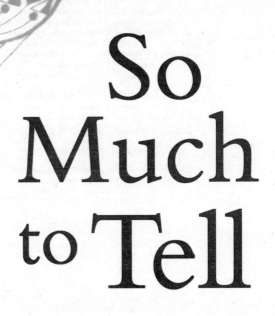

So Much to Tell

The biography of
Kaye Webb
by
Valerie Grove

VIKING
an imprint of
PENGUIN BOOKS

VIKING BOOKS

Published by the Penguin Group
Penguin Books Ltd, 80 Strand, London WC2R ORL, England
Penguin Group (USA) Inc., 375 Hudson Street, New York, New York 10014, USA
Penguin Group (Canada), 90 Eglinton Avenue East, Suite 700, Toronto, Ontario, Canada M4P 2Y3
(a division of Pearson Penguin Canada Inc.)
Penguin Ireland, 25 St Stephen's Green, Dublin 2, Ireland (a division of Penguin Books Ltd)
Penguin Group (Australia), 250 Camberwell Road, Camberwell, Victoria 3124, Australia
(a division of Pearson Australia Group Pty Ltd)
Penguin Books India Pvt Ltd, 11 Community Centre, Panchsheel Park, New Delhi – 110 017, India
Penguin Group (NZ), 67 Apollo Drive, Rosedale, Auckland 0632, New Zealand
(a division of Pearson New Zealand Ltd)
Penguin Books (South Africa) (Pty) Ltd, 24 Sturdee Avenue, Rosebank, Johannesburg 2196, South Africa

Penguin Books Ltd, Registered Offices: 80 Strand, London WC2R ORL, England

www.penguin.com

First published by Viking 2010
Published in this edition 2011
001 – 10 9 8 7 6 5 4 3 2 1

Set in Bembo MT Std
Typeset by Palimpsest Book Production Limited, Falkirk, Stirlingshire
Printed in Great Britain by Clays Ltd, St Ives plc

British Library Cataloguing in Publication Data
A CIP catalogue record for this book is available from the British Library

ISBN: 978-0-670-91908-6

www.greenpenguin.co.uk

Penguin Books is committed to a sustainable future
for our business, our readers and our planet.
The book in your hands is made from paper
certified by the Forest Stewardship Council.

Mixed Sources
Product group from well-managed
forests and other controlled sources
www.fsc.org Cert no. SA-COC-1592
© 1996 Forest Stewardship Council

To Kate and John Searle

Contents

List of Illustrations ix

Foreword xi

Preface xiii

1 The Time Capsule 1

2 What Kaye Did at School: 1914–30 11

3 What Kaye Did Next: 1930–39 25

4 Kaye's Lilliputian War: 1940–45 38

5 Enter Ronald Searle 52

6 Becoming Mrs Searle: 1946–9 65

7 High Circles: 1950–55 84

8 Social Whirl: 1955–8 104

9 Which Way Did He Go?: 1958–61 123

10 Nuffin' Like a Puffin: 1962–6 147

11 Sniffup Spotera!: 1967–70 162

12 Mission Completed: 1971–5 186

13 The Succession: 1976–9 209

14 Post Puffin: 1980–85 228

15 'I like things to end happily': 1986–96 243

Afterword 265

A Postscript 269

Bibliography 273

Acknowledgements 275

Permissions 277

Index 279

List of Illustrations

All images are from Kaye Webb's own collection, courtesy of Kate Searle.

1. Ronald Searle's letters to Kaye after he was released from Changi were illustrated with his enchanting little drawings.
2. Ann Stevens, née Fahy, Kaye's mother: red-haired, glamorous and theatrical.
3. Arthur Webb, Kaye's journalist father.
4. The toddler Kaye, 'Princess Sunshine', at the seaside.
5. John Webb, Kaye's younger brother, killed in Burma in 1944.
6. Bill Webb, Kaye's elder half-brother, sporting journalist.
7. Miss Webb of *Lilliput*, everyone's favourite wartime magazine.
8. Kaye with Wing-Commander Keith Hunter, who became the second of her three husbands in 1942.
9. Kaye sailing home from the US on the *Queen Elizabeth* in October 1947 with her twin babies.
10. The twins, Kate and John Searle.
11. Ronald Searle and Kaye Webb in Ronald's studio in Bedford Gardens, Notting Hill Gate.
12. The happy Searle family at Westgate-on-Sea, *c.* 1950.
13. Kaye and Ronald at Le Lavandou, in the South of France, 1955.
14. Kaye's TV debut, 1955.
15. The Searles at the Chelsea Arts Ball, New Year's Eve 1954.

16. The Searles dining with screenwriter Arthur Sheekman and his actress wife Gloria Stuart, 1954.
17. 'Handsome goat assists': Kaye at the Young Vic theatre in January 1968.
18. Kaye joining in Puffin Club adventures.
19. 'Kaye's girls' at a bedside editorial meeting, c. 1977.
20. Kaye with violinist Yehudi Menuhin, a patron of the *Young Elizabethan* magazine, who remained a lifelong friend.
21. Kaye and her brother Bill at St James's Palace in November 1974, when she was awarded her MBE.
22. Kaye always blossomed in the Mediterranean sun.
23. Kaye at a party with the poet Roy Fuller and the perennially popular writer Noel Streatfeild.

Foreword

(from Kaye Webb's radio talk 'Learned from Life', 1958)

I think the chief reason for living is learning: perhaps 'discovering' is a better word. We are born nothing. We arrive full of innocence and curiosity, and if we are lucky, we keep the curiosity. Wouldn't it be dreadful to wake one morning and feel that there was nothing left you wanted to know about, or, even worse still, that you knew everything? I'm not talking about knowledge of course, but wisdom.

And the idiotic thing is that even the wisest parents quite often try to kill this curiosity. It begins in tiny ways: because they want to spare their children pain, they start warning them off things – 'Fire burns'; 'Knives cut'; 'Friends change'. Of course, we end by discovering these things for ourselves, just as later on we find out such truths as 'Laugh and the world laughs with you; weep, and you weep alone' – and all those other wise sayings we have come to call clichés.

But just think if we listened to these warnings and didn't find out some things for ourselves! We'd be unable to make real contact with our fellow-men because we would not have shared any experiences with them. We would not understand them. We would be shut away from life. Love and friendship both grow out of shared feelings.

When our children come home with wounds, we sympathize because we've had them too, and can imagine their pain. When, later, they have disappointments or heartaches, we can offer them comfort. But supposing we had not suffered either ourselves because our parents had taught us to avoid them, we would not know what on earth they were talking about.

And since, inevitably, I've got on to the subject of children, another thing I have learned from life is that the really worst service we can do them is to teach them to care what people think ... to train them to behave in this or that way, not because it is fundamentally right, but because of outside opinion.

And we are almost all guilty of this. We say that manners have to be better in front of strangers, faces have to be cleaner, and so on. How often have I heard myself saying, 'I don't know what Mrs Thingumajig must think of you!' or 'What sort of a home must they think you come from?' It's the right thing for the wrong reason, and can end by our carrying around a terrible old man of the sea on our backs, governing all our actions for the benefit of anonymous outsiders instead of our own consciences. Incidentally, if you can learn from life that it does not really matter what people think as long as your own heart is serene, then you suddenly discover, as a sort of bonus, that you have also learned tolerance as well.

Preface

Kaye Webb sometimes said, looking back, that her professional life had worked out beautifully, with perfect timing; her private life had been the reverse. She blamed herself for her husband's sudden departure, when their twins were fourteen. The pain of that emotional disaster never left her. Yet to the world at large she remained forever warm and vital, a life-enriching force. She erupted into the world of children's books during those decades of the twentieth century (1960–80) when a literate, curious, imaginative young readership was avid for sustenance, guidance and instruction – from books. For three generations of children, the words 'Editor: Kaye Webb' on the title page guaranteed quality within.

Through the Puffin Club, by inventing ways to make books exciting, Kaye Webb inspired generations of writers, illustrators, publishers, critics and book-lovers.

'Kaye had many abilities (including some she didn't know she had),' wrote the late Naomi Lewis, children's author and anthologist. 'But what was outstanding and, indeed, unique in her, was a kind of flame, the power to rouse the hidden gift in anyone around her – sometimes to the point of genius. In the Puffin Club, all that was magic in her had full range. The whole thing was a feat of creation which no one else could have realized.'

1 : The Time Capsule

First came the Penguin. Penguin Books was launched by Allen Lane in 1935 with the aim of making literature affordable by anybody with sixpence to spend. With their orange covers and distinctive modern design, Penguins were an immediate hit. When the war came, despite severe paper rationing which meant that books were pulped and re-pulped, and with half their staff away in the forces, Penguin published 600 titles. The pages were of thin, greyish, straw-based paper, stapled together because of the shortage of machinery and manpower in the printing industry. But Penguins were pocket-sized and portable, and became a national institution, essential to servicemen with hours to while away in camps, barracks and troopships, to volunteer fire-watchers, and to civilians huddled in air-raid shelters. The bombs of the Blitz destroyed millions of books in publishers' offices – six million were lost one night in 1940 when Paternoster Row was struck – but the war encouraged the reading habit.

Practical books sold best: titles like *Keeping Poultry and Rabbits on Scraps*. *Aircraft Recognition* by R. A. Saville-Sneath remained the all-time bestselling Penguin, until *Lady Chatterley's Lover* in 1960.

Penguin's founding genius, Allen Lane, had left school at sixteen and joined his uncle John's publishing firm, the Bodley Head. He was still a bachelor at thirty-eight when his friend Noel Carrington (brother of the Bloomsbury artist Dora, and a father of three) dreamed up a series of low-priced books that would gratify a child's need for information, with colour illustrations, which Carrington had pioneered. Lane displayed 'a childlike enthusiasm' for Carrington's picture-books and distributed them as Puffin Picture Books in 1940. The four titles were *War on Land*, *War at Sea*, *War in the Air* and *On the Farm* – ideal for children being evacuated from cities to the countryside.

As it happened, Lane had already discussed a children's list with Eleanor Graham. She had written four children's books, including *The Children Who Lived in a Barn*, had reinvented the children's department at Bumpus Books, and reviewed for the *Sunday Times*. Lane and Eleanor both remembered, from their childhoods, W. T. Stead's 'Books for the Bairns'. Stead, the great Victorian crusading journalist, wanted to see every child provided with books that reflected Christian values, devotion to the monarchy and goodwill to all. The first Book for the Bairns was *Aesop's Fables*, which was published in 1896 and was an instant success, selling 150,000 a month. It was followed by *Brer Rabbit*, *Mother Goose*, *Grimm's Fairy Tales* and *Great Events in British History*. In his prefaces, Stead delivered homilies, such as 'Try to love the boy or girl you dislike most and crush the nasty feeling of grudging envy, for LOVE is the Good Fairy of Life.'

In 1940, during an air raid, Eleanor Graham took the Underground from her office at the Board of Trade to Hounslow West station. She was driven to Silverbeck, Allen Lane's William IV mansion in Middlesex, two miles from the Penguin office at Harmondsworth, an area of decaying farms and market gardens. Having supplied librarians for years, Eleanor knew what children liked to read. Lane had decided on the name of 'Puffin' for Penguin's junior imprint. The penguin was a bird that had both dignity and gaiety; the puffin was short and round and comically top-heavy, like a child's toy. Puffins, Lane agreed with Eleanor, should not just reprint traditional classics, but find the best new fiction, history and poetry. Noel Carrington had already bought the first fictional Puffin Picture Book, *Orlando's Evening Out*, by

Kathleen Hale, and Eleanor now set about acquiring full-length fiction for Puffins.

'*Probably if it had not been for whooping-cough, John and Susan would never have seen the scarecrow who stood in the middle of Ten-acre field.*' So began the very first Puffin novel: *Worzel Gummidge*, by Barbara Euphan Todd, in 1941. Along with the tale of the talking scarecrow they published *Cornish Adventure* by Derek McCulloch (Uncle Mac of *Children's Hour* on the wireless), *The Cuckoo Clock* by Mrs Molesworth (a Victorian tale of lonely little Griselda, sent to live with two old aunts), *Garram the Hunter* by Herbert Best (an African adventure story) and *Smoky*, 'the story of a cow horse' by a former cattle-rustler, Will James.

These were not Eleanor's first choices. But librarians and schoolteachers were snooty about paperbacks. Nor did hardback publishers thrill to the idea of cheap editions, on inferior paper, with an advert for Kiltie Shoes on the back. They were reluctant to sub-lease rights to their established titles, just as they had initially resisted Penguins. Jonathan Cape refused to release Arthur Ransome's *Swallows and Amazons*, or Hugh Lofting's *Dr Dolittle*.

But by dedication, persistence and gentle persuasion, Eleanor built up a children's paperback library. Two decades later there were 150 Puffin story books, including *Ballet Shoes* by Noel Streatfeild, *The Incredible Adventures of Professor Branestawm* by Norman Hunter, and *The Family from One End Street* by Eve Garnett. When Eleanor retired in 1961, her baton passed to a woman who blew into the children's book scene like a tornado: the former journalist Kaye Webb.

Under Kaye Webb's eighteen-year regime, from 1961 to 1979, Puffin Books really did overturn children's publishing in terms of sales, enthusiasm and influence. By the end of her time, other publishers had leapt on the bandwagon and started their own children's paperback imprints. But the brand name of Puffin was the one several generations of children had come to depend on, and more than 200,000 of them had joined Kaye's pioneering Puffin Club, which brought living authors out of their eyries to meet their readers, and arranged activities and holidays so that they associated books with fun and adventure.

Since the early 1960s, television had become so much part of children's lives that books were under threat of becoming a secondary distraction. Children born in the 1970s were the first generation whose parents had themselves grown up watching television. Infants were now introduced to the screen long before they learned to read print. Literacy itself seemed imperilled, and how to reach the non-reading child became a preoccupation of the 1970s. The moment had come, Kaye Webb decided, to celebrate the mind-expanding, eye-opening world contained in children's books of the past century – while they still read them. Kaye's fiction editor, Jane Nissen, remembered from her American childhood that the New York Natural History Museum had created a 'Time Capsule' in the 1950s. Kaye seized the idea. She would gather the best Puffin books, and record messages from children's authors, and from their devoted readers. These would be buried underground, to be dug up either fifty or 100 years hence: the heirs of the 'Puffin Guardians' would decide which.

Kaye and her team chose 176 of the '*nicest*' children's books to bury: a significant choice of adjective in 1978. Books for children had been published that Kaye did not think particularly nice. At her annual Puffin Exhibition, illustrator Quentin Blake once heard her ask a ten-year-old child what she thought of a new book. Kaye took it back with the words, 'Yes, it's bloody awful, isn't it, darling.' She preferred the canon of classic works she had published because she admired them, by authors she revered. She was not a sociologist who believed books must reflect current society; she was a showman, and the Time Capsule would be her showcase. Books by living authors were inscribed with a message inside, among them Nina Bawden's *Carrie's War*, Richard Adams's

Watership Down, Philippa Pearce's *Tom's Midnight Garden*, Noel Streatfeild's *Ballet Shoes*, Roald Dahl's *Charlie and the Chocolate Factory* and K. M. Briggs's *Hobberdy Dick*. Other books, by dead authors, were included to give a complete picture of twentieth-century children's literature: C. S. Lewis's *The Lion, the Witch and the Wardrobe*, Frances Hodgson Burnett's *The Secret Garden*, etc. To these were added thousands of messages from members of the Puffin Club, collected at the Puffin Exhibition.

How to preserve the books in the capsule? Microfilm, they were told, would not survive for a century. They consulted Professor Akers of Camberwell School of Arts and Crafts, who welcomed the project as an experiment in preservation. Printed pages were copied leaf by leaf, by Xerox on to Archive long-life text. The books were rebound to the original format, their covers re-attached with adhesive of polyvinyl acetate. The books were shrink-wrapped and packed tightly, to be buried in a brick-lined hole, covered with heavy-duty polythene under a layer of concrete 'like a damp-proof course in a house'. As some remarked at the time, Penguin offices were full of books fifty years old, in a state of perfect preservation; but Kaye's capsule would survive even an atomic bomb.

The burial took place in the grounds of Penguin headquarters in Bath Road, Harmondsworth, Middlesex, on 5 August 1978, the occasion recorded at the Science Museum, the V&A, and the British Museum Library. It would be regarded in 2078 as Buried Treasure, said the press release, 'and may even be the means of reviving interest in a skill that, heaven forbid, could have fallen into disuse'.

The day was sunny, and Kaye and her team wore pink tabards with the Puffin logo over their summer frocks. They were preserving, said Kaye, 'a complete and unique record of what the best authors are writing for children nowadays. There . . .

never has been such an inspiring and exciting time for children's literature as the last twenty years. And perhaps it may never be as good again. For who knows what the future holds in store? If by any awful chance writers stopped writing, or stopped writing so well, and children stopped reading, or only read fearful comics or just looked at pictures . . . why then, when this is dug up we might just be the means to revive a lost art!'

The astronomer Patrick Moore, a large man with a large personality, performed the burial under a cherry tree on a fake hill. (When people asked Kaye, 'Why him?' her reply was, 'Why not?' He had presented the moon landing on television in 1969; he was a popular figure, eccentric, right-wing, cat-loving, who had been a self-taught authority on outer space at the age of eleven.) Moore drove up from Hampshire despite having just had a car accident. Kaye recalled that his words were 'perfectly judged, instinctively apposite and right' but few in the crowd could hear them, because at the precise moment when Moore lowered the box on a rope down the hole, there was a mighty roar and, as if on cue, Concorde soared overhead. 'Here's the future!' cried Moore.

'It is a pity that none of us who helped put the capsule together will be around for the Great Exhumation in 2078,' Kaye said in her speech. 'Still, it's good to know it will happen, and to think it will make a serious contribution to the future. As the buried messages from the authors have suggested, not to have books to read would be worse than never having tasted chocolate or ice-cream. Let's just hope that the children of the future appreciate that not all buried treasure is gold and precious jewels.'

Penguin's modernist offices were laid out on a campus with Japanese-style courtyards, fountains and Oriental trees. That day it looked like a garden fête, with bunting, stalls and games. You could do face-painting and draw round your friend on the ground, and play 'Pot a Puffin'. The atmosphere was typical of Puffin events, with children flocking round their authors, among them Nina Bawden, Leon Garfield, Helen Nicoll, Joyce Lankester Brisley, Norman Hunter and Ursula Moray Williams; and at the centre, the magnetic figure of Kaye Webb.

The twenty Puffin Guardians who attended received a certificate from Patrick Moore ('towering above us like a colossus, and heartily shaking our hands') and solemnly committed themselves to guarding the contents of the box, promising to appoint their children or grandchildren as heirs. Principal Guardian was Sir Allen Lane's granddaughter Zoë Teale, aged ten (who was to publish her first novel in 1995). The youngest was 'Chico', the baby son of Alison Rosenberg, designer of Puffin exhibitions. There was also Nina Bawden's nine-year-old granddaughter Jessica, and Puffineers Paul Godfrey (future playwright), Alison Cartledge, Philip Geddes and Vivien Moir, who had travelled with her grandmother from the west coast of Scotland.

One of the Guardians' promises was that whenever the Capsule is unsealed, it will be 'in the presence of distinguished authorities in the world of Children's Literature'. Among the messages in the books inside the exhumed capsule, they would find:

Tom's Midnight Garden by **Philippa Pearce**:
Like the old woman in this story, I stretch out my hand to touch the children of the future: for a moment I touch you with these words of mine.

I send you my love. Neighbourly love is what, now, we need much, much more of: I wish you may have it.

I wish you happiness.

Do you still read books? I hope so. I wish you that joy, among many others.

Ballet Shoes by **Noel Streatfeild**:
Imagine: this was written for you by an author old enough to remember Queen Victoria's coffin drawn by a steam train.

Warrior Scarlet by **Rosemary Sutcliff**:

Dear children

It seems odd to be writing this to you, who will not be born for another ninety years or so. Odd but nice.

I wonder what your world is like, and I hope that by reading the books and letters and such like things that we in 1978 are sending to you, you will come to know a little more what our world is like, and the things in it that we think are worth sending on to you. My love to you all, Rosemary Sutcliff.

Borka – the Adventures of a Goose with No Feathers by **John Burningham**:

I hope the grass is still green and the birds are singing.

You are probably blaming our generation for mucking up your world. Sorry. Try to make a better job of it than we did. Best wishes from the past. John Burningham.

The Seas of Morning by **Geoffrey Trease**:

Were we so quaint, in nineteen seventy-eight?
We too had friends, and fun. We drank and ate.
One thing we much enjoyed was called a book.
You don't know what that was? Here – have a look!

The Adventures of Robin Hood by **Roger Lancelyn Green**:

I pray that, were I able to be with you in 2078, I could say, with Shakespeare –

'Oh wonder!
How many goodly creatures are there here!
How beauteous mankind is! O brave new world,
That has such people in it!'

Silly Verse for Kids by **Spike Milligan**:

To tomorrow's children –

I think the world population (if there's no war) will be massive.
I did warn people when I was alive. I hope your world is tolerable.
Live – Light – Peace
Spike Milligan, July 1978.

The Puffin Book of Magic Verse, **edited by Charles Causley:**
> Life is magic,
> Love is a spell;
> Guard both well.

The Dolphin Crossing **by Jill Paton Walsh:**
Whatever the most dangerous crossing in your time may be, I wish
you may set out bravely, and safely return.

Kaye herself wrote a message inside *The Crack-a-Joke Book*:
'This was the 1,000th Puffin to be published while I was the
Editor in charge. We wanted to create something very special
which would make children laugh, but also help other children
who were having a bad time.

'In the years before 1978 and in this year too, all sorts of dreadful
disasters have happened in different parts of the world. People, and
their children, have been made homeless and hungry, because of
physical disasters, like floods, fires, earthquakes and stupid wars.
So people from countries all round the world united to rush aid
to them when things were desperate. One of the charities formed
was called OXFAM, and we are specially proud because we sold
so many copies of this book that we were able to give nearly
£10,000 to them to pay for things like food and blankets.

'I wonder whether you will be doing the same sort of things
in 2078. Although it would be wonderful to think that a hundred
years from now all such problems will have disappeared.

'I wonder, too, whether you will be laughing at the same sort
of jokes. I wish I could be there to see you open this book and

start telling them to each other, but whatever happens, this and all the other books in this special legacy we have left you have been chosen with our love and wishes for your happiness.'

Today, thirty-two years on, the Time Capsule's voice already belongs to another era, before the computer revolution. It is no longer entombed at Harmondsworth, as the old offices were razed to the ground in 2003. The Capsule was lifted and transported (unopened) in 2005 to the Centre for Children's Books at Felling, near Newcastle upon Tyne, to be part of its treasury of children's book archives.

What would Victorian writers have written, in messages to future children? They might have conjured up a world in which change would mean improvement, progress, invention, better education, and alleviation of poverty and misery. The Queen's Silver Jubilee Year of 1978, despite street-parties and jamborees across the land, was a more sceptical time. There was high inflation, high unemployment, a plethora of strikes, international unrest and a widespread sense of disillusion.

The writers' messages of 1978 mostly recognize this. They did not seem to cherish a hope that the future might really be an improvement on the present. But they managed to voice a wary confidence that children, at least, arriving in the world not knowing what terrible things can happen, would continue to possess an inborn capacity for love, friendship and goodness.

2: What Kaye Did at School

1914–30

There is a noted link between bookishness and a sickly childhood. Kaye Webb was eight when she contracted rheumatic fever – commonplace among children in the early twentieth century, before antibiotics – and was confined to bed for many months. How else could a child in 1922 be entertained, except by reading? 'My mother wheeled her bookcase into my bedroom – so I went straight into Thackeray, Scott and Dumas,' Kaye would recall. She read few children's books, except for *What Katy Did*, which she read 'at least six times'. An ideal choice, since the heroine of Susan Coolidge's character-forming story is confined to bed after falling out of a tree. She is (temporarily) a wheelchair-bound paraplegic. Crotchety and self-pitying at first, she becomes by degrees a model of patience and unselfish good humour, so noble and kind that people flock to visit her. Kaye – baptized Kathleen and sometimes known as Katy – could identify with her quick-witted namesake, whose creator wrote, 'There were always so many delightful schemes rioting in her brains, that all she wished for was ten pairs of hands to carry them out.' Those words might have been written about the woman Kaye grew up to be.

The Webb family had an old connection with the world of children. Today, toy theatres survive chiefly in Pollock's Toy Museum; but a century ago, every middle-class child owned a toy theatre, with tin footlights and green calico curtains, opening up a world of make-believe, of brigands and bandits, pirates and soldiers – 'an absorbing recreation, the delight of countless evenings by the fireside'. The theatre sets and one-shilling playscripts were published by either Pollock or Kaye's great-great-grandfather, William George Webb. He was born in London in 1821, the artistic son of a City wool merchant. At fourteen, W. G. was apprenticed to a publisher of theatrical prints, and began sketching, engraving, colouring and publishing his own work, making Webb's Toy Theatres a leading name in the business. He specialized in patriotic plays: *The Battle of Waterloo, Union Jack, The Rifle Volunteers* and *Robin Hood*. His pantomimes had 'many tricks and changes of scene', and 'some wonderful spectacular effects'.

Victorian artists and writers – Dickens, Frith, Millais, Chesterton – loved their toy theatres. The actress Ellen Terry had one, and so did Henry Irving. The impresario Charles B. Cochran and his friend Aubrey Beardsley, sharing a study at school, concocted their own dramas, Beardsley drawing the figures and sets. Robert Louis Stevenson, not yet a household name, wrote a magazine article, 'A Penny Plain and Twopence Coloured' (the Penny Plain sets were preferred, for the child to paint himself), illustrating it with Webb's scenes and characters. But during his research, Stevenson fell out with W. G. Webb. Webb had made helpful notes, and asked for some remuneration. Stevenson rebuffed him; Webb tore up his notes; Stevenson stomped out of his shop and inserted, out of spite, a crushing reference to Webb in his text, before departing for the South Seas. A. E. Wilson told this story in his 1932 book of the same title, *A Penny Plain and Twopence Coloured*.

'I believe Webb knew many secrets of the trade now for ever lost,' wrote Wilson.

W. G. Webb lived to lament the fading popularity of the toy theatre: 'Our children in these days have neither the patience nor the time necessary to colour and ornament the sheets.' In Kaye's childhood Webb's son Henry James Webb, her octogenarian great-grandfather, still kept the little shop at 124 Old Street, Finsbury, which remained 'a wonder-house of quaint treasure', with a display of toy stages, tinselled pictures and sheets of characters. H. J. Webb's customers included Charlie Chaplin, Diaghilev, the theatre designer Gordon Craig, the Sitwells, and the actress Gladys Cooper. The young Winston Churchill, a 'jolly and impulsive lad', would burst into the shop and vault over the counter. Webb, a gold-mine of memories, traditions and history, sat in a corner, painstakingly colouring his prints; in earlier years he had employed twelve people to do this. He told Wilson he had personally witnessed Stevenson's spat with his father.

But by the time the next generation of Webbs left school, toy theatres were no longer 'the national pastime of the British child'. Instead of joining the family printing business, H. J.'s son set up on his own. And his eldest son, Kaye's father, became a journalist. Arthur Webb was, at seventeen, inquisitive about everything and everyone (something he passed on to his daughter) and passionate about politics. Reporting for the *Football Star*, he was first to telephone his reports direct from the grandstands. In due course Arthur encouraged his wife, Ann, and their three children to earn their living in Grub Street.

'Mothers are the most difficult members of a family to describe,' Kaye wrote, 'perhaps because their moods are often changing – sometimes patient and loving, sometimes irritable and cross about things which don't seem important to their children, but usually turning up trumps on important occasions.' Ann Stevens was just such a mother. 'For almost half my life I rarely did anything without seeking and needing her approval,' Kaye wrote, 'or in unconscious imitation of her.'

Ann was red-haired, glamorous, generous, flirtatious, flamboyant, slightly scatty, witty and theatrical, with a penchant for stylish clothes with beaded embroidery. Her daughter would inherit many of these characteristics. As a girl, Kaye would 'chalk up' her success with young men, for Ann's pleasure. Her mother, Kaye thought, would have been a courtesan in an earlier era. Her life-story 'read like a romantic novelette'. Ann began with nothing, as the third illegitimate daughter of Kate Fahy, an attractive mill-girl of Irish stock who had caught the eye of the mill-owner. He bequeathed her two houses in Islington, where Kate took in lodgers. One of these apparently fathered Ann in 1885. Kate's three children all bore her surname, Fahy, until she became housekeeper to George Stevens, a widowed Islington building contractor with six children, and married him. Thereafter her children took the name Stevens.

It is unlikely that Ann Stevens had much schooling, but a little went a long way for children then: elementary pupils left school at thirteen, literate and grammatical, able to spell and punctuate properly. Ann, intelligent, lively and rebellious, was apprenticed to a dressmaker. According to family legend she was working in the City when she met a well-born Anglo-Irishman known as 'Pasty' Fitzpatrick, and became pregnant by him. Fitzpatrick was sent off to Berlin with a family retainer as chaperone, but when her baby son was born in 1912 Ann received a letter from him saying he was willing to marry her. She jumped on a train with her baby – named Louis but later known as Bill – and followed him to Berlin, only to be waylaid at the station by the retainer, who said her lover regretted his promise and gave her £200 cash to go away. Whereupon the resourceful Ann sent telegrams to two other suitors, saying she was destitute with her baby. Both agreed to marry her (she claimed), but only the jovial Arthur Webb, by now twenty-four and a reporter on the *Islington Gazette*, turned up with a licence, salvaging her reputation.

Who knew how true Ann's story was? To her grandchildren, 'Nan' was a mesmeric teller of tales. 'It was always a treat, when Granny turned up.' But that was the view of a grandson, and 'Nan' was always nicer to men.

In January 1914, Ann and Arthur's daughter Kathleen was born at 34 Flanders Road, Bedford Park, Chiswick. Large, smiling and healthy, she was greeted by her grandmother Stevens (after whom she was named) as 'Princess Sunshine', and called 'Kayki' by her two-year-old half-brother Bill. During the Great War, Arthur joined the Inns of Court OTC near Fleet Street, and from 1917 was commissioned in the 4th Ox and Bucks Light Infantry, serving in Northumberland. Meanwhile Ann took her children to live in Landseer Avenue, Hove, in Sussex.

The marriage of Arthur and Ann was not harmonious. At one point, Ann threatened to leave Arthur, taking Bill with her. Kaye overheard this, and not yet knowing that her brother was not their father's son, divined that Bill was her mother's favourite, as was indeed the case. 'She never did go away; my poor wretched father went instead, to Ireland, to the *Irish Times*,' Kaye wrote. During the 1920s, the years of the Troubles, Arthur was held up at gunpoint twice, by both sides. He stayed in Dublin until 1929, when he came home with a clock inscribed 'To Arthur Webb as a token of esteem from his colleagues on Irish Times, 14 June 1929'.

While Arthur was in Dublin, Ann and her three children – another baby, John, had been born in 1918 – lived in the north London suburbs, first in Mountview Road, Crouch End, then in Aberdeen Park, Highbury. Kaye attended a little dame school, and went briefly to Hornsey High School, where she won a prize, Oscar Wilde's *The Happy Prince*, for recitation. Ann was, in Kaye's view, an admirable mother, 'marvellously loving and sweet'. 'With the skimpiest of education and no advantages, she became a film and theatre critic, and tried to include all that was new and interesting in her lifestyle. As children we had a long period of going barefoot, and sleeping on wooden boards, while she bobbed her hair and won difficult crossword competitions – a very new development in 1920. We also had dancing and elocution lessons far beyond my poor father's means, and were taken to theatres and ballets (at ten, I saw Pavlova in *Swan Lake*) and had long holidays in Sheringham with our own beach hut.'

Arthur Webb had that vital personality trait in the old-fashioned journalist: intense curiosity. Malcolm Muggeridge described him as 'a short, energetic, eager, immensely shrewd and kindly man, quick-witted and quite fearless'. In 1926 the *Irish Times* sent him on his first visit to America. 'Went to the Winter Garden theatre and had seat in stalls so changed into dinner dress,' Arthur wrote in his notebook. 'Unlike Londoners, New Yorkers do not dress for the theatre! Would have enjoyed the show more if I had worn a lounge suit like most of my neighbours. Was told that only out-of-towners would think of dressing up to go to theatre.' He watched astonished as the managing editor of the *New York Times* ordered whisky, champagne, wine and gin from his bootlegger, telling Arthur, 'Prohibition is for the other feller.'

In Washington DC, Arthur recorded: 'Well, I have shaken hands with the president of the United States. I suppose I should be thrilled.' At a press conference, Calvin Coolidge was asked his view of a new book on American history. His reply was: 'Well, I think we should all read history to understand the present.' 'Three minutes later we were all in the street, as he had dismissed us with "I think that's all, gentlemen." Yet even his banal words had to be attributed to "a White House spokesman".' Washington, Arthur decided, was 'a dull town with sleepy people. Everything closes down at lunchtime.'

In 1926 Kaye was enrolled at the co-educational Ashburton School in Devon, where her brother Bill was already a pupil. Ashburton was an ancient country grammar school, its tower dating from 1304. Roll call and prayers were held in a lofty hall with elegant cornice mouldings and elaborate coats of arms. 'Fides probata corona' (Tried loyalty is the crown of excellence) was the school motto. Ashburton had all the pretensions of a minor public school: a hockey team report in the school magazine would end, 'Play up, play up and play the game!' and when Lord Fortescue came to present the prizes in 1926, he delivered a homily based on Lord Cromer's advice: 'Love your country; speak the truth; be punctual.'

At twelve, Kaye travelled to Devon by train, arrived before term began and, when offered a choice of beds, chose the one by the window, which was already taken, causing mutiny in the dorm. She was ostracized by the girl boarders of Class IIIA, and was conscious of her 'London accent'. In the first term she missed her first Latin lessons, having a bad attack of jaundice, and never caught up. But she did make friends: one Violet Chivers threw pasties up through the window of the sick bay. On Friday nights there were dances at the boys' house, and there was much competition to be invited. Kaye was automatically asked, because Bill was there.

Kaye's own résumé of her 'not very distinguished' schooldays simply says: 'bullied, miserable, had jaundice'. But she looked back with gratitude on 'marvellous Mr Gibbs', her dynamic young English master, 'such a rare and wonderful teacher that he made the whole of the rest of the school acceptable'. Ben R. Gibbs, Welsh by birth, wrote textbooks such as *History Through Literature*, and *Children in Dickens*. Under his influence the drama and debating societies and school magazine flourished. He organized an Eisteddfod, at which pupils sang, read and put on plays, which 'gave the term a bit of impetus'.

There is almost an element of parody in Kaye's school reminiscences, with herself cast as the Madcap of the Fourth. She was sent to the headmaster, Mr Naylor, for scattering sneezing powder, and never forgot the church parade when the headmaster's unpopular wife, Ma Naylor, led the procession with her dress tucked into her pink woolly knickers. The schoolmates' names she always remembered included the twins Pixie and Piers

Pidgeon, Spenwyn Daw, Harold Palk, Hubert Nosworthy, Clifton Huddy, and a boy named Billy Ross, who was later hanged for shooting dead his fiancée and her mother. 'A very nice boy, and a good artist,' wrote Kaye, to an old school friend. 'I think he must have been unbalanced at the time.'

Kaye soon began speaking in debates. She supported or proposed 'That there is too much attention paid to sport at the present day', 'That the world gains more from the ordinary man than from the man of genius' and carried the motion 'That the thinker is of more value to mankind than the man of action' by twenty-seven to twelve. In the mock election of 1928, fourteen-year-old Kaye stood as the Liberal candidate. 'Having held up her hand for silence in a most ecclesiastical way she delivered her address,' reported the school magazine, 'and hastily left the platform before heckling started.' She won narrowly, with twenty-five votes against twenty-three for the Labour candidate (glamorous Susannah Suter from Monte Carlo, 'the star of our house, talented and funny and sang well'), while the Tory, Harold Palk, trailed with nineteen.

When Mr Gibbs showed the class how to write a sonnet, and asked for first lines, Kaye 'offered six lines, to everyone else's intense irritation – I must have been odious'. Mr Gibbs told Kaye she was a natural writer, and published her essay on 'The Romance of Waterfalls'. 'How great and magnificent is a waterfall as it crashes down the rocks bearing with it all that can be captured from its pathway . . . It fills one with admiration at its never-ending energy, its glittering pureness, its happy conception of its daily task.' In her fancy it was a fairies' bathing pool, a nymph rising from its depths – 'but no, it is just the sun shining . . . just the fall of the water as it chatters away when it joins the running brook'.

The Ashburton Book of Verse, published in 1928, prompted approving letters (no doubt solicited) from the writer John Buchan, the Devon novelist Eden Phillpotts, and Walter de la

Mare, who wrote to Mr Gibbs: 'There is a poem I particularly liked, by someone called Kaye Webb. I think she really is going to be a poet.' This was her poem:

> I found a friend in solitude today
> Before the frisky fawns commenced to play,
> 'Ere the blackbird's whistling call,
> Dew at my feet.
>
> We peeped into a nest where thrushes bide,
> We plucked a bud, and pressing by my side
> In a voice of happy ecstasy, she cried
> 'Is this not sweet?'
>
> Then through the hushed air of the morning
> We heard the owl's shrill cry of warning,
> In rapture was a fresh day dawning,
> The night was dead.
>
> The leafy treetops rustled and a bird began to sing,
> The cockerel in his pleasure told the world that he was king,
> From the old church on the hillock came the bells' sweet
>   piercing ring,
> Solitude fled.

De la Mare's approval made him Kaye's hero. 'I kept his picture in the lid of my desk and used to gloat over it.' He looked 'rather like a benevolent Roman emperor', J. B. Priestley once said, and she agreed.

After 1930, when Kaye left, the school reverted to being a minor boys' public school. Mr Gibbs, promoted to Second Master but out of sympathy with the new ethos, died in 1934 aged only thirty-seven. He might have made a great headmaster, said the school magazine's obituary. 'No boy or girl could come under his influence without being the better for it, and that, perhaps, is the greatest tribute that can be paid to a schoolmaster.' Long afterwards, in 1992, Kaye wrote to Myfanwy Knight, Mr Gibbs's daughter, about 'your dear father' and her private lessons with him. 'We read all the way through *Memoirs of a Midget*, and he transferred to me his love for Walter de la Mare, and years later when I was doing some broadcasting for the BBC *Woman's Hour*, I got to know [de la Mare] very well, and he gave me all his books, and spoke with affection of your father . . .

'I would like you to know that he was the one good thing about the Grammar School – he taught both my brother and me to really care for poetry, and he taught me a lot about my writing. He could be quite fierce with a classful, but he was always nice to me.'

Mr Gibbs had said Kaye should aim for Oxford. It rankled, much later, that she had not done this, not had a 'proper' education. She always felt inadequate and ill-read, compared with graduate employees.

Because Kaye fancied being an actress, and was good at reciting, her mother contacted her friend Lilian Baylis at the Old Vic, who offered to take Kaye on as a trainee. But Mr Gibbs told Kaye she should aim to write her own plays, and act in them later, so she turned down the chance. But 'from the age of 13, the stories and plays I planned to write remained unwritten because her life [i.e. Ann's] and its incidents so absorbed me'. Later, she did do some amateur acting, with Alec Clunes at the Tavistock Theatre in Southampton Row, 'and I was quite good, but they'd always give me comic parts'. Besides, she said in 1979, 'I've always been fat' (not so, in fact) 'and my mother told me if I was an actress I'd have had to stay on a diet all my life.' In a later era Kaye would have sailed into university. Instead, she came home from Ashburton to find her parents together again. Her father was night editor of the newly revived left-wing *Daily Herald*, for which he designed the original layouts. 'But it was an unhappy time,' Kaye wrote, 'as there were so many rows, and I prayed one or other of them would break it up.'

In 1930, she was taken by her father to be 'finished' in Belgium, deposited with M. Raymond Burnier and his wife at 24 Place Ste Anne, Bruges. 'It was,' wrote Kaye, 'an excruciatingly boring time.' At sixteen she was the epitome of girlish charm, with a mischievous come-hither look in her grey-blue eyes. The loving letters from Ann to 'My own darling baby' and 'My darling babe' were punctuated with what was then new-fangled advice about resisting chocolates and pastry in favour of fruits and salads. 'Take care of your diet – don't overdo the "eats",' Ann would write. 'Remember that "what you eat, you are". If you eat salads, fruits, drink water and lemonade etc, you'll feel fresh and energetic – while if you eat sweets – pastries – drink sweet drinks etc you'll get fat and feel lazy – 'nough said.' There was also more general advice. 'I want you to have a very happy as well as a profitable time. I want your outlook to broaden and your mind to be cultivated in the best way of all – by observation and good reading.' She wasn't to let learning French or anything else worry her. 'Don't get all hot and bothered if you are headachy. Just tell me and I'll write Madame.' Kaye was soon writing to her mother in shorthand and keeping her supplied with 'just the sort of letter I like receiving from my kids – bright and happy and full of information'. Ann was cheered and sent a ten-shilling note when she heard Kaye was playing tennis, swimming and cycling: 'Think how slim you will be!' But Kaye must not forget her 'Williams' Pills for Pale Girls' when having her period, and to 'tell Madame you have to keep quiet for a day or so'. Ann's earnest hope was that Kaye should meet an eligible young man. Having met such a chap in London, Ann wrote: 'This is the type of young man I like you to know, my dear.'

Like many daughters, Kaye became her mother's confidante. Ann reported that her little brother John 'is going to be a considerable worry to me I'm afraid . . . his report last term was shocking – shocking – I really don't know what to do to buck him up.' Also, she'd heard that Bill, who had gone to Paris on leaving school, to be a photographer's assistant at Pacific & Atlantic Photos in the rue Lamartine, still couldn't speak any French. He was in Paris 'for the express purpose of learning the b . . . y language'. Should she summon him home? 'He can learn the news-business in London, and it won't cost so much.' One day while in Paris, Bill went to Longchamps racecourse in the Bois de Boulogne and won a wad of francs; from then on he was hooked on the horses. One weekend he left Paris, arrived at his mother's house without warning, explaining that he had won a bit on the Derby, and whisked her off to see a show called *Petticoat Influence*. 'Wasn't that a wonderful surprise?' wrote the doting Ann.

As for Kaye's father, he was finding his *Herald* job 'rather trying'. So was Ann, since Arthur was under her feet all day. 'I get a good bit of Dad these days. He doesn't go in the office until 6 o'clock and hangs around all the afternoon – I do wish he would play golf or do something – it is getting on my nerves.' Other family members were also irksome. Ann's elder sister Mabs and her daughter Kitty were constantly bickering, and Ann, who had some inherited money, sent them to live on the Continent. 'I'd rather pay than have them with me.'

Ann was always busy – with bridge, theatre-going and film reviewing ('I have to get my Racy Reviews off today') – and always opinionated. When Princess Margaret was born, she commented scathingly, 'What do you think of the little Duchess? Keeping all the world waiting for three weeks on the tiptoe of expectation of an heir to the throne – and then producing another daughter!' To Ann, only boys mattered.

She did try to boost Kaye's social confidence, even if it

conflicted with her warnings about starch in the diet, which only exacerbated Kaye's anxiety about her figure. 'Now my dear – don't start worrying about being fat and comparing yourself with Peggy Endicott because she happens to be slim. You are different types entirely. If you try to emulate her you'll lose your particular charm – which believe me is just as potent as Peggy's – if not more so.' Slender herself, Ann assured her daughter that she was 'a sweet kid, and bonny too'. She sent her a beach hat, silk suits, a tennis dress ('I will mark it "worn and soiled" so you won't have to pay any duty') and material for making beach pyjamas: 'You have to make the legs very wide and a loose little bodice with braces'.

In July she was advising Kaye to be discreet when flirting with someone named Fred, 'not to offend Madame'. Another young man named Peter had already claimed her daughter's affections, which Ann encouraged. 'Peter sounds an absolute darling – isn't it delicious being "in love". Tell him to phone me – Hampstead 5635 – if ever he is in London and I'll be delighted to see him.' In striped blazer and white flannels, Peter survives as a small black-and-white snapshot signed 'With dearest love to Kaye – Peter' in April 1930.

In September, Ann told Kaye that Dad was keen for his daughter to enter a contest in the *News Chronicle*. She must write an essay on Mr Churchill's articles in the *Daily News*.* 'I think you might stand a chance,' Ann wrote. 'It might tell in your favour your being only 16.' She was sure Peter would be thrilled if Kaye landed a job on the paper: 'I'm sure, from the way you describe his type, that he wants more in a girl than mere good looks.' Ann would 'try and think of an arresting way of beginning it. Something that will strike the examiners as being original.' So what, if rules

* The national newspaper founded in 1846, originally edited by Dickens, and shortly to be merged with the *News Chronicle*.

stipulated that parents guarantee the essay to be 'the unaided work of the entrant'? 'I can do that as I shan't materially alter anything you write. Anyhow, I couldn't improve on your work – you are much better than I am nowadays.' Nothing came of this plan, however, as Kaye was too young to enter. In the meantime Ann urged Kaye to emulate herself, rather than Arthur.

'Both you and I, darling, love to be liked. We would do quite a bit to create good impressions . . . but we both have a fundamental honesty . . . Don't, my dear, like your father, just make a contradictory statement, in a boorish manner, so that you become intensely disliked.'

Ann had mapped out Kaye's life on her return. 'I think you should have a couple of weeks shorthand every day – then try for a job somewhere and join a literary society for one evening, music for another, dancing for another, pictures with your Mummy for another and bridge or something that turns up for the other two. I should like you to take a course in cutting out – so that you can make your own gowns with a touch of distinction. I feel sure that you and I are going to have a happy life together dear if only we are left in something like peace.'

Towards the end of Kaye's time in Bruges, Ann sent word that Arthur wanted a few days in Paris with his daughter. 'I wish he had not asked but he has been alone all his hols and seems to think nobody loves him etc. You know what he is!' Kaye demurred, and Ann's next letter insisted that Kaye ditch a date with Peter and go to Paris instead. 'Dad makes few requests of you and after all he does <u>everything</u> for you.' On the journey through France, she warned: 'I trust you will be a cautious girl and not speak to a soul or allow anyone to stand you a drink or café etc as you never know – that is the way girls are lost for ever.'

3: What Kaye Did Next

1930—39

Both parents steered Kaye towards journalism. In an astute move, Ann got Kaye to do her film reviews while she visited Bill in Paris. There wasn't much to it, she told Kaye: no need even to see the films. 'Only a few lines each, about the story. Get the stuff from KL weekly.' 'That gave me a kind of confidence,' wrote Kaye. But at sixteen, she still hankered after a stage career. Ann's friend W. Macqueen Pope, author of many books on the theatre, wrote a letter of introduction to the leading actor-manager Sir Gerald du Maurier, and Kaye was told to turn up at the St James's Theatre★ on a certain day. She arrived at King Street, feeling she was at the crossroads of her life. Several hundred young men and girls were already there for a mass audition. The doorkeeper assumed Kaye had come to join them, so she did. As she got within earshot of the stage, her self-assurance evaporated. 'I watched magnificent young women swing confidently on to the stage and start tearing themselves to tatters, only to be interrupted in the middle of a sob with a "Thank you, dear, that'll be all." Delicious little creatures played through whole comedy scenes, then stood in a circle of light while another voice from the darkness said, "Can we see the legs please?" followed by a "Thank you, dear".' Kaye wrestled with cowardice and panic. But if she backed out now she would lose her chance of glory. So when her name was called, she stepped from the wings.

★ A fine Victorian building, demolished in 1957 despite dramatic protests by thespians.

'I felt like a child just born, like a criminal about to be condemned, like the most alone person in all the world.' Around her was the empty stage, the footlights illuminating her wrinkled stockings, her tidy blue suit and flat-heeled shoes: she felt 'charmless, powderless and speechless – absolutely sick with fright'. 'Make me a willow cabin at your gate,' she began. She managed to recite twelve lines of Viola's speech to Olivia from *Twelfth Night* before a voice said, 'Thank you, dear' (with a hint of laughter, she suspected). They hadn't even asked to see her knees ('which were quite good, if I bent them a little'). And so she learned that miracles don't happen, went back to her shorthand and typing lessons, joined an amateur dramatic society, and answered an advertisement in *The Times* for an office girl.

The office had a Fleet Street address. Fleet Street was then the centre of the printed world, home of national papers, news agencies, the regional press and humble trade journals. The *Paint Manufacturing Journal* placed her on the lowest rung of the ladder: 15s a week to tie on labels, and deliver parcels and messages. But it was Fleet Street. 'Just walking down Fleet Street, thinking "I'm actually here" and getting a poached egg on toast for fourpence-ha'penny at the ABC' was thrilling. She branched out into *Mickey Mouse* magazine, writing letters signed 'Mickey' to the child readers, at twopence a letter. 'Hello everybody! Mickey has shown me so many clever poems, drawings and riddles from our readers that we have decided to give you all a chance to prove what you can do! Here are four splendid competitions with first-rate prizes . . . So "pull up your socks" and "get down to it"!' Then she became editor's secretary at the weekly magazine *Picturegoer*. Rossiter Shepherd obviously wanted her, because he ignored her poor shorthand skills with 'Brush it up and start next week.' She was 'George the Inquiry Man', answering movie fans' queries about their favourite stars. She also answered readers' letters as a sob sister, though she hardly knew herself what they meant – especially if they asked, 'Could I be pregnant?' – and she had to enlist Ann's help.

In 1933, aged nineteen, she was asked to produce *The Picturegoer's Who's Who and Encyclopaedia*. This was advertised as having '2,000 biographies of British film stars' – which it was up to her to provide. At that time 2,000 British film stars did not yet exist. So she contacted every single name on the cast list of every film, including obscure walk-on players, who were gratified to be included. This is now a highly collectable book, with red cover, gilt lettering, and ninety-four photographs.

On *Picturegoer* she got office passes to every cinema, and met her first film stars. Leslie Howard told her all about Hollywood, when she went to show him the proofs of an interview. She called on Ivor Novello and found him sitting on a sofa holding hands with a man: her colleagues hooted with laughter at her embarrassment. In the next few years, in the offices of Odhams Press in Long Acre, Covent Garden, she worked at *Kinematograph Weekly* and *The Broadcaster*, then *The Sportscar*; and at twenty-one, she was Lady Editress of *Caravan World*, though 'I'd never been in a sportscar or a caravan in my life'. She often had to get help on layout from her dad, and from kind bosses. 'Life,' she said, 'was a series of bluffs.' What was it about Kaye that always made people want to help her? 'Well, I work very hard, and I think they sense that, and I'm pretty conscientious,' she later said, 'and I'm hopeful.'

Her brother Bill was also at Odhams (later absorbed into IPC), which owned the *Daily Herald*, the *People* and *Sporting Life*, the paper where Bill, the racing fanatic, found a natural home. In July 1933 Kaye was on holiday in Guernsey when he wrote to say 'the office seems an awful bore without you' and to tell her Odhams were planning a woman's paper: their first colour weekly, *Woman*, was launched in 1937. But Kaye never did work

on 'a woman's paper'. Instead she joined two magazines that
furnished her with an education in politics and literature, a lively
social life and an introduction to some of the finest writers and
artists of the day.

Her twenty-first birthday party in 1935 was 'cataclysmic on
mother's side, too detailed to explain, but felt guilty'.* Kaye had
got engaged for the first time at nineteen, but broke it off; she
continued to 'get engaged now and then', her mother's example
doubtless leading her to encourage multiple admirers. It did not
protect her from falling for a complete rogue.

She succumbed to the dubious charms of a boyish-looking
paint salesman named Kit Brierley, spoiled son of well-to-do
parents, whom she met in some kind of club on 27 September
1937. Something about the bullying, petulant tone of the letters
which began arriving from his various addresses (a bedsitting
room in Marylebone, a boarding-house in Maida Vale, a hotel in
Liverpool, a Soho club) instantly suggests a shady operator. Kit
professed himself jealous of her other suitors, but from the first
he was determined that she was 'THE girl for me' and he was in
deadly earnest. 'I have kicked about the world for too long, &
have experienced too much, to dive wildly into something that
might so vitally affect not only my happiness but yours as well.'
Soon he was calling her 'Sweetheart' and reacting huffily to her
suggestion that he should use Nivea for his complexion. His face
might not have launched a thousand ships, he retorted, but 'it
has faced the battle and the breeze. It doesn't want to resemble a
lady's lily-white hand, it is proud of its natural rugged beauty.'

Ann smelt a rat, and discouraged the romance. 'I do think

---

*Late in life Kaye Webb made some notes on her youth but never wrote a
memoir. She leaves us no further information than Ann's insistence that her
old lover Fitzpatrick, Bill's father, be among the guests.

though,' wrote Kit peevishly, 'that she might have given a bit more weight to the fact that you are no longer a child and also that, if I were the sort of person who might do anything to hurt you, I would not have been open enough to write to her as I did. After all – if you and I had decided upon a certain course of action, we would have plenty of opportunity of carrying it out without spending the weekend together.' Within a month he had proposed and was accepted, though the image he had of her ('My darling little sweetheart', 'my precious') suggests that he barely knew her. 'Oh darling, I can't tell you how I feel when I think of you being my Darling little wife with your sweet nature and your adorable ways and all the other lovely things that go to make up you.' At the register office, he was asked if he was really over twenty-one. 'I am going to write to my Mum this evening and tell her all about it.' His mother in Cheltenham sent a cheque for £25 as a wedding present. His father clearly voiced disapproval, necessitating a response 'couched in no uncertain terms . . . which will either calm him down or result in my being cut off with the proverbial shilling'.

Never mind – how happy they were going to be! They would never have any really serious rows, Kit was sure. They were meant for each other; he had never doubted it since the moment they met. So Kaye was married to Christopher Eustace Desmond Brierley at Hendon register office on 27 December 1937. Nine weeks later, in March 1938, Kit went off to India to sell his paint. He promised he would soon arrange to send for her. But almost at once, his letters stopped. No money arrived. Kaye realized that Kit was 'not quite honest' and possibly 'a bit alcoholic'. Had she already been pregnant when they married? She certainly had an abortion (or a miscarriage, she later said), soon after Kit's departure.

Luckily for her, she had landed on her feet professionally, in two pioneering magazines, *Lilliput* and *Picture Post*, whose offices were a nest of singing birds. *Lilliput*, pocket-sized and irreverent, was launched in August 1937 by a young Hungarian refugee, Stefan Lorant. Lorant was a gifted photographer who had already pioneered photo-journalism in Germany. He claimed to have given Marlene Dietrich her first film test and had been imprisoned by Hitler for six months in 1933. The ideas for *Lilliput* were Lorant's, but its title, and the £1,200 cash, came from a petite, elegant, keen-eyed young woman named Alison Blair, née Hooper. She had been to Girton, Cambridge, married, and had two children. Her father had edited the *Calcutta Statesman* and she had the distinctive upper-class manner and accent of one raised under the Raj. She was also Lorant's lover, and became Kaye's confidante.

Lilliput was an immediate success. While a highbrow readership was served by Stephen Spender and Cyril Connolly's *Horizon*, and Claud Cockburn's *Night and Day*, *Lilliput* was in Kaye's words 'a magazine for fairly intelligent people, the duffel-coat brigade'. It reflected a nation fighting for its life against the fascists, but made light of gas-masks, blackouts, rationing, all the dangers and discomforts of civilian life in wartime. It laced its mockery of Hitler, and its warnings about the threat of war, with drawings by the cartoonists Anton, Brockbank, David Langdon, Vicky and David Low, and soon overtook *Punch* in circulation. Each issue cost more to produce than the selling price – sixpence, like Allen Lane's early Penguins. Within months Blair and Lorant were out of cash. Their saviour was the South African-born Sydney Jacobson, later a war hero, Labour MP and life peer, who arrived in October 1937 to be assistant editor and invested his gratuity in the magazine.

Lorant had brought to *Lilliput*, from the German magazine *Der Querschnitt*, mischievous and ironic photo juxtapositions: a picture of Dr Goebbels at home was printed side by side with a lemur and her young; Hannen Swaffer in dressing-gown, with fag in mouth, next to a film extra in friar's outfit, also with fag; an aged crone next to a newborn baby; a bug-eyed Belgian grison dog, juxtaposed with a bug-eyed South American general with identical expression; Neville Chamberlain displayed alongside his lookalike, one Cyril Herbison, 'a Lancashire man'. Every photograph made some kind of statement, even the rumps of horses in statues and in real life, and the cleavages and naked breasts of exotic dancers or bathing beauties with healthy smiles – something for soldiers to pin above their bunks. (It always irritated Kaye that this feature was what people most mentioned about *Lilliput*.)

In the summer of 1938, Hultons bought *Lilliput* and launched *Picture Post*, a large-format photo-journalism magazine, with Lorant as first editor. It too was an instant success, soon selling two million copies a week. From the start, *Picture Post* campaigned against the persecution of Jews in Nazi Germany. In November 1938 they ran a picture story entitled 'Back to the Middle Ages': photographs of Hitler, Goebbels and Goering were contrasted with the faces of the scientists, writers and actors they were persecuting. At *Picture Post*, Kaye briefly became secretary to Lionel 'Bobby' Birch, a dashing and legendary Fleet Street figure. But within months she moved to *Lilliput* to become Sydney Jacobson's secretary – and quickly proved she had editorial skills. In May 1940 she suggested that the captions to a series of photographs on the theme 'The Promise of Spring' (to take people's minds off war) might quote from a letter D. H. Lawrence wrote to Lady Cynthia Asquith in 1916. D.H.L. wrote: 'When I see the lambs skip up from the grass into the sharp air, and flick their legs friskily at the sky, then really, I see how absurd it is to grieve and persist in melancholy . . .' Kaye's suggestion 'made Lorant decide that I could be trusted'.

Lorant edited the two magazines in tandem until July 1940, when, having failed to get British citizenship, he emigrated to

Massachusetts, followed by his lover Alison Blair.★ Sydney Jacobson and Lionel Birch volunteered for the army. 'So there was a gap,' wrote Kaye, 'which I would fill.' But there was no question of her becoming editor. A letter from Maxwell Raison, general manager of Hulton Press, dated 16 August 1940, denied that Kaye's meeting with him had been 'stormy' but said he could not agree to her taking the editorship of *Lilliput*. 'It was certainly a surprise to find your name on the paper as assistant editor because the appointment had not been mentioned to anyone, but I cannot blame you for that, and I certainly wish you well with the job.' An acting editor would be appointed shortly, 'pending further news of Mr Lorant'. Tom Hopkinson, a blue-eyed charmer newly divorced from the novelist Antonia White, and an inspired editor later knighted for services to journalism, duly took over Lorant's role, with Kaye as his assistant. 'And what incredible chances and challenges that offered me,' she wrote. She was the only girl in the office, after Alison's departure, and 'a lively and attractive girl' too, as Hopkinson remembered. They nurtured new artistic and literary talent, regular contributors including Honor Balfour, Macdonald Hastings (who wrote the witty 'Lemuel Gulliver' column), Anne Scott-James and Charles Fenby. Forty-five years later Kaye edited *Lilliput Goes to War*, an anthology which conveys the freshness and exuberance of the magazine.

While Kaye settled into this professionally fulfilling office – just off Fleet Street, at 43 Shoe Lane – her private life was a mess. Her cables to Kit Brierley were ignored. Then a letter arrived from Corstophans Hotel, Simla, dated 3 October 1938. Kit said he kicked himself for being such a fool, but he had been through 'absolute hell'. In Lahore, he had entrusted his letters to a hotel

---

★Lorant pursued a successful writing career in the US and died in 1997. Alison Blair wrote a fictional account of their affair, *Of Former Love*, in 1951.

bearer who must have pocketed the stamp money ('the swine'). His firm's Bombay office wanted fuller explanations of 'various schemes I was initiating'. Kit was indignant: he had been 'slaving away for 12 hours a day in the hottest part of India at the hottest part of the year' and had written 'an absolute stinker' to head office 'who know nothing of life in India'. The stress had given him a nervous breakdown: 'I lay in bed or sat on a chair for hours on end without being able to bring myself to talk to anyone, or read or write or do anything at all; and then, for no particular reason, I would burst into tears – most humiliating.' A doctor friend brought sedatives, and he was fit again now.

'My troubles were not at an end though because, shortly after leaving Lahore, I had an accident with the car, knocking down an Indian woman.' He had taken the woman to hospital, driven the police to the scene of the accident, and tried to collect witnesses. A doctor said the woman, having only a broken leg and slight concussion, would probably recover. But while they were talking, 'somebody came along to say that she was feeling worse: we rushed to her bedside and, to my horror, were just in time to see her die (from shock). I can't tell you how awful I felt.' Luckily, the local magistrate sympathized with Kit. The dead woman's middle-aged sons were sent for, agreed to accept 200 rupees in compensation, and made no claim against him. So there would be no court proceedings, 'but the whole thing was such a nightmare that I still dream about it'.

He was still promising to send for Kaye. It was the anniversary of their first meeting on 27 September the previous year. 'Did you remember? I thought of that first meeting in the Club and the funny feeling I had that you were the only girl in the world and would eventually be my Wife.' He recalled 'that day at Brighton and our first weekend at Nettlebed, when I felt so awful at having offended you and yet couldn't bear the idea of being away from you even for a night: and then our wedding and the flat at the St Regis – oh beloved, why do we have to be away from each other like this.' He sent 'a piece of paper' (a 10s note) and was sorry it wasn't more.

The war had begun, more than fourteen months later, when Kit, now a Lieutenant in the Royal Indian Navy, wrote from HMIS *Hiravati*, c/o the Navy Office, Cochin, to Arthur Webb. It was a letter of hollow contrition. 'I can't tell you how ashamed I am at the way I've treated Kaye,' he wrote. He had 'got in with the wrong sort' in Bombay, drank too much, got into debt, couldn't afford to bring Kaye out to join him, 'and then hadn't courage and was too ashamed to write to Kaye and explain what was the matter.

'I would like to apologize to you and to Mrs Webb for behaving like a cad and causing so much worry and unhappiness. I would do anything to put things right again . . . If I say that I still love Kaye and have always loved her, I expect it will be dismissed as nonsense in view of what I have done.' He had also treated his own parents badly 'through my own stupidity and my habit of trying to evade unpleasant facts'.

That, mercifully, was almost the last the Webbs heard of Kit Brierley. But marriage is harder to get out of than into, and it took Kaye three years to ditch him. Brierley was served with divorce papers (through the Admiralty) in June 1941 in Bombay. On 12 August that year came a mysterious reply to Kaye from her solicitor, Theodore Goddard: 'Dear Miss Webb. The answers to the points which you raise are as follows. (a) You cannot. (b) Yes, but I think you would be unwise to take that step.' Not until 13 July 1942 was a divorce granted to Kathleen Brierley on the grounds of her husband's desertion without cause for three years. Expediting the decree absolute cost her £275 7s 10d and an extra 6 guineas, the King's Proctor's fee. The intervention of the King's Proctor was necessary because she was already living with the man who would become her second husband.

She wrote to thank her barrister, Victor Russell, who responded warmly, wishing her happiness. 'My clients are like ships that pass in the night but you are one of the ships I shall remember and I shall look forward more than ever to future *Lilliputs*.' She was hoping to wrest some of the divorce costs from Kit. Her brother John, who had been a golfing correspondent on the *Evening Standard* until he joined up on the day war broke out, was now serving in India. He promised to 'do my damnedest to collect something from the devil'. A year later she was able to tell her father, 'Great news – J. managed to extract some dough from Kit. I've never been so surprised in all my life. But gather it took a lot of time and trouble, bless his heart.'

Letters of congratulation on her divorce came from Kit's own family in Cheltenham, guilty about not having warned her off their ne'er-do-well son. Kit's mother wrote: 'I needn't say how much we rejoice to think you are free of such a worthless person as Kit. Whatever else I forgive him, I will never forgive him his treatment of you . . . But I doubt if we ever see or hear anything of him ever again. I have schooled myself to feel <u>nothing</u> where he is concerned – almost incredible (but a fact) when you think of the heartaches he's given me. Well, you'll understand, if no one else does . . . Think I told you we've cut him off in our wills, except for the little he must have under settlement.

'Well Kaye dear, I do hope much happiness is just round the corner for you. Choose warily this time!!' (She adds that she sends the 'first-rate' *Lilliput* to her daughter Ursula, who sends it on to the troops, 'so I feel the expenditure is more than justified'.) Ursula too wrote to Kaye: 'It seems kinda funny to be congratulating someone so heartily on getting free from one's own brother, but that's how it is.'

The new man in Kaye's life was Andrew Keith Hunter, a fellow old pupil of Ashburton, two years her junior, who had won the school prize for English in 1933. One day in the summer of 1937, just before she met Brierley, Kaye was on a bus when Keith, an engineering student at London University, recognized her distinctive voice. The following summer, when Kaye was already despairing of hearing from Kit, Keith was in the RAF, recovering from a plane crash off Portland Bill, his hands badly burned. Kaye rushed off to visit him in hospital.

Keith was the antithesis of Kit. At nine, he had been shipped home (from India, where his father was a journalist) to board at Ashburton, and to fend for himself. He was blessed with a warm, happy, inquisitive nature, instantly liked by everyone, with a dazzling smile and gentle manners. He wrote to Kaye in May 1938 from the Officers' Mess at RAF Hullavington, Chippenham, Wilts. Her letter, with a snapshot that hardly did justice to her 'distinctive and very attractive personality', had made 'my already cheerful spirits soar to those rare heights which made mere existence seem a privilege'. He said her busy life reminded him of Finals, and enthused about the pleasure her letters gave, having 'natural warmth, with a hint of impulsiveness! Which is typically Kaye.' In March 1939 she sent him an inscribed copy of *The Yearling* by Marjorie Kinnan Rawlings, and their romance began. That summer they drove to the south of France, returning via Paris, where they stayed at a small hotel which, they realized after a disturbed and noisy night, was actually a brothel. She became 'My Darling Kathleen', 'My darling beloved', 'Darlingest'. 'You know I love you,' he wrote, 'you know I adore you, but I wonder if you know how essentially you are a part of me.'

Just after the 'phoney war' began, he was writing her loving letters from various RAF stations. 'There is hardly need to ask of the quality or quantity of our happiness compared with the "poor wretches" now rushing into these "war weddings" . . . thinking about the heavenly nights we've spent together . . . I could go on and on and on raving about your perfection.' Her letters left him 'spellbound' with their 'expressions of such perfect love'. 'How perpetually fresh the word darling remains between us, doesn't it?'

4: Kaye's Lilliputian War

1940–45

On 15 July 1942, at Hendon again, Kaye became the wife of Wing-Commander Andrew Keith Hunter. He was twenty-five, Kaye twenty-eight, a handsome couple whose smiles, as they gaze at each other in photographs, are unmistakably adoring.

'Hoohrah! Cheers! Good egg!!' brother John wrote from Bangalore. Brother Bill, who remembered Keith from school as 'a dear fellow', was sure Kaye would be happy this time 'and even if it did cost a lot of dough I expect it was a sound investment. You should get a good marriage allowance and a decent pension if Keith should happen to get knocked off. Which is very unlikely of course, at the Wing-Commander stage.' Bill himself had married and was, since January 1940, the father of a baby boy, John Patrick, known as 'Dumps'.

Kaye lost weight, thanks to gastric flu, and managed only 'a vain attempt to have a honeymoon' which was 'not exactly restful'. Although she dutifully darned Keith's socks, which bore her trademark green wool for years afterwards, the bride and her Wing-Commander had no more than a few days together before he was sent overseas. Keith proved a brave airman: he was awarded the OBE during the war and was mentioned in dispatches on three occasions.

The war, as Kaye wrote, put a rocket under her career. *Lilliput*'s popularity enabled her to 'ring up anyone I liked and invite them to contribute'. She approached all the literary luminaries of the day, including George Bernard Shaw, Ernest Hemingway, C. S.

Forester, Osbert Sitwell, John Betjeman, H. G. Wells and Max Beerbohm (who said yes because he 'couldn't resist' her letter). In May 1942, from his cottage near Dorking, Beerbohm wrote: 'Dear Miss Kaye Webb, Here is my little thing about Caran d'Ache. It is just about 870 words. Will you please specially endorse my direction to the printers about my punctuation and my division of paragraphs? – things which I hold sacred.' The PS to this letter is 'Do forgive me for having thought you were a man.'

Everyone wanted to appear in *Lilliput*. '*Punch* still didn't use by-lines, and writers would always rather have a shop window,' Kaye wrote. 'We like our cartoonists recognizable – we like to be able to say "That's a Langdon" or "That's a Searle".' A young soldier named Ronald Searle had sent in some schoolgirl cartoons in 1941, which everyone liked. Franta Belsky was another new cartoonist, a young Czech whose English wife Margaret did the drawings. Gerard (then Gerhard) Hoffnung, 'a fat boy with a very gruff voice', aged fifteen, son of affluent Jewish parents who arrived in London from Berlin in 1939, sent in drawings from Highgate School. Kaye didn't really like them, 'but Tom insisted he had genius,' she wrote, 'which indeed he had, so we kept on using him'. ('I am all excited,' young Hoffnung wrote to Hopkinson, 'and I keep on jumping about in the House.')

Ideas poured into the office, and Kaye noted how they tended to come in waves. 'We have had twenty cartoons of a BBC announcer sitting in front of a microphone wearing a sou'wester while he says "And here is a gale warning", or some variation on the idea.' It happened with stories too: one month a load of tales about a talking horse, or a singing dog; another month a spate of mysterious train journeys that don't stop at the usual station but roll on into ghostly country.

But Kaye had to be tenacious to cling on to her job. An unsigned letter dated 19 November 1942 states, regarding 'Mrs

Kathleen Hunter (Kathleen Brierley)': 'Mrs Hunter is Assistant Editor of *Lilliput*, and she also assists with editorial work for *Picture Post*, the staffs of the two papers having been merged since the war. Mrs Hunter is the only person remaining on our staff who has had long contact with *Lilliput*, and who is able to deal with the photographs and with the handling of the magazine for press. In present circumstances Mrs Hunter is indispensable to *Lilliput* and we wish to make the strongest possible claim for retaining her services. There would be practically no possibility of replacing her in present conditions.'

Contributors wandered into the office in Shoe Lane. 'Stevie Smith brought in her poems. V. S. Pritchett was nice enough to allow me to reshape one of his articles because it wasn't what Tom wanted, and he said my name should be on it. John Pudney would come in and talk about ideas, and we would go on to the rooftop and pretend there was no war on at all.' It was an agreeable time. She was in the centre of a vibrant, talented coterie of poets, writers and artists, who flourished in the hedonistic wartime atmosphere of blacked-out Soho and Fitzrovia.

'If only I had kept a diary of those days,' she later wrote. She took the sculptor Henry Moore to lunch, to discuss the captions to his powerfully moving drawings of people sleeping in the Underground bomb-shelters, later bought for the nation. She cabled a young poet named Laurie Lee, then living in a caravan in Sussex near the grand home of his rich, married, well-connected mistress, Lorna Wishart, to tell him they were sending Bill Brandt down to photograph him. (It was a poetic portrait, Laurie seated under a tree looking dreamy and smoking a pipe. 'Saw your phiz in *Lilliput*,' his fond mother Annie wrote, from Slad.)

She invited Dylan Thomas, whose *Portrait of the Artist as a Young Dog* she had just read, to write picture captions; he was thrilled to get £15, and offered to do lots more. His wife Caitlin having decamped to Wales, Dylan was free to roam the bars of Soho, and he took Kaye to the French pub (the York Minster), the Swiss, the Gargoyle and the Colony Room. Drunken binges, which had already so damaged his liver that he was unlikely ever to be called up, did not deter Dylan from being an incorrigible seducer, but Kaye was warned off him by *Picture Post* colleagues, who told her he had venereal disease. 'So it ended as suddenly as it began,' said Kaye.

Dylan introduced her to the poet and artist Mervyn Peake, a striking figure, with dark eyebrows beetling over wary, watchful eyes. When Kaye later tried to marshal her memories for possible memoirs, she was vague about dates. 'I think it was the year 1941, and I think the Soho pub was called The French House,' she wrote in 1986 to Brian Sibley, who sought recollections of Peake. 'Dylan, with whom I had first visited The York Minster, said: "Kaye, you must meet this chap, he's a marvellous artist and I don't know why you aren't using him in *Lilliput*" or words to that effect, and I found myself looking at a long, thin, disorderly looking man, with intense eyes and very black hair, who was both excited and embarrassed by the introduction and immediately tried to brush it off.

'However, we went on talking, until there was a Dylan-triggered skirmish, when Mervyn broke off to go to his aid, but by that time I had his address. Next week I sent him a story to illustrate, and by return came a haunting drawing of a drowning man. After that we became friends. One memory I have is of sitting with him in the Café Royal (in those days you could stay there for hours with one sandwich and a drink) while he talked about his plans for *Gormenghast*, and another when we were both suddenly intoxicated by the general excitement, hopelessness and danger of the time we were living in, and literally achieved a sort of waltz all the way down Regent Street. It must have been pretty late at night, so nobody stopped us. Perhaps that was the night

when he was AWOL from his barracks in Chelsea and went back
to find part of the floor on fire. He told me later that he'd left a
cigarette burning and was punished for it.'

Peake was as gentle and chivalrous as Dylan was priapic and
volatile. She would invite them both for Sunday lunch of steak
and kidney pudding, consuming several weeks' meat rations. One
night at the Café Royal she was with Dylan, his wife and *Lilliput*'s
editor, Tom Hopkinson, who, an impeccably neat man himself,
was aghast to see Dylan in battered corduroy jacket, with dirty
fingernails. Caitlin, in red taffeta evening dress and gorgeous
flowing hair, ordered plovers' eggs and champagne, and whisked
Hopkinson off to dance, though obviously drunk, 'unsteady on
her feet, raucous and throwing bread about'. A nightmarish evening,
Kaye recalled, after which they had to give the Thomases money
to get back to Putney. Dylan needed a winter coat but hadn't enough
coupons: Kaye said her father had left behind a coat when he went
off to America, 'an evening coat with exaggerated puff sleeves,
which Dylan wore all through the winter with great charm'.

In another reminiscence, shared in 1982 with Hopkinson, Kaye
recalled 'Bobby' Birch: 'Do you remember that occasion when
we were all in the car together going back to either your home
or his, and I was staying the night with him – he was doing his
little amorous fumblings in the back of the car and suddenly said
to me, "Who are you?" I replied, "Kaye," and he said, "Oh,
you're staying with us, you'll keep" and turned his attention to
whoever was on the other side! He always did everything with
such charm and niceness, and he really was such a romantic,
wasn't he?' (Birch was at the time married to the second or third
of his seven wives.) Kaye may have been a left-behind wife, but
she had no shortage of male companions.

One young man she met through *Lilliput* was Maurice
Edelman, who arranged her first broadcast in 1942, interviewing
him about his book *How Russia Prepared*, a Penguin Special. Forty

years later Edelman's sister Sophia told Kaye she had always been curious about her: 'I know there was a special friendship between you and Maurice and your name floated around my visits to London.' Yes, Kaye admitted, their relationship was 'quite an emotional one', but she could never write about it as it would offend Edelman's wife, Tilly. 'I don't have to tell you how very attractive he was to women. He really only had to lift an eyebrow and think up some suitable compliment to be successful!' (Edelman did have dark and eloquent eyebrows.)

'He also taught me how not to split my infinitives, and for about three years we were really great friends. I used to go down to Amersham sometimes, and of course, sometimes ended up in air-raid shelters.' Kaye 'really adored' him, she said. Together they wrote an adaptation of Alfred de Musset's play *On ne badine pas avec l'amour* (No Trifling with Love). But then Edelman left for North Africa as a war correspondent. Kaye offered their play to the Arts Theatre, without success. She and Edelman had parted as friends, she said, and she hadn't seen him much after the war. 'We once met and had a nice walk in Hyde Park and exchanged memories.'

In December 1944 she befriended the handsome, urbane actor James Mason, educated at Marlborough and Peterhouse, Cambridge, and possessed of a uniquely mellifluous, languid voice. He submitted an article entitled 'Yes, I Beat My Wife', a jokey account of a film star's life. Kaye found it on the reject pile, where a colleague had thrown it, never having heard of Mason. They ran it, illustrated with his own self-caricature, and so began a long friendship with (briefly) romantic overtones.

'I entered a complete new world, a silly girl who really didn't know anything, and I had power, because everyone wanted to be published in *Lilliput*.' It was also Kaye's own chance to learn journalistic skills such as accuracy. Misnaming a Chelsea street in a picture caption of 'London by Moonlight' gave her sleepless nights. Martha Jordan, who had been the Webbs' maid-of-all-work in Hampstead before the war, caught sight of Kaye's name in *Lilliput*. 'Good going Kaye,' she wrote. 'You have gone a long way from the Job you had then, do you remember (Let George Do It★) *Picturegoer*.'

Tom Hopkinson later summed up *Lilliput*'s wartime appeal. 'It made no demands. It did not attack or criticize. It simply made one laugh, providing a couple of hours of easy enjoyment. Writers, artists and photographers seemed happy to work for it despite the ridiculously low fees it paid, and the sales soared.' George Lansbury, the veteran Labour leader, wrote of the pleasures of old age, at eighty-one. Hopkinson found that 'all kinds of well-known people who don't normally write articles – archbishops and admirals, sportsmen and scientists, film stars and prime ministers – have some personal interest they will be happy to write about if asked'.

Kaye, industrious and ambitious, also broadcast book reviews for the Home Service, and snippets for the Ministry of Information entitled 'The World and His Wife'. She wrote to her father about her first broadcast to America, in 1942: 'I know the script was incredibly coy and I thought the recording sounded frightful.' Her voice seemed 'a bit "classy" and completely unlike my own idea of the way I spoke. And it comes out a tone higher.' She wrote for the Middle East edition of *Gen*, a forces newsletter. Her London Letter, at five guineas a time, 'just rattling on about things that were happening in London', was voted its most popular item. 'Wouldn't mind doing something for the American papers,' she told Arthur. 'D'you know anyone who wants a fortnightly or monthly column from England?'

Shortly before Arthur Webb left for the USA in 1941, he had pressed the case for America's entering the war, and invented a name for the document drawn up on an American battleship

★ Kaye's column answering moviegoers' queries.

somewhere at sea by Churchill and Roosevelt, declaring their common principles. Arthur suggested calling it the Atlantic Charter, and under this name it became known to historians. After Arthur left for Washington, Ann lived in Pattison Road, Hampstead, two doors from their former address. 'It seems odd to see the Lenhoffs sitting out in our old garden at 44. Painfully nostalgic,' wrote Kaye to her father. She told Arthur about the England he'd left behind, the 'laughable' train journeys, the country a mass of Canadian and American uniforms. She had been to a Fabian Society summer school at Frensham, an idea she approved of, 'although I'm not, as none of our family are, a great lover of organized fun'. (This statement is rather extraordinary in view of the organized fun that became such a feature of Kaye's Puffin Club life.)

In her free evenings, she did voluntary work: as gas-mask fitter, fire-watcher, and server in the canteen for the troops at Charing Cross station. She was third best shot in the Fleet Street women's rifle brigade – the legendary journalist Evelyn Irons was top – and somehow drove an ambulance, though she never did master reverse gear. She was responsible for 'Street Savings' in Pattison Road, collecting £500 for the Great Savings Week, remarking to her father, 'Did you know there was that much money about?' But she disliked knocking on doors. 'You know how much I liked meeting people and entertaining and so on. Now I actually loathe it . . . Every Sunday morning when I set out with my stamps and my smile to gather in the sixpences my heart sinks. They all want to talk.' War tragedies were coming closer to home. 'Remember nice old Col Thompson? His daughter's fiancé was killed flying four days before they were due to be married. And yesterday they had notification that the eldest daughter's husband was killed, and a few months ago his favourite nephew got it. Mummy said it was like that in the last war. Some families had all the loss and others, like yours and hers, were marvellously lucky. One feels almost apologetic about it.'

Lilliput, she said, in jaundiced mood, 'drags along, I must say without much joy. Tom is really rather difficult to work for (there is no suggestion of working "with"). I, or rather he, has a new man* starting next week, whose function is to improve the literary standard of the paper. I rather dislike the look of him . . . very flabby and ill-looking, another ineffectual' (family code for intellectual) 'unless I'm much mistaken. He is to share my room. Oh lordy me . . .'

'Poor darling mummy' was working for the WVS, despite a weak heart. She became a star of WVS quizzes, and got into the London final – a signal achievement, said Kaye: 'I rather gathered she carried them along.' Ann was also paying the family's former housemaids, Elsie and Kath, on what Kaye termed 'the Webb pension list'. One of them 'does odd bits of dressmaking and comes over for dinner at least once a week and it's my guess Mummy pays her rent . . . and even then she rings and asks if we can spare 4s.' (Her brothers both felt people took Ann's largesse for granted.) 'It's really getting to be a bit of a drain on Mummy.'

Arthur wrote cheeringly to his 'darling daughter'. He told her he'd given President Roosevelt a copy of *Lilliput* during a White House press conference, and the president laughed happily at David Langdon's drawing captioned 'Is your journey really necessary?'† Delighted by her remarriage, Arthur hoped Kaye would soon get a passage out to join Keith; but she was not to get despondent if

---

* John Symonds was the biographer of 'the wickedest man in the world', Aleister Crowley. Later Symonds wrote children's books, published by Kaye in Puffins, including *Elfrida the Pig*, illustrated by Edward Ardizzone. He died aged ninety-two in 2006, still jogging on Hampstead Heath.

† It showed a queue of commuters at a railway ticket office, spying the notice on the wall 'Is your journey really necessary?' and adopting attitudes of deep thought, obviously pondering whether or not they really needed to go to the office. Kaye later included the drawing in her *Lilliput Goes to War* anthology.

she couldn't. 'We can't all get what we want in this world . . . Just think how much worse things might be than they are . . . I have had more disappointments than most. I never got what I wanted out of life. And now I never shall. But what does it matter, there is a job to be done, and events are bigger than us.' He apologized for this ad hominem advice. 'But I always got an extra job to do when I felt most blue and most despondent about things. It didn't solve anything of course but one hadn't time to brood about things one couldn't alter.'

Kaye's two brothers, both serving abroad, in Ceylon and India, kept her informed of their feelings about the war. Bill's letters were long, charming, philosophical, self-deprecatory about getting stout – his pre-war thirty-eight-inch waist now measured forty-three inches – and his hair going white: 'Alas that spring should vanish with the rose . . .' With the RAF in Ceylon he had plenty of time to listen to classical music and to read. 'Go to library and get out the short stories of Saki (H. H. Munro),' he told his sister. 'If you want to forget the war read Balzac's *Splendours and Miseries of a Courtesan*, or *Père Goriot* . . . either of these will make you forget everything.'

One letter from Bill was an essay on whether dramatists' and novelists' work endured if they wrote propaganda rather than about broad human issues: he had read Voltaire, Dos Passos, Sheridan, Shaw, Racine. He congratulated Kaye on doing a brilliant job at *Lilliput*, 'way ahead of your rivals'. But what would become of their generation of Webbs? he wondered. 'I am concerned with the world these days, Kayki . . . We are in the midst of a great struggle, but one places oneself and one's people mentally in place of the Russians and one wonders. Aren't most English people of our generation Kayki too pleasure loving? . . . younger people should discipline themselves, go without the cinema for odd months, pioneer.' Kaye's left-wing sentiments naturally supported the peoples of the Empire, regarding British imperialists as exploitative. Bill took issue with her. 'Remember Empire Builder winning the Molyneux Cup at Ascot?' he wrote. The empire-builders had had no easy task, he declared, and 'pleasure was forfeit'. 'You say these men exploited coloured populations, the material was there beforehand awaiting native development.' Bill thought he knew better. 'The Brown races seldom have sufficient strength of will to inaugurate, conceive anything. Frankly since I've lived abroad in these countries, I haven't much use for them . . .'

Brother John too, now a Captain in the 1st Punjab regiment, found India 'a lousy country and very corrupt'. He wished he could write about it for Percy Cudlipp, his editor at the *Evening Standard*. 'Gandhi is a mental case and damn-fool politicians should come out and spend six weeks here before talking of "promises" and "self determination",' wrote John. After the war, he thought news reporting for the BBC would be 'just my line, what? Who do you know there now, & what are the chances of a little spade-work early on? I think I could be quite good at it.' He'd like to have a settled future, to 'assist early marriage' despite his sweetheart Marjorie having broken it off – 'I would have gambled on it being the real thing, never was so attracted to a girl – oh well!!' In 1943 John was in Lahore, writing to Arthur about the future, and the need for political leadership. Arthur, like Kaye, urged John to think carefully before dismissing the Indians' desire to run their own country. 'Pop I do think about matters very seriously,' he said. For himself, he was just hoping to see some action. 'Three years now and I've not fired a shot in anger at less than 5,000 feet.'

Kaye confided to their father that she hoped John would not 'go getting married or anything on leave'. (Keith's sister had just married 'the "flashest" looking guy I ever did see'.) But John got exactly what he wanted in February 1944: he was appointed adjutant to General Orde Wingate in the second Chindit campaign. 'Whoopee!' he cabled a friend, and assured Arthur: 'I'm not going to be doing anything all that dangerous.' But a month later came another telegram. John had been hit by a grenade while his battalion came under heavy fire, on 22 March 1944 – two days before the death in an air crash of General Wingate. So the Webbs were not, after all, immune from loss. John was buried in a military cemetery in Burma.

The family heard nothing of this for four weeks, but on the night John was killed, Ann Webb had woken up and said, 'One of the boys is calling me, and is in terrible pain.' 'John was the very dearest person in my life,' Kaye wrote – but not until 1975, in a letter. Kaye guiltily recalled that a friend of John's had come to tell her more details of his death, 'but I'm afraid I behaved rather badly because I found everything about it rather unbearable, so I sort of cut him short and turned "social" and I always felt he got the impression that I didn't care . . .' Arthur Webb was in Washington when he heard the news. Arthur regarded his only son as the one likely to follow in his own journalistic footsteps. 'My dears,' he wrote to the family. 'There is no need of words to say what we all feel. All over the world there are families with empty chairs like the one where John used to sit so carefree and happy.' His letter became a diatribe against power-crazed despots, and the stupidity of Britain's having missed its chances of stopping this war 'when Japan invaded China, when Italy went into Ethiopia, or when Franco raped Spain, we had another chance with Czechoslovakia, we missed them all'.

Arthur persuaded himself, as do many parents after such a loss, that some good must come of it. 'I can't help thinking that John's loss isn't just a personal one. He and all those like him who have laid down their lives cannot have done so in vain. Out of it all must come some good for little mites like Bill's child.' Arthur later fulfilled his noble intention, privately financing the training of two young journalists who showed the kind of promise John had.

In July that year Arthur left Bretton Woods, where Maynard Keynes and the bankers were planning 'an International Bank &

Monetary Fund', and headed off to spend his fifty-sixth birthday in Berlin: 'First British correspondent to get there since war started!' Days later he was in Washington reporting the arrival of de Gaulle, striding out of the White House 'stiff-necked and unsmiling'. The General might, Arthur predicted, be 'a thorn in the side of the Allies when victory is won . . . He reminds me of Oswald Mosley who also thought he had all the answers to the world's problems. Both men are dangerous egotists. They are little Hitlers and miniature Mussolinis.'

Arthur never lost his ebullience, or his lively interest in more frivolous topics. That November, he was at the Washington Press Club for a lecture by a Professor Higgins type who could discern, from an accent, exactly where any American was born, even which town. The Prof divined that Arthur's English companion was 'a Middlesex man' – 'How right you are, I was born in Brentford!' – but was entirely stumped by Arthur's diction. He failed to detect 'Islington, or accents acquired in Northumberland with the army, or during my seven years in Dublin, and those picked up wandering round Washington and other American cities. He decided I was English, and had no fixed abode!'

Back home, the war over, Kaye wrote to Sydney Jacobson congratulating him on his MC. 'Kaye, don't get too het up about the gong,' he replied. 'It happens to a lot of other blokes, & it doesn't happen to a lot of other chaps who deserve it more.' He was still in Germany, on the Ruhr. 'A weary, dreary job this, at the tail-end of a war. I'd rather fight the Japs.' Kaye was preparing election leaflets for colleagues standing for Parliament, Maurice Edelman and Tom Driberg.★ 'Tom Driberg has my blessings, Kaye,' wrote Jacobson, 'and you may work for him as hard as you like.'

★ Tom Driberg, later Baron Bradwell, Labour MP for Maldon 1945–55 and for Barking 1959–74.

An article Kaye wrote called 'Peace Comes to Lilliput'
expressed her first peacetime wish: to have an office of her own.
But in every professional respect she had to admit that the war
had been a blessing. True, she had lost her beloved brother, and
the family house had been bombed. 'But I would never have got
to be an editor so quickly, or started broadcasting. The war
opened doors to me, they were looking for talent – and your
adrenalin runs faster when you're frightened.' She had felt guilty
to have such an interesting job, 'while my girlfriends were
yawning their heads off on night duty in the RAF Operation
Rooms, or getting chilblains on Ack Ack sites', and had tried to
atone for it 'by spending my evenings washing mustard off dirty
plates in station canteens'.

'Oh yes,' she would say, 'I was a war profiteer.'

5 : Enter Ronald Searle

Ronald William Fordham Searle was born in Cambridge on 3 March 1920. His father, William, a soldier in World War I, was then a porter on Cambridge station; later he was a post office engineer, and an amateur boxer known as 'Buller' Searle. He had met his wife, who had been in domestic service, in Ireland.

At the age of five Ronald was already a natural artist who found drawing came as automatically as breathing. He drew the family pets – a lurcher, two cats, pet mice, rabbits and a goldfinch – and the milkman's horse. Number 107 Newmarket Road was a cluttered though not a bookish home, but they had a gramophone, and he observed the popular prints on the walls: *When Did You Last See Your Father?*, *The Boyhood of Raleigh*, and *The Porteous Mob*, a vivid scene of an angry crowd. Ronald and his sister Olive, born in 1922, were fascinated by the exhibits in local museums, especially of anatomical peculiarities, the displays of Egyptology, the relics of classical antiquity. In the chalkpits of Cherry Hinton, they collected their own private museum pieces.

Ronald was a good-looking boy, good-humoured and serious, and able to concentrate: the kind who, in a later era, would have been an enthusiastic Puffineer. He became head prefect at his grammar school, worked as a butcher's boy, and sang in the choir and as a soloist. He saw his first copies of *Punch* in the free library in Mill Road, and began to collect comic art and books on draughtsmanship, and Spielmann's *History of Punch*; he spent hours gazing at the Blakes and Turners in the Fitzwilliam. He was one of those rare beings who are, from childhood, focused on a single ambition. Sketching into the night by candlelight, he already displayed a penchant for the grotesque, transfixed by sickening images of surgery and madness.

Later he wrote:* 'I had the inborn advantage of the eccentric, the abnormal seeming to me, as well as to most of those around me, perfectly normal . . . for the first time since the Searles had plodded their way through the bogs to escape the Vikings, a left-handed Searle was proclaiming that he had to be An Artist, instead of a gravedigger, or whatever.'

Further education was out of the question financially. But he paid his way through evening classes at the Cambridge Art School by parcel-packing, and offered his services (at fifteen) to the *Cambridge Daily News*, who accepted his drawings at half a guinea each: more than his week's wages at the packing house. His early drawings were H. M. Bateman influenced, with a touch of Low in the political caricatures and a glance at W. Heath Robinson. His political views were inspired early, as he observed, at home, the parents of the Searles' student lodgers politely patronizing his parents when they collected their offspring.

He depicted himself as The Artist, a bearded youth in sandals, long hair and a battered hat, but infiltrated with ease the gown, as opposed to town, side of Cambridge. He joined the Students' Sketch Club and drew for the undergraduate magazine, *The Granta* (edited in 1938 by Charles Wintour, later editor of the *Evening Standard*), borrowing a gown to infiltrate university meetings. Eric Hobsbawm, *The Granta*'s 1939 editor, says Searle easily blended in with the undergraduate editors on equal terms. 'He had skills we didn't have, and was the only one of us who couldn't be replaced.' He drew the composer Ralph Vaughan Williams, the violinist Fritz Kreisler, the writer Dorothy L. Sayers, and Winston Churchill addressing the Guildhall. He illustrated Arts Theatre programmes. He co-produced and starred

* In *Ronald Searle in Perspective*, New English Library, 1984.

in a revue show, and drew caricatures for an audience of children in the Robins' Club, run by his newspaper. He lugged his portfolio round Fleet Street, without success. In the summer of 1938 he was awarded a scholarship at the art school, where 'it was drummed into us that we should not move, eat, drink or sleep without a sketchbook in the hand'. He enrolled there on 15 September 1938, the day Neville Chamberlain arrived in Berchtesgaden to meet Hitler.

His happy art school life lasted just three terms. A recruiting campaign was launched in Cambridge, and Ronald joined the Royal Engineers as an architectural draughtsman. He was issued with a rifle, keeping a sketchbook in the knee-pocket of his battledress trousers. 'Everything was very black and white. You were anti-Mussolini, you were anti-fascist. When Chamberlain came back waving his piece of paper saying "peace in our time" everyone started digging trenches like mad. No one believed it for a second.' He drew a cartoon of a man in a gas-mask trying to smoke a pipe and eat a sandwich. And he had his first drawing commissioned by a Fleet Street paper, the *Daily Express*, an illustration for a short story called 'The Refugee'.

From 1941 he was stationed (with Hobsbawm) in Scotland, at Kirkcudbright, which had a thriving artistic community that included the Polish-born avant-garde painter Jankel Adler. Here Ronald met two schoolgirls, Cecile and Pat Johnston, daughters of a local artist. They were pupils at a progressive academy, evacuated from Edinburgh for the duration, called St Trinnean's – an old Gaelic name – inspiring his drawings of wickedly delinquent young girls. (St Trinnean's closed in 1946 but its former pupils were forever dogged by the later association with his St Trinian's cartoons.) And in July 1941 he sent some cartoons, by registered post, to 'Miss Kaye Webb, Assistant Editor, Lilliput, 43 Shoe Lane, EC4.' Kaye sent her usual charming reject letter to the first two packages, with the encouraging note, 'I do hope you will send anything else which seems suitable', but she did accept three cartoons, 'including the one about the schoolgirls'. He sent samples of his other drawing styles with a note saying, 'I can draw like this, and this, or this' to show how versatile was his talent. 'If ever you are in London, I do hope you will come and see us,' Kaye wrote, so one day while he was in London that summer, with only two hours before taking his train back to camp, he arrived at Shoe Lane. But Kaye was 'in conference' and her secretary said she saw nobody without an appointment. So he wrote again, to say he was being sent abroad but would send in work whenever he could. Ten years later, in a broadcast, Kaye said it still made her 'hot all over' that she had been oblivious of this thwarted first meeting. 'I had always liked the idea of him,' Kaye said. 'I liked his jokes, and I loved his handwriting.' The handwriting, spidery and italic, and much imitated, has been part of Searle's signature style ever since.

Ronald had embarked, with 5,000 others, on the Polish ship *Sobieski* from Gourock in Scotland, bound for an unknown destination. From Halifax, Nova Scotia, they transferred to an American troopship, and set off on a mysterious three-month circuit taking in Trinidad, South America, South Africa, Kenya, and finally Singapore, arriving in January 1942 to the sound of Japanese planes attacking. Under heavy bombardment, the Malayan mainland had been surrendered to the Japanese, and Singapore island became a temporary refuge, soon encroached upon. During the terrible battle, under fire in a Singapore street, Ronald found in the debris a copy of *Lilliput*, containing his St Trinian's cartoon. The surrender came on 15 February. Ronald became a prisoner of war, one of 50,000 who were marched the fourteen miles to Changi, where they were left to moulder in disease and near-starvation.

At home, Kaye and Tom Hopkinson realized they had not heard from him for some time and had no more of his cartoons in stock. Kaye wrote to the address he'd left and was told that he was missing, believed killed in action, during the fall of Singapore. Kaye remembered feeling acute sorrow, even though they had never met. Even his family in Cambridge knew nothing of his survival for two years.

In the prison camp, Searle carried on sketching, and designed sets for the prisoners' Christmas show. They started a magazine called *The Survivor*, which branded him and his colleagues as trouble-makers, and they were all removed – Searle to Ban Pong and 'The Railway of Death', the Siam–Burma railway, 'and a life of horror'. He was only twenty-two.

Still, he managed to scrounge paper and produce drawings, bribing the guards by promising to draw pornographic pictures. In the jungle, he suffered not only gastro-intestinal illnesses, but ulcers and manges, and later beri-beri, from malnutrition. Many comrades died. He drew the sadistic cruelty of the guards, before the start of each day's eighteen-hour slave labour on the railway, and was often beaten with a pickaxe or bamboo stick. Cholera was a worse threat. One day he woke from a fever to find that the comrades on either side of him had died, and there was a snake under the bundle on which he had rested his head. Tropical ulcers destroyed the flesh on his ankles and hands. His legs were paralysed, he weighed seven stone, and then he got malaria, and was covered in running sores. Everyone thought he was dying. Astonishingly, he kept on drawing. He captured the savagery and squalor of camp life, hiding his drawings, of which 300 survived, under the beds of prisoners suffering from cholera. Luckily guards avoided entering their tents. 'I thought it was important to record what was going on, even if the drawings were only found later,' he said. 'To know what it was like to have been cut off in the jungle thousands of miles from anywhere.'

'When you are shut up in the jungle, your body is so disgusting that you can only live in your head,' he said. 'I remember when we were doing the basic slave labour of carrying stones from one point to another and throwing them over the edge, everyone was chanting nursery rhymes. It was stupid and banal, but it was a way of forgetting what was going on around you. If you had enough imagination to realize what was really happening to you, you'd drop dead immediately. One thing that saved me was a total lack of imagination.'

His incarceration was generally thought to be the key to his bleak humour. His experiences as a PoW never left him. 'These drawings were not a means of catharsis. Circumstances were too basic for that,' he wrote in *To the Kwai – And Back* (the collection of his war drawings, published in 1986). 'But they did at times act as a mental life-belt. Now, with the perspective and detachment that a gap of 40 years or so can achieve, they can be looked on as the graffiti of a condemned man, intending to leave rough witness of his passing through, but who found himself – to his surprise and delight – among the reprieved.'

In 1944 he befriended the Australian cartoonist George Sprod. Together they designed a prison show at the Barn Theatre (Hut 16) where *Cinderella and the Magic Soya Bean* and other shows ran for five nights; Ronald himself played the Ghost in a revue sketch called *Hamlet Goes to Hollywood*. Transferred to Changi Gaol, crammed with 10,000 prisoners in a space built for 600, Ronald was stricken with dengue fever and then malaria again, his fifteenth attack. He drew a kindly portrait of a guard named Ikada, who allowed him to wander to the seaside to draw the natural scene. Sprod reintroduced a camp magazine, *The Exile*, with Ronald as art editor: they produced ten issues, containing many of his cartoons. He had jaundice and hepatitis. Meals might be boiled dog, boiled cat, and – on Christmas Day – three kittens, fried. ('Like rabbit, but more delicate.') In the final months, four years into his incarceration, he lost two of his closest friends and got an abscess in his left calf which grew into a huge ulcerated crater, requiring an operation under anaesthetic.

His good friend and fellow survivor, the Australian writer Russell Braddon, said of him: 'If you can imagine something that weighs six stone or so, is on the point of death . . . calmly lying there with a pencil and a scrap of paper, drawing, you have some idea of the difference of temperament that this man had from the ordinary human being.'

Rations, mainly rice, were reduced still further as the war in Europe ended. The men in Changi felt dispirited and abandoned. Then came the dropping of the atomic bombs, and at last the official surrender, in September 1945, and freedom. Ronald was invited, as the artist behind *The Exile*, to accompany the Mountbattens to Government House, where the port flowed and Lord Louis committed some of Ronald's prison camp stories to his diary that night. On 27 September they set off for home, again in HMT *Sobieski*.

On 5 July 1945, Kaye was sitting in a deckchair among the honeysuckle and rambler roses in her mother's garden at 4 Carlton Road East in Westgate, Kent, typing a letter to her father for his birthday, in a brisk breeze 'that the rhymesters call "playful" and is whisking typing paper about the lawn'. She had been having a hectic time, printing *Lilliput* in Northampton, and editing election papers for the Labour candidates in Coventry East (Richard Crossman) and Coventry West (her friend Maurice Edelman), for whom she was canvassing. She had made the printer re-do Edelman's election address. 'And stuff has got lost on the railways and everywhere everything is in such a muddle one could weep,' she told Arthur. 'However, the spirit of the Labour party people up there is terrific . . . and I think Maurice will get in.' (He did.) 'Heaven knows what my paper will look like if it ever comes out . . . I've been horribly tied . . . I've learnt a great deal about newspaper makeup, even if it is only for a column job. Feeling slightly hag-ridden and will be glad when it is all over.' By 7 July, when the election was over, everyone would be feeling flat 'after all that excitement and hard work and then three weeks to wait for the results'. Ann was helping the local Thanet candidate, addressing 2,000 envelopes. But nobody was sure whether the soldiers would vote Labour as expected.

Their house was 'in a frightful mess' after bomb damage, filthy and chaotic. Keith's father and stepmother were living in Kaye's brother Bill's wife's flat; nobody had any money. Bill hoped to be out of the air force by Christmas. Kaye's car, missing bits which had been pinched, was in Coventry, ready to drive people to the polls on election day. 'I disgraced myself and the family this week,' Kaye told Arthur, 'by broadcasting in a Quiz and not being able to answer the simplest questions, all because of the damned election.'

One Sunday morning later that summer, she read in Tom Driberg's column in *Reynolds News*: 'I have just found Ronald Searle of *Lilliput* in Changi Gaol where he has been a prisoner of the Japanese for three and a half years.' Kaye was ecstatic, 'as excited as if he had been an old friend'. She rushed to tell her mother, who said, 'That's nice, darling, but who is he?' Miss Webb of *Lilliput* was Ronald's best potential contact. He had seen her byline in *Gen*, the forces newsletter, in the prisoners' hospital. A fortnight later, Kaye had a letter saying he would come and see her as soon as he was out of hospital, adding that he had about 170 cartoons from his PoW days.

He then telephoned, but they couldn't meet because it was Kaye's turn to be rushed to hospital, in Canterbury, with acute appendicitis. Ronald sent her a 'really HUGE' bunch of yellow chrysanthemums, with a little card 'to wish you better – R.S.' Next day came a parcel containing 'a batch of absolutely perfect books', ranging from Lear's *Nonsense Poems* and *Struwwelpeter* to Impressionist reproductions, and a soft toy, 'a foolish stuffed kangaroo named Ermintrude, from the Suez Canal'.

The illustrated letters he wrote her that November and December were a chaste form of courtship. They had not yet met, but there was an immediate bond between them. His letters were boyish, eager, spattered with exclamation marks. From his parents' house at 29 Collier Road, Cambridge, he sent sympathy for her appendectomy. 'I hate operations, I always have such surrealist dreams when I am "under", and when I come round and try to remember what they were about (to draw them) I forget – and that makes me mad!' He had been for his medical board. 'There was a doubtful moment when he tested my legs for reflexes and found I hadn't any! Apparently there is still a little beri-beri lurking around. It was rather a draughty experience wandering about long corridors in the nood!' (He did a drawing of his naked rear view scampering down a corridor.) He expected his discharge in the first week of December – 'O happy day!' There was, he told her, to be an exhibition of his PoW drawings in Cambridge, December 3–8, after which 'I will dump them on you for you to do as you are told – before they go off to the War Artists' thing.' There were also the issues of *The Exile* produced in Changi. He had never dreamed that *Exiles* would get back to England. 'Yes, all the layout was mine but as you may notice, quite a bit of it was cribbed from you.'

Kaye wrote an item in *Lilliput* about Ronald's return. 'Thank you, Kaye for that "belated" little piece; to know that perhaps it has meant something to one person at least makes these struggles against mental suicide worth while. There were times when it seemed eternal – that we should never see England again, there was no future, each day brought something more ghastly than the one before, we began to think – maybe death would be easier – more comfortable, at least it would bring rest . . . I was lucky, I had my sketchbook to help me twist my mind away from it. But some had nothing. So you see it had to be done – to try and help the rest of them through too. All my friends died . . .

'Oh God, this letter is supposed to brighten you up a bit – and by now you should be feeling thoroughly depressed! So I'll leave you alone and pack a few books for you. Can I help at all – is there anything you want? Take care, and don't start doing handsprings yet! Yours, Ronald.'

The next night he wrote again, from 7b Edith Grove in Chelsea, where he was trying to cook, over a 'stinking wisp of gas', a soufflé that had turned into a cheesecake. This letter has a drawing of himself looking sad alongside two mice saying, 'What? No crumbs?' He was going to Shoe Lane to see if *Lilliput* would publish his 'scribbles' entitled 'Studio Life'. 'I produced three more lots of schoolgirls last night. You are doomed to see these in due course. Did you ever run around like this – looking hearty? ("Hurrah for St Trinians!")' Alongside is a St Trinian's schoolgirl with a hockey-stick.

Kaye was recuperating in Margate Hospital when John Symonds sent her galley proofs of articles. 'Yes ops are bloody,' he wrote. 'The only satisfaction I got from my last one was kicking a nurse down, or so they told me, as I came round – she had to wear a bandage on her leg for a fortnight.'

Ronald sent Kaye clippings about his exhibition at Cambridge School of Art, 'Life as a prisoner in Japanese hands, recorded by a Cambridge artist', with its unforgettable and disturbing images: executed heads displayed in a Singapore street, glint-eyed grim-mouthed guards, a British officer being beaten for failing to salute in Changi, the cholera victims, the agonizing labours in the jungle. Attendance had been higher than at most exhibitions in Cambridge – 'out of morbid interest', he felt.★

★ Looking back on those drawings in 2009, when some of them were shown at the Hayward Gallery, Ronald said: 'It was all baby stuff really as I was still learning to draw. But the subject matter was so mind-popping I had to get it on paper, regardless of the lack of ability.' He realized that 'the experience made me into a good draughtsman'.

He found himself shying away from meeting people. He had been to a 'stewy' party 'in a moment of weakness', and lasted eleven minutes before having to come up for air. 'Either I am suffering from claustrophobia or else the artificiality of it all makes me sick.' He was glad she liked the books he sent: 'I love "pampering" people – especially people having their "interiors explored"!' and was finding it exciting to get back to work. He'd been to *Lilliput*'s office and had met 'your friendly and rather vague John Symonds'; they'd taken half a dozen 'Studio Life' drawings. A telegram came to say that 'the Chelsea Housing Board has an unfurnished room for my inspection' in Tite Street, which he would take, until a studio in Bedford Gardens fell vacant. He ends with love to Ermintrude the kangaroo.

Ronald duly installed himself at Tite Street, at 15s a week, plus threepence for use of iron, and sixpence for his radio, for a large room with 'a lousy view but no mice,' a gas fire but no phone, plenty of storage space and a couple of gas-rings. If Kaye wanted to give him a Christmas present, a cookery book would be welcome. He was having the room distempered and painted and stained and scrubbed, and would move in in the new year. (Years later, the Searles returned to Tite Street and found that a plaque had been put on the wall: it was Oscar Wilde's old house.)

He needed furniture: he had been 'lurking in hardware shops gazing at potato peelers'. He had a couple of divans, and would get bookshelves. The *Lilliput* money would pay for a teapot. He needed 'feeding things, or a curtain length'. Might Kaye go along to the auction she had mentioned, and if she saw an easy chair, 'raise your arm feebly and grab it'? 'At that time furniture was quite scarce,' Kaye recalled, 'and it says a great deal for the relationship we had built up by letter, that I went off to Canterbury as soon as I was allowed out, and found him a chair in a second-hand shop for £7. I sent him a letter describing it, and he wired back "buy it". In a way we fixed ourselves up sight unseen, for we were both deeply interested in each other.' (The chair proved highly uncomfortable, but it remained in his studio.) He told her that when she got back to *Lilliput*, she 'must save up something nice and horrible for me so that I can do a morbid illustration for a change and make everyone depressed!'

A new editor, Richard Bennett, had been appointed at *Lilliput*. On 21 December 1945, the general manager at Hulton Press had again summarily rejected Kaye's suggestion that she might be joint editor. So she was in a gloomy mood as she approached her thirty-second birthday that January. 'My dear Kaye! Fancy getting depressed in your youth,' Ronald wrote. 'You talk about 32 as if you were a wizened old witch or something. Although there is very little for me to go on I feel that despite a fairly strong change between 20–25 there is very little between 25–30 that changes a person. I feel completely different from the person with my name who left Art School for the army way back in '39, and I have a feeling that from now on I shan't change a great deal. That's probably why we are both feeling so youthful whilst our bodies waste away. Actually the whole thing is a fallacy, 32 is no age, you are very attractive and that together with a personality with which you should be able to do anything with anyone, you should have no cause for misery.' His illustration shows himself in a vast ornate bed, with half-finished letter on the counterpane, and cigarette ends on the bedside rug.

The next page illustration is himself in uniform, apprehensive as a menacingly bulge-eyed and moustachioed dentist peers round the door wielding a spanner. He had a dental appointment in Wimpole Street for 9 a.m. Monday morning. 'Could you imagine a worse time of the week to do anything, let alone visit that den of horrors?' Beri-beri, he explained, since she had asked, was 'a vitamin deficiency malnutrition arising from an almost entirely polished rice diet'. The wet type caused you to blow up (oedema), your flesh tissue turning to water; the dry type caused you to waste away. 'The wet type I had/have/don't want sometimes appears in the legs, sometimes in the face, sometimes in the stomach' (each with illustration). 'With it comes paralysis of the muscles affected. The only cure is good food, plenty of vitamins especially B, and rest. The main thing is exclusion of rice – it is peculiar to rice diet and the east, and I believe the western parallel is pellagra . . . it is not likely to affect me unless I go back to the east and live on a handful of rice (which I've definitely no intention of doing!)'

He was getting more commissions, but hoping to steer clear of stuff 'that is liable to destroy my "straight work" – if that is the side that is ultimately to triumph! I must get down to some life.'

6: Becoming Mrs Searle

1946–9

Eventually, in the new year of 1946, Ronald Searle arrived at the *Lilliput* offices in his oversized army clothes and baggy trousers, clutching his drawings. Despite their correspondence Kaye felt 'appallingly shy and embarrassed' and couldn't face being alone in her office to meet him 'in case, in spite of his jokes, his handwriting and his taste in books, he turned out to be quite awful'. So someone else showed him in, and she followed. He wasn't awful at all. She suggested they repair for lunch to the Gargoyle, the raffish Soho hangout where she had been with Dylan and Co. 'I wanted to show off. He says I ordered a double whisky, which I rarely drank, and then said, "Will you have another of this gut-rot?" ' He'd been told that Kaye was 'plump and jolly', and because of a misleading line in one of her cabled 'London Letters' ('My dispatch case is full of fag ends'), he mistakenly assumed her to be a heavy smoker, and kept offering cigarettes which she refused. He noticed 'with great dis-appointment' that she wore a wedding ring. But they went off to dinner 'and we talked our heads off'.

'He was so gentle. I felt he was a sort of saint really. We were all obsessed with what people had suffered.' He showed her his aide-mémoire from Changi, and the drawing of his meeting with Mountbatten. The next day he wrote suggesting that Kaye should be his agent. 'It was a charming thought, and there was no way that we were not going to go on seeing each other.' And so their love affair began.

He was so young, he had been through so much, his war was so different from hers, he was so enthusiastic about launching himself into Fleet Street, no wonder Kaye found him 'cherishable – even noble'. It was plain, she said, that he wanted her to be his wife. (Like Robert Browning, who arrived at Wimpole Street and declared that he was in love with Elizabeth Barrett having only read her poems.) Her marriage to Keith was 'not working out, probably because of knowing Ronald' ran Kaye's understatement. She went to Tite Street often, and Ronald would cook a cottage pie on his little gas stove.

Despite her two husbands, Kaye had little experience of married life: only brief interludes with both incumbents. She told me, in 1981, that she really ought to have stayed married to Keith, a good man who always remained a friend. Keith was listening, in 1946, to 'Stormy Weather' on a distant gramophone when he wrote to Kaye, 'Well, stormy weather it is, isn't it? When me and my gal ain't together.' It was a good-natured letter about a standing order that he wanted to clear up 'on punctilious businesslike lines' with no ill-feelings. 'After all, very few people could have so much real understanding between them as we have had in our time, and I think it's a memory worth honouring. Mark you, this finance-management is the one thing on which our mutual understanding has most often found itself not-so-mutual.'

In June 1946, discharged from the army, Ronald settled into his London life, attending art classes and producing a book of theatre sketches for a French publisher, *Le Nouveau Ballet Anglais*. *Illustrated Weekly* had published his opus of his four captive years, 'Artist Triumphed Over Prison Camp Life', on 9 February 1946. His first cartoon to be published in *Punch*, drawn in Changi, appeared on 20 March. *Lilliput* published another St Trinian's cartoon ('Hand up the girl who burnt down the East Wing last night'), again drawn in Changi, in April.

Despite paper rationing, newspapers and magazines needed drawings to enliven current affairs, and Ronald's illustrating career took off. He went with Tom Driberg to the Labour conference in September, for *Reynolds' News*, and to a rope-works in the Old Kent Road, where the hangman's ropes for the Nuremberg trials were being manufactured. He illustrated Patrick Campbell for *Lilliput*, and plays for the *Radio Times*. Colin Eccleshare, whom he had met on *The Granta*, was now at Cambridge University Press, and published *Forty Drawings* by Ronald Searle in November. The poet Frank Kendon, who wrote the introduction, wrote to Ronald urging him to cherish his gifts ('seriously valuable to humanity') and to reserve his time and leisure to do so. But Ronald was seduced by the demand for his cartoons. His fellow *Punch* cartoonist Michael ffolkes remembered, 'Ronald Searle was like a human factory.'*

In July, a studio became vacant. Bedford Gardens, off Kensington Church Street, was an artists' colony inhabited at various times by the painters John Minton, Keith Vaughan, Jankel Adler and 'the two Roberts', Colquhoun and MacBryde. Studio 2 was large, with a passage to a bathroom, and beyond that a small kitchen-cum-living room, and a communal lavatory. It was permanently cold. 'But we were extremely happy there,' wrote Kaye. ('We never lived there as a couple, although the children were conceived at that time,' Ronald told me. 'Kaye was still living in Hampstead with her mother.') There were sometimes noisy orgies in Colquhoun and MacBryde's rooms. One night Ronald went out late to post a letter, and returned at 3 a.m. 'Guess where I've been – with the boys downstairs,' he said. 'And guess what they were doing? Scottish dancing!' Hence the wild whoops and stamping about. Russell Braddon came over from Australia and stayed at Bedford Gardens; so did Syd Piddington,

* Michael Bateman, *Funny Way to Earn a Living*, Leslie Frewin, 1966.

who had shared a hut with him in Changi; and Bill Williams, former cabaret entertainer, so Kaye learned their songs from the prison camp.

She still had her job at *Lilliput*. Max Beerbohm declined her 'charming and amusing' request for a Christmas piece: 'I am afraid Dickens didn't leave anything for anybody to say about Christmas.' In the autumn of 1946, *Lilliput* sent her to Paris to see French photographers; she would also prepare a broadcast about café society (the Flore was the favourite of Sartre and Picasso, she reported) and the impact of clothes rationing on Parisian chic. Ronald joined her for the weekend. (In her notebook, in his unmistakable handwriting, Ronald wrote 'French for: "Down with the Eiffel Tower! Remove this monstrosity! We artists protest! Lift not working. Out of order."') A torn-out page is headed 'Kayki Webb, Paris,' with his drawing of a smiley frog, dated 21 October 1946, and a message: 'I love you sined seeled delivered Ronald Searle.'

They planned to hasten her divorce proceedings by 'starting a baby', and soon after the Paris weekend, Kaye found she was pregnant. 'We probably started our twins' life together full of good food for the first time,' she later wrote. 'At any rate, the dates coincide.' This light-hearted reference to gourmet fare (in fact there were still food shortages in Paris) hardly reflects what both felt about the life-changing step they had so precipitately taken – especially when Kaye found they were expecting twins. Ronald was astonished. PoWs had been advised that they would probably remain sterile for at least three years. The sudden prospect of double fatherhood was a source of utter amazement.

On 17 December 1946, Keith petitioned for divorce, on the grounds that his wife had 'frequently committed adultery with Ronald Searle' at Bedford Gardens, Notting Hill Gate. By the time this was granted the following summer, Keith too had a new love, the beautiful and effervescent Barbara Woosnam, aged twenty, who occupied the bedsitter across the landing of his Maida Vale flat. One day, Keith accidentally locked Barbara in his flat when he went to collect his mother-in-law, Ann, who was coming for tea. Ann reported back to Kaye: 'There was a very pretty girl there, and he's going to marry her.' Barbara seemed 'a nice lass, even if she has grabbed him on the rebound', Ann later wrote to Kaye. 'Good luck to both of them.'

Ronald was not Kaye's only suitor. The columnist Patrick (Paddy) Campbell, who shared her office, was 'wooing hard'. Campbell, thirty-three and married, was the son of Lord Glenavy, Ireland's Lord Chief Justice. After Oxford and wartime naval service, Campbell had become 'Quidnunc' on the *Irish Times*, first of many humorous columns. (Later, his stammer made him a star when he captained a team on the TV panel game *Call My Bluff*.) Campbell wrote to her, as 'Dear dear Kate', on Christmas night 1946. 'I can wait now. What I have I can remember for a year. You need only look at me sometimes, and it will be Christmas Eve again . . . You fill my heart, so I sit looking at nothing, seeing your face . . . Goodnight, dear darling. Let's see who can do the best waiting.' In the next letter he persisted: 'I can literally see you everywhere – an extra cornea on the eyeball. Now, you go and paddle at Margate. I'll get you in the end.' He signed himself 'Your Boy'. A further declaration came: 'Don't ever think that I am not determined that we shall be married. You are the only woman I'll ever know who has everything that I want in a woman. It's better for us to be apart for a while now, my darling.' But in June 1947, Campbell wrote to tell her he had 'found the one I've been looking for all my life'. 'She's called Cherry, and she's about five feet high and she's come to live with me until we can get married. She, of course, has a nice young husband, and what has been happening in the last few weeks has been a severe trial for all concerned.'

He did not unsay anything he had written; he thanked Kaye for the cigars and shirts she sent for his birthday. He was writing from *Lilliput*'s office, where, in conference, someone had said, 'Could we not get one of those ideas of Kaye's?' 'And all of us sitting around, quite helpless. You're badly wanted around here, Katie. Your soap and towel, untouched, are still in your drawer, and the rug and rubber boots in your cupboard.' He knew about Ronald – who would illustrate his new book – and about her now advanced pregnancy. 'Katie,' he told her, 'you go on sitting in your garden, just waiting nicely and peacefully and proudly. When you come back you won't have any closer friend in England. If it's any consolation to you I, in my way, have reached a perfect peace at last. A very special kind of love – Paddy.'*

Kaye carried on editing and broadcasting until she was seven months pregnant. Arthur, still in Washington, offered to pay for her confinement, and her mother – who had already, at sixty-two, had a mild stroke – was convinced that Kaye, 'poor darling', would be better looked after in America, which was assumed to be 'the best place for everything'. Kaye told herself she should seize this chance to see America, so she agreed, with many doubts, to leave in May for Washington. She suspected that Ronald was not that keen on getting married, though at the last minute he had proposed. In America she would register the twins as her husband Keith's, otherwise they would be regarded as 'stateless'.

It was a muddled arrangement, undertaken in great stress, after much family confabulation, and greatly regretted later. The correspondence between Kaye and her mother reflects how little they had thought through the consequences. Ann said she had been 'an absolute idiot' not to realize how much she would miss her Kayki at this crucial time. She fully intended that afterwards,

* He married Cherry, the second of his three wives, later that year.

Kaye and her twins would live with her: she would reorganize her house in Kent to include a nanny's bedsitting room next door to the twins' room on the first floor. 'Searle', as she called him, had told Ann that the *Lilliput* office was dull without Kaye. 'What a personality my girl has to be sure!' Ann wrote. 'Good old Kayki.' Kaye had work to do in New York, for Tom Hopkinson: he wanted her to find the photographer Gjon Mili, 'an off-hand and indolent sort of chap', and 'tear a pile of Kodachromes away from him'. *Lilliput*'s editor, Richard Bennett, sent her the news that other babies had been born to colleagues, so 'the case for a Hulton crèche is building up'. Bennett had dined with Ronald ('He really is as nice as he is talented. You seem to have a very good taste in men') but he was in danger of 'dissipating his talents on jobs that are well beneath him'.

Whether Kaye really would marry Ronald was unresolved. 'Only a very young and unknowledgeable man would have bound you with a last minute promise Kayki,' Ann wrote disapprovingly. 'You take your time my love and don't be bulldozed ever again into making a decision against your real instinct and will.' Yet almost in the same breath she was writing, 'Now then you will have to stay married and make the best of it, whichever way it goes, as you will not be able to get away with it again my darling.' Soon after Kaye's departure, she even wrote hoping that Kaye might 'meet a wealthy American – (whom you fall for) – then you could fly over to fetch me back with you. This, of course, is nonsense darling – I'm just wandering!!'

It is hard today to imagine an intelligent thirty-three-year-old woman enduring homilies from a mother with a poor track record in marital matters; Ann's arbitrary, repetitive and often contradictory advice would enrage most women. But she could sometimes dispense maternal wisdom. She advised Kaye to wait a while before marrying again, and to 'wipe Paddy right off the slate'; he was 'a man of straw' and 'a menace to your peace of mind'.

About Ronald, she wavered. 'Take Searle,' she wrote one day. 'He is a good chap – he will get on, undoubtedly, he has many fine qualities and yet Kayki, I don't know – when he was down here shades in his voice – bad manners – an absorption in himself to the complete exclusion of others – I really would think very seriously about marriage with him. It seems to me that you would have to endure continuous pinpricks. Stay friends with him but gradually I should try to think in terms of complete independence.' But three days later a letter from Ronald charmed Kaye's mother. He was 'packed out with work – seems frightfully bucked with life and says he can keep 19 bairns let alone twinnies', Ann reported. He had drawn her 'a beaming little fat mother with nine children each side and one in her lap and storks flying all around'. . . 'He is certainly rather sweet Kayki and so thrilled about being a father – I don't believe he will be able to keep quiet about it to anyone.'

On practical and professional matters, Ann was firm. Kaye must tell Searle to save for the expenses ahead, and for Kaye's divorce. Kaye's brother Bill, who was staying in Ronald's flat, often 'sharing a cuppa' in the evening, told Ann that Ronald's values were all wrong, and that he 'doesn't deny himself a thing'. 'That is rather reprehensible in so young a man . . . But it is a good trait and I prefer that to meanness,' Ann typically added. 'Please do not think I do not like him. I have rarely met anyone <u>more</u> loveable but like all artists, I think he is best living alone . . .' Bill, Ann reminded Kaye, had a lot of sense, 'whereas you and I are inclined to judge on sentiment, gifts, charming letters and so on'. She was also rightly concerned, three decades before maternity rights were granted to women, that Kaye might not get her job back if she stayed away too long. She might have to find another job, or exist on freelance work. 'Actually, I believe you should be back at the office by the 10th of October,' Ann said firmly.

Kaye reported that Washington, like Britain, was having a baby boom; one in every five women on the street seemed to be pregnant. By mid-July the twins' birth was imminent, indeed overdue. 'It's a bugger Kaye darling,' wrote Ann, 'this extra waiting. I have had it with both boys and when I was alone waiting for Bill, I <u>really</u> used to look at the big lake and wonder whether it was worth going on – but you see it <u>was</u>, and I was alone. I had no husband, no job to go back to and I did not speak to a friendly soul for months. You remember all that when you are inclined to get fretful.'

In the same letter Ann reported a conversation with Ronald. 'I said to him yesterday, "have you met any pretty girl you have taken a fancy to or would prefer to Kaye" and he looked completely startled and said "I don't know what you mean Mummy. There is only Kaye and work and work and Kaye and if I didn't have Kaye, then there would only be work for me, ever".'

Kaye went into labour on 16 July, 1947: a hot summer day, 96 degrees Fahrenheit in the shade. There was no air-conditioning in her hospital room and a jug of ice melted in minutes. John and Kate were delivered after a twenty-four-hour labour, on 17 July. Ann could not sleep until she received Arthur's telegram reporting that all was well, whereupon she and Ronald 'had a little drinkie or two, & went for a walk and "nattered"'. Kaye later wrote an article (and a broadcast) about giving birth in America. The hospital was comfortable but expensive (seven dollars a day, 35s); the obstetrician (£50) vanished after the birth, when she had to engage a paediatrician; all these services had to be separately paid for. The nurses were undisciplined, chewed gum and ate one's grapes, and mothers were rationed to twenty-minute interludes with their babies. There was no free orange juice or baby clinics such as our Welfare State already provided. Above all, Kaye had felt lonely, as any expatriate new mother would.

The twins were registered as the children of Andrew Keith

Hunter. He was in America at the time, and visited the hospital, carrying home a trunkload of Kaye's maternity dresses for his future wife Barbara, who was already pregnant. Showing the babies to her former husband brought it home to Kaye that the man she should be with at this moment was Ronald. 'It was a great mistake,' Kaye often said later. 'The first of many. It didn't help Ronald to become bonded to the children as he should have done. I feel that if he'd been with me when I had them, he never would have left them. It was really the first serious mistake in my life.'

Ann sent flowers, and advice about breast-feeding and resting while her stitches healed. Kaye sent her news to James Mason (who had emigrated with his wife Pam to New York, and was shortly to depart for Beverly Hills), asking him to be godfather. 'Splendid, splendid,' he wrote. 'We would be delighted to be godparents. But are we sufficiently reliable? I mean are we ever likely to see them? If you are satisfied to have me teach him his catechism by long distance telephone, well and good.' Mason decided that baby John looked like Mr Molotov (Vyacheslav Molotov, Stalin's foreign minister). 'The girl looks very pretty,' he wrote. 'I guess Molotov looks alright too tho' it was difficult to recognize him without the moustache.' Pam's own baby, now imminent, would be 'first lady president of the US, better even than Evita'. When Portland Mason, later famed for her precocity, duly arrived he wittered on like every other new father about her brilliance, weight gain, etc. He had plenty of time to dote: his role in his latest film, *Madame Bovary*, took one and a half days.

Back in London, once he knew the babies had safely arrived, Ronald set off with Paul Hogarth for a trip to Yugoslavia. The Communist Hogarth was invited to bring artists to witness its reconstruction. Kaye's pressing need was to secure her job for her return. Although Richard Bennett had written to tell her he had just taken on a new writer, Maurice Richardson, it was a bombshell when two weeks later Maxwell Raison wrote to say *Lilliput* was now fully staffed. 'Bennett tells me he wrote to you some time ago telling you he felt that *Lilliput* no longer offered any opportunity for you. I am afraid you must take it as settled that we cannot offer you your old job on this magazine.' *Picture Post* too was 'out of the question' and frankly the prospects were not too cheerful. 'Furthermore, Bennett tells me you wrote to say that you would expect a lot more money on your return, and there is no prospect at all of that.' Perhaps she should try to get work in the United States?

Kaye, aggrieved and wounded, wrote to Raison reminding him that she had been assured she would not be the loser on her return, that the management 'had plans' for her. 'I am chagrined to remember that, just over a year ago, I asked to be transferred to the *Leader*, or rather Charles Fenby asked for me. Then I was told to stay where I was because I was needed. When I first knew about the babies and that I had to have time off to produce them I offered to resign and was again told I was "needed". When I came over here in May, on my last conversation with Bennett I asked him if I could be sure of having my job to come back to and he told me it was "mine as long as I wanted it". Of course situations change, and nine years is perhaps overlong to stay on one paper, but at any rate it shows loyalty; there were quite a few good jobs available in Fleet Street even as little as a year ago and I have twice refused outside offers. To be turned loose in this particular way is not at all pleasant.' She would never have pressed her salary claim to the extent of losing her job 'since I now have a family to support'.

In this uncertain state Kaye sailed home in October on the *Queen Elizabeth* with the babies, whereupon Ronald had the unsettling experience of meeting his three-month-old son and daughter for the first time. Kaye took them to her mother in Westgate ('and dumped us', in her son John's view), visiting them at weekends, while she negotiated her new job with her old friend Charles Fenby, editor of the *Leader*, a popular family weekly. Her twins were barely six months old, and living with Ann, when she was appointed the *Leader*'s show-business editor.

There was no time to ponder on whether they were doing the right thing. Both were thrust on to a treadmill of deadlines. Ronald's first cartoon album came out, *Hurrah for St Trinian's*, although only a dozen St T's drawings had appeared, and it was already a chore he felt trammelled by. Kaye had her weekly column to fill, and did so with enormous panache. Unlike other showbiz journalists who meet only stars and celebrities, Kaye looked for the peripheral characters of theatreland. She interviewed stage doorkeepers, publicity agents, theatrical wig-makers, dressers, box-office managers, and the people (a company called Windrams) who supplied artificial flowers. She sought out 'The Producer's Wife', 'The Director's Daughter'. She wrote about what actors do when they have a cold. She covered the *Gang Show* comics, Billy Smart's circus, fairgrounds, pantomimes, end-of-pier shows, and music-hall artistes such as Buster Shaver and his troupe of performing midgets. (Three of the midgets, Olive, George and Richard Brasno, were siblings. Their six brothers and sisters were normal-sized, and so were their parents. 'Every third child Mr and Mrs Brasno had was a midget.')

On 7 February 1948 she interviewed Thora Hird, a Morecambe girl who was now a film star: an interview which utterly conveys the personality of the subject. Thora was packing a West End theatre in *No Flowers for the Living*, in which she had originally been offered, at thirty-seven, the part of a fifteen-year-old girl. She'd said to the producer in her forthright Lancastrian way: 'Look at me, gentlemen. I know a bit about makeup, but I can't look like a fifteen-year-old girl. And if someone had made love to me on a bombed building I shouldn't have had hysterics – I probably would have encouraged him.' So they asked her to read for the Mum instead, and no acting was required: she *was* Mum, 'in character, in every word and gesture', Kaye wrote. She'd just been turned down, Thora said, for another stage part as a Lancashire woman. The producer felt that her accent wasn't genuine enough. 'Happen if I'd come from Devonshire,' said Thora, 'he'd ha thowt I was graand.' W. Macqueen Pope – 'Popie', an old friend of Ann's – was now PR for the Theatre Royal, Drury Lane, a real showman whose parents and grandparents had acted in the same theatre. He thanked Kaye for a splendid article, 'brilliantly written and observed'. Kaye had joined one of Popie's tours under the Drury Lane stage, 'like the bowels of a ship', where he mixed theatrical anecdotes with his reminiscences of joining Drury Lane as errand boy, and becoming an actor himself. He showed them the Royal Box (6 guineas to hire), Queen Mary's footstool, Henry Irving's mirror; he told of squabbles over stars' dressing rooms, and panics when the hydraulics didn't work; of Nell Gwynn, of the Drury Lane ghost, and of Edmund Kean, who had arrived at the theatre starving, and was ignored 'until the night he started playing Shylock to a half-empty and indifferent house. In the interval the audience rushed into the street and begged passers-by to come inside and see this great new actor. He finished with a packed house.'

She also did straight interviews, with Laurence Olivier, Ralph Richardson, Loretta Young, Mrs J. B. Priestley, Flora Robson. Kaye was no hatchet-wielder. But her notes for a Peter Ustinov profile show how perceptive she was: 'Mother: he mentions her often . . . stories about her?' 'Character: is he really shy?' 'His quips come so quickly . . . Foreign languages in and out all the time.' 'Talk to him about international affairs and they suddenly get clearer.' 'Likes Camembert and red wine and beer and thick Turkish coffee. Impossible not to treat him like a visiting troupe of entertainers just as it is impossible for him not to give a performance of some kind.' (This fact was noted by everyone who ever

interviewed Ustinov.) He was 'enormously generous with his
advice and time and praise for others'. 'He clowns so much and yet
his face if he leaves it alone is charming and rather touching.'

Ronald felt, in retrospect, that he was thrust into becoming a
family man when he had barely come to terms with his return to
civilization. One of his 'Studio' cartoons in *Lilliput* in March 1946
was acutely prescient of his later experience of trying to work
with small children underfoot. 'Life in a studio' showed a bearded
artist, like himself, advancing with a noose upon a small boy who
has just scrawled over the painting on the easel. 'I was simply
totally unqualified to be – so rapidly – a husband and father.'

And yet, Kaye wrote, 'It seemed to me that we were settling
down to a happy domestic life. We did have ten really marvellous
years. I thought it a very good marriage, and he was a wonderful
husband.'

The amicable divorce from Keith Hunter became absolute, a
civilized process, both parties using the same solicitor, Terence
de Wolf. So Kaye and Ronald were married at Kensington register
office on 12 March 1948. Despite Kaye's uncertainty about
Ronald's commitment, the notes he wrote to his bride, constantly
referring to himself as her husband, were sweetly loving.

> Diddle diddle dumpling
> Your husband Ron
> Went to bed singing this song:
> I love Kayki
> Wherever I may be
> And I wish she would maykmi
> A nice cuppa tea.

He was an assiduous sender of flowers, or drawings of flowers
on little cards:

Some flowers your husband lays at your feet, my sweet.
Some flowers your husband puts in your arms to mirror your charms.

> A garland of flowers to brighten your morning
> From seed to blossom they've grown for you
> I can't find a word except dawning for morning
> But the other bit rhymes with I love you!

Three months after her third wedding, Kaye had a letter from Kit Brierley, confessing to joblessness and 'pretty dire financial difficulties'. He had taken out an insurance policy in 1938, naming Kaye as beneficiary, and could no longer keep up the premiums. Would she consent to his realizing the present value of the policy – 'about £90 I believe'? And if she let him know what he owed towards their divorce, 'I will do my best to settle in full.' Kaye leaves us no record of her response.

Keith Hunter duly married Barbara, who got accustomed, at the Searles' parties, to introducing herself as 'Kaye's second husband's second wife'. (She had just had her second baby in 1949 when a knock came on the door and she was informed that Mr Ronald Searle wished to become the adoptive father of his own twins.) Barbara, who knew many PoWs, says they all needed motherly warmth and security, and this Kaye could give. Ronald was still having nightmares about Changi. 'But he didn't want to talk about it,' Kaye said. 'It did obviously affect him. Nobody who came out had a happy marriage, I think. You can't blame anyone who suffered for anything they did emotionally after. They must have been so damaged. Friends dying around him – how can you endure that?'

Just after the twins' first birthday, in August 1948, Ronald set off with Paul Hogarth to draw the rebuilding of Warsaw. He wrote while en route for Prague, when he was unable to leave the train while officials rubber-stamped their passports, and their currency was checked for the umpteenth time. '"ZMRZLINA" says the notice on the platform – and I'm inclined to agree!'

He was shocked by the desolation of Nuremberg, 'acres of rubble and hollow shells with unnecessary windows framing the sky'. Walls and floors hung down the gashed sides of buildings 'like hair-combings'. From Ghent he wrote, 'Am expecting good news to come from Aix any moment' (illustrated with a rider on a galloping horse). 'Few people smoke, fewer still smile, and the wind blows over the waste and the grit crunches constantly under our feet.' He drew ruined streets, piles of debris, a roof of gothic vaulting revealed by a bomb crater. He added 'Big Kisses to you and the babes from their wandering Pop,' and lovingly signed off 'All my love for you, Ronald', with a drawing of a limpid-eyed rabbit.

His trip took in Paris, Venice, Cracow, Gdansk, Warsaw, Wrocław (the former Breslau). From Prague – 'awakened by the dustmen who bang the bins like anywhere else in the world' – he sat in a beer-garden and wrote: 'At the Polish consulate we were met at the door by a stuffed wolf and a quartet of stuffed bears.' They were visa-less until an English-speaking Pole who read *Lilliput* recognized Ronald's name. This was Ludwik Perski, a buddy of the war artist Feliks Topolski, who persuaded the vice-consul what great journalists and artists Searle and Hogarth were. 'Prague is really a magnificent place architecturally. A mass of palaces – dripping with baroque and all peculiarly individual. There was an almost deserted atmosphere – which they call the cucumber season – everyone is away and the cucumbers are being pickled.'

In Warsaw there was 'appalling devastation'. He drew it, to give Kaye some idea. It reminded him of the back of St Paul's: 'heap after heap of brown and grey rubble supporting the tottering shells of what is remaining upright'. But at least there was street life, peasant women in pleated skirts and kerchief headdresses, 'the old and rather thin droshky horses are clip-clopping over the cobbles, sounding very much like the BBC's coconut-shell hooves'. It was hot, they had to get some zlotys, Hogarth was accosted by a fiery-looking woman who flopped about like a puppet, reeked of whisky and shouted 'Tovarich!' The Ministry of Culture took them to see a tunnel being reconstructed, and Ronald left his folding stool on an escarpment there, 'blast it'. In the castle courtyard they were shown wooden figures by Wit Stwosz (aka Veit Stoss), the German sculptor, from the high altar of the Church of the Virgin Mary, 'and what a sight it was, all part of a 20ft triptych, a dozen or so figures up to 12ft tall looking like wax Holbeins. And several hundred smaller figures, lying in rows on racks . . . and all carved, down to hairs on beards, in the 1400s from a linden tree 500 years old. It was a chance of a lifetime seeing the finest example of wood carving and perhaps the most intact of the 15th century.'

The air was thick with religion, Ronald said. He was struck by the sight of the Madonna in the eaves of every roof, and in almost every house a little shrine with a light permanently burning. 'You've only got to see the faces of some of these illiterate old peasant women before an altar covered in mumbo jumbo of candles and ikons and statues and jewels to realize how they saturate themselves in it.'

Poland was Topolski's homeland, from which he had fled thirteen years before. The war, he wrote, hung 'like a cloud of bomb-dust' over massacred Wrocław, where they were holding an International Congress of Intellectuals for Peace, and Topolski inveigled Hogarth and Ronald into the throng, so they heard interminable speeches calling for intellectuals to defend peace and culture from the new fascism that threatened in Spain and South America. Also present were the historian A. J. P. Taylor, the novelist Aldous Huxley, the *New Statesman* editor Kingsley Martin, the writer Richard Hughes, the poet Paul Eluard, and Picasso. It was worth being there, Ronald said, to meet Picasso.

He wrote loving verses home to Kaye:

Although the wynds blowe cold
Although the skyes are greye
My heart is warme for you my love
Although I'm far awaye

Your wand'ring husband's almost back
With his scribbles in his pack
His feet are sore – his nose is blue –
And he is calling, I love you!

In October, the Searles went to Portofino, where Jenny
Nicholson, daughter of Robert Graves (and godmother to Kate),
took them to visit Max Beerbohm in Rapallo. Kaye photographed
Max at his home, Villino Chiaro. Kaye persuaded Max to write
a preface to Ronald's second cartoon collection, *The Female
Approach*, which came out for Christmas 1949. And in Portofino,
Ronald completed ten fine paintings, exhibited at Wolf
Mankowitz's Little Gallery on their return.

They had just missed seeing Noel Langley, whose bestseller
The Inconstant Moon (about Dante and Beatrice) Ronald had
illustrated. Langley was in Rome on a movie location, suffering
from a director who 'rewrites everything himself secretly by
night, like the mice in the Tailor of Gloucester'. The female lead,
Sally Ann Howes, he told them, 'is the mistress of two expressions:
one, a horse, and two, a horse upside-down'. He added, 'I see
Campbell is bringing out his stories in book form. Is he keeping
Ronald's drawings?' (Yes, he was: Paddy Campbell's book was
one of the deadlines filling Ronald's impressive 'Deadlines chart'
on the wall of his studio.)

In fact Ronald was working flat out, for Shell posters, for
Robin Jaques at *The Strand* magazine, and – from May 1949 – for
the new editor of *Punch*, Kenneth Bird, alias the cartoonist
'Fougasse'. Ronald became *Punch*'s theatre caricaturist, which

meant accompanying their amiable critic Eric Keown, a striking six foot seven inch figure, to the theatre several nights a week, which he did for the best part of the next decade. Luckily, he enjoyed Keown's company.

Kaye's columns for the *Leader* lasted just over a year. In her valedictory piece she said how approachable theatre people had been. 'Despite a childhood spent on the edge of "the business", I had thought of theatrical people as a race apart.' She was surprised at how actors would praise friends in work, but did little to help those without jobs. ('In my world of Fleet Street this is actually in reverse.') Managements cast plays only from inside the circle they knew, and ignored actors' creature comforts. Kaye had spent hours hanging about draughty stages, huddled in an overcoat, watching leading actors 'gradually congeal with cold and hunger as dress rehearsals go on half the night'.

Despite her freelance schedule, she wanted to bring the children home. 'After weeks of wooing the estate agent', they found a mansion flat. Number 30 Burnham Court, in Moscow Road, Bayswater, was big enough for the family and a Norland-trained nanny, Rosemary. Ronald kept his Bedford Gardens studio, and they were installed by Christmas 1949. Kaye adored the paraphernalia of Christmas. A photograph shows Kaye and Ann (now 'Nan the Gran'), and the eighteen-month-old twins with their presents, two toy wire-haired fox terriers on wheels, beside the lavishly decorated (by 1949 standards) tree. From America, grandfather Arthur sent turkey and plum pudding, and James Mason, who was finding Hollywood 'the darnedest place', every film involving 'endless finagling', sent a smoked ham.

7: High Circles

'We move in very high circles nowadays,' Kaye wrote to her father, with just a touch of irony, as the new decade began. The Searles found themselves at the centre of British life: guests of honour at the Lord Mayor's reception, at a Foyles literary luncheon, and at King George's opening ceremony of the Festival of Britain. ('Send as many Americans as you can,' Kaye told Arthur, 'it is really worth coming to.') Ronald's 'dynamic' interpretation of Cowper's *The Story of John Gilpin* was judged the best liked of the Festival's 'Painter and Poet' films. In 1950 Ronald had attended the Old Bailey trial of Klaus Fuchs, the German spy who handed Britain's plutonium bomb plans to the Russians. Hartley Shawcross, late of the Nuremberg trials, prosecuted. Within ninety minutes Lord Chief Justice Goddard was pronouncing sentence of fourteen years, telling Fuchs he had betrayed British hospitality with the grossest treachery. Sketching in court was still illegal, but Ronald had trained his visual memory to reproduce scenes after the event.

A career woman with small children was a fairly rare specimen in 1950. Her column 'Kaye Webb Reporting . . .' in *Everywoman* magazine was peopled with her friends (the playwright Christopher Fry, the Labour MP Barbara Castle, the actor Peter Finch, the painter Mary Fedden, the bookshop owner Christina Foyle, the cartoonist Nicolas Bentley and Christian Kunzle, the creator of Kunzle cakes). She told readers she had engaged a Sunday cook from a company called Solve Your Problem, so that

she could go with her husband and twins to sail boats on the
Round Pond in Kensington Gardens. And Kaye was always keen
to accompany Ronald ('Change blouse, bring petticoat, corset,
ear-rings') to important first nights – to Gielgud in *Lear*, Peter
Brook's latest at Stratford, *Hamlet at Elsinore* – and to the opera,
dances and parties.

In the spring of that year came an alluring project, and she
dropped *Everywoman*. The publisher Tony Godwin invited the
Searles to do a joint book 'purely for pleasure', about any city
they liked. They responded in unison: 'Paris', scene of their
romantic weekend in 1946. For five weeks in May and June, they
stayed at the Hotel de Pavillon and covered 'this adorable city'.
They were welcomed by the illustrator and political cartoonist
André François, given a party by the weekly satirical paper *Le
Canard Enchaîné*, wined and dined nightly. 'Ronald settled his
tiny stool on the paving stones of the Quai d'Orsay, where he
looked rather like a disciple at the feet of Minerva,' wrote Kaye.
They sought the Paris of Wilde, Sartre, de Nerval. They plunged
into Left Bank life, sitting for hours at the Café Flore or the Deux
Magots: 'Paris is the best city in the world in which to be poor.'
They took a *bateau mouche* down the Seine, strolled down the
Champs-Elysées, discovered the Musée Rodin, went to Dior and
the Paris Fair, to Les Halles, to Delacroix's studio, to Saint-
Sulpice, and spent Sunday morning at the *marché aux puces*. They
went to Fouquet's café, where Edith Piaf was discovered, and to
the Lido at the Arc de Triomphe end of the Champs-Elysées, and
to the Folies Bergère to see the Bluebell girls. 'In Paris,' wrote
Kaye, 'it is impossible to forget the feminine bosom.' Also, 'In
Paris, lavatories are as conspicuous as letter boxes are concealed.'
Ronald's streetscapes – detailed, alive, exciting – gave a complete
impression of the city. Paris offered him scope for meticulous
detail, with its rococo architectural and sculptural extravagances,
its awnings and wrought-iron lamps and railings and balconies.

He drew unmistakably Parisian characters – *bouquinistes* and *boulevardiers*, fishermen and lovers, distinctive individuals at tables in the Café de la Paix, and a sad couple at the Porte de Vanves, selling their few pitiful possessions including a knife, a fork, a door handle. He drew the statues of the Père Lachaise cemetery, the cabaret at the Bal Montagne and its enormous blowsy *proprietrice* Georgette, who told them, 'Faites-moi de la publicité, n'importe laquelle.' ('Madame est servie,' wrote Kaye.) Juliette Greco ('long black hair and unsmiling black eyes') sang at midnight at La Rose Rouge. Kaye fell in love with a young comedian at the Club Fontaine des Quatre Saisons. They went to the rue Pigalle and Montmartre, and the Théâtre du Grand Guignol, and discovered secret alleyways like the rue de Beaujolais. A Russian-French gypsy fortune-teller named Nina in Clignancourt predicted that the book would be a success.

Ronald drew whatever caught his eye; Kaye jotted down notes, adding whatever factual information she could not resist passing on. Their book was not about famous people, except the toothy comic actor Fernandel, who made them laugh so much they could not bear to leave him out. They also included Kiki de Montparnasse, model of Picasso, Derain and Modigliani, relic of old bohemian Paris. Both were intoxicated by the city, and decided they must return for another long holiday, making their base on the Île St Louis.

Ronald's drawings were ready when they got back on 3 June (and were exhibited in October), but Kaye's text wasn't written until she was on the train from the Edinburgh Festival in August. Later, when Basildon Bond asked Ronald for a sample of his handwriting for an advert (with a drawing of him by E. H. Shepard), he wrote: '*Paris Sketchbook* was the best assignment of all – my wife was doing the writing!' Kaye said she had 'made Ronald's life a bit of a misery' by ringing home every night to check on the children. When *Paris Sketchbook* (a title first used by

Thackeray) was published at Christmas 1950, it carried the dedication 'For Kate and John who were left behind'.

Ronald threw a celebratory dinner on Monday 11 December, in the Mikado Room of the Savoy, and designed the placement with 'Miss Kaye Webb (Mrs Ronald Searle)' at the head of the oval table. On her right sat the great sculptor Jacob Epstein, on her left the Comte Adalbert de Segonzac.* Around the table sat the actress Diana Graves and her husband; Frank Waters, managing director of the *News Chronicle*, and his actress wife Joan Maude; Epstein's mistress Kathleen Garman, one of the seven beautiful Garman sisters; the actor Alec Guinness and his wife Merula; and Ronald's friends from Changi, Russell Braddon and Syd Piddington and their wives. (The Piddingtons performed a famous stage telepathy act, and were the subject of Russell Braddon's first book.)

The Paris book led to other *News Chronicle* commissions: they left for Tangier, Fez and Marrakesh early in 1951, arriving in the middle of an uprising; Ronald drew Allal el Fassi, the outlawed leader of Morocco's Istiqlal independence party, while Kaye conducted an interview in French, which consisted largely of her horrified reactions: 'C'est vrai? C'est affreux!'

It was again a wrench to leave the twins. Kate was prettier by the day, with an entrancing smile; John prattled away in cute baby-talk: 'Wot is dat Mama? Wot are you doin' Mama? Where Kate gone?' He said 'My' instead of 'I'. 'My 'bedient boy now Mummy.' 'Pop in 'Merica over the sea-water. My go to see him in 'Merica one day.' They were taken to the park daily by the nanny, Rosemary, loved drawing and being read to, and fast outgrew the American zipper suits sent by Arthur. Could he get

---

* Adalbert de Segonzac was London correspondent of *France-Soir*. He had served with the RAF, attached to a Free French air unit, took part in the invasion of Normandy, and was shot down over the Rhine, spending the rest of the war as a prisoner.

them pretty swimsuits from Macy's, Kaye asked, if he had any dollars? ('Why not give your friends lemonade one evening instead of bourbon?') And she yearned for nylons – sick of wearing lisle stockings – and often ran out of still-rationed sugar, 'because of making cakes for kids'.

The Moscow Road flat was six floors up, and sometimes they left the children alone. 'One day our parents came home and there was no sign of us,' John recalled. 'Mum did her big hysterical number – and we were watching all the time, hiding under the bed. After that, they put bars on the windows – but didn't stop leaving us alone.' Ann, already frail and weighing under seven stone, often had the twins to stay. John remembered those Westgate episodes as idyllic for him, but hard on his sister, because 'Nan', having preferred her sons to Kaye, now made a favourite of her grandson too. In John's bedroom at Westgate were John Webb's army uniform, boots and bayonet: Nan constantly told him he was the reincarnation of his dead uncle. Shutting the door on Kate, she would say, 'We don't want to play with her, do we, Johnny?'

Kaye confided her guilt to Arthur. 'I really feel I ought to be with the kids more now. Nurses are all very well but the best of them can't tell stories and play like a mum. Rosemary is good but they are handful for one person . . . and I hate to leave them with strangers at Westgate all through the summer.' Yet she took another job, as assistant editor of Lord Kemsley's new travel magazine called *Go*, 'aimed at the higher middle class with big incomes', with an office in the *Sunday Times*. 'Isn't GO a damn silly name? I'm trying hard to persuade them to drop it. They are giving me £1,000 a year for a six-month contract and I have a strong feeling that by then I'll give it up' – which she did. The magazine was altogether too chi-chi for her liking, and the editor, Leonard Russell, kept rejecting pieces by her old friends. Besides, Russell started work at 6 p.m., 'and I never saw the kids'. But she had to work: although Ronald's show at the Leicester Galleries had done well, attracting buyers like Alec Guinness, Ingrid Bergman and Christopher Fry, the cost of living had risen 'frighteningly'. When the children were almost four, they were enrolled in a Chelsea nursery school with thirty pupils, their fees seventeen guineas a term.

The collaborative Searles became a fixture in the *News Chronicle*. In October 1951 they covered Dr Edith Summerskill's election campaign in Fulham, and Herbert Morrison's in Lewisham South; in February 1952 they reported on George VI's funeral cortège at Paddington station. And they embarked on a series called 'Looking at London'.

Such a weekly interview, which may take seven minutes to read, involves background research, approaching and cajoling the subject, arranging the rendezvous, recording the interview, transcribing notes and (most time-consuming) crafting the finished article. Kaye never lacked ideas: she was naturally inquisitive and industrious. Ronald came along with his sketchbook and pens. Anyone who did anything interesting in every corner of London yielded a piece. (John once told his mother a man was playing a harp on Queensway, nearby; Kaye rushed out to interview him.) Together the Searles explored secret turnings off the Old Kent Road or St Martin's Lane or Farringdon Street to find 'real Londoners': a rat-catcher, a sewer-flusher, a book gilder, a fiddling busker, a manufacturer of corks, the silver-men of Chancery Lane, Mr Phillips the lamplighter of SW7, a man who made a ladder for Nelson's Column, a traditional nanny, a Victoria station ticket-collector, the mink-skinners of Garlickhythe in the City, a gamekeeper in Richmond Park, a tattooist, a flag-maker, a taxidermist at the Natural History Museum, a maker of piano hammers, a dealer in Oriental antiques, the bargees on the canal at Little Venice, the Searles' own jobbing gardener, who was a connoisseur of Dickens, and Ada Smith the gypsy lavender-seller (one of fifteen daughters herself, and the mother of eleven sons), who gratefully accepted a cigarette and a glass of whisky. They wrote about barrel-organs, Sotheby's, horse auctions at the Elephant and Castle. They penetrated World's End, and Shepherd Market in Mayfair. When they talked to the sentries outside Buckingham Palace, Ronald's friend Clement Freud turned up in his car, an old London taxi that had cost £50, and fed them a three-course meal with a whole carp as pièce de résistance. To facilitate their excursion to Portobello Road, Freud and his then more famous wife, the actress Jill Raymond (drawn by Ronald when she played Beauty in *Beauty and the Beast* in 1950), set up a stall in the antiques market, so that Ronald could draw while the Freuds sold their old junk. To their amazement they made easy money. Freud had just lost his job as manager of the Arts Theatre Club, so for three months they kept on the stall every Saturday. Later, when Freud opened his first restaurant, in the Royal Court Club, Ronald designed his menus.

Charles Fenby, who had moved on from editing the *Leader* and was now editor of the *Birmingham Gazette*, wrote congratulating Kaye on one of her 'quite brilliant' interviews. 'You are the new Henry Mayhew! I know how this sort of piece in which the subject appears to be doing the talking means all the more work for the writer. You have brought it off perfectly.'

Fenby's great friend at Oxford had been Cecil Day-Lewis, the publisher and poet. Day-Lewis had just moved into Bedford Gardens, at number 73a, with his new love, the young actress Jill Balcon. At her first breakfast with Cecil, she had shown him Ronald's *News Chronicle* cartoon: 'our first shared memory'. Now they were neighbours, and often sang together – since Day-Lewis, like Ronald, had a beautiful singing voice. On Day-Lewis's birthday in 1951, 27 April, he and Jill were married at Kensington register office. When they returned to their flat, having left the door unlocked for the cleaner, they found that Ronald had propped on a chair a St Trinian's drawing of a headmistress with a cringing new girl by her side: 'Prudence is new to St Trinian's. I want you to take care of her, girls!' Below this Searle had written 'For Prudence read Jill.'

But Ronald was already jaundiced about St Trinian's. D. B. Wyndham Lewis's book *The Terror of St Trinian's*, under the pseudonym Timothy Shy, was an instant bestseller of 1952. It was publicized by a stunt in which an army of young ladies, led by Hermione Gingold, smashed in a window of Foyles bookshop (who were forewarned), while Clement Freud drove his taxi with his wife Jill playing 'Miss Desirée Umbrage', head of the school, bound and gagged on top. The whole setup was filmed by Pathé News: 'a cretinous publicity stunt,' Ronald commented to me last year. Max Parrish wanted another St Trinian's book at once, but Ronald resisted. Instead, he published *Souls in Torment*, an explicit farewell to St Trinian's, in which the school is wiped out by an atomic bomb. Words (preface and dirge) were by C. Day-Lewis, who told Kaye he would be 'delighted to do a short solo on the Bones for an intro to Souls in T. A fee of 25 guineas would be OK.'

Ronald's routine was to walk to his studio each morning, returning for an early supper at Burnham Court, before leaving to meet *Punch*'s critic Eric Keown for their work at the theatre. But the winter of 1951 had been 'harder and more miserable than any I have known,' Kaye told her father. The time had come to consolidate family life and studio in one place, so a search began. 'We were on our knees with pounding around Paddington and Bayswater for weeks,' Ronald recalled. The trek brought them to a unique house in Bayswater, 32 Newton Road, built in an uncompromisingly contemporary steel-and-concrete style. 'As soon as we went through the front gate we fell in love with the house – as odd as it seemed in a street of early Victorian villas,' Ronald says. It had been designed in 1938 for two bachelor artists, 'unknown artistically, but extremely wealthy' (the sculptor

Robert Conway and his friend), by the young architect Denys Lasdun. There was a vast studio on top, where Ronald could work, with a north light and a fine terrace. The wall by the front door was of glass bricks; upstairs was a thirty-foot stretch of plate-glass window. The cellar was full of stuff left by the previous owners (including several Lucian Freuds, which they returned).

'The only problem was, we had no money,' Ronald recalled. 'Well, just about enough to put down the deposit. The price was unbelievably expensive for a couple of freelancers at that time' (it was £7,000), 'and the banks felt that it was an unsaleable modern horror – pity that it had no Elizabethan timber on the façade, or something.' Eventually they got a £5,000 mortgage from Lloyds Bank, Notting Hill Gate, at 4.5 per cent, Arthur Webb guaranteeing the deposit. 'And we did manage to pay it off, by agreeing to perpetrate untold rubbish over the years,' Ronald told me. 'It turned out to be perfect for all our working space and living needs.'

Lasdun became one of their 'People Worth Meeting' in the *News Chronicle*. Without divulging that it was her house, Kaye interviewed Lasdun about 32 Newton Road, which was in fact the prototype of Lasdun's current project, the Paddington Housing Scheme. Both were heavily influenced by Le Corbusier. 'Historians interpret a people by their architecture,' Lasdun declared, 'and it is our business to interpret people's desires', the most important being to raise the spirits, and induce a feeling of well-being. 'A family's life must take root in a house. When a man comes home at the end of the day and is face to face with his front door he should be able to feel, quite genuinely, "I'm jolly pleased to see you!"' The Searles did feel that. The house made passers-by stop in their tracks. Visitors stepping inside would gasp at the space and light. It proved an ideal party venue, and Kaye set about organizing parties. One of the first was a welcome home to Arthur Webb in March 1952. (He stayed for three months. 'It was wonderful having you for such a long stretch,' Kaye told him, 'to enjoy the first fruits of our Studio Folly!')

Ronald gave Kaye a leather-bound ledger and inscribed it

Kaye Searle
Visitors
30 Burnham Court W2
32 Newton Road W2

They had already had a party in Burnham Court for *The Naked Island*, Russell Braddon's book about the fall of Singapore and life in Changi, illustrated by Ronald. One night in March came Peter Finch, Geoffrey Willans (creator of the comic schoolboy Nigel Molesworth), Peter Ustinov, Franta Belsky, the Alec Guinnesses. If guests failed to sign their names, they would be listed in neat feathery pencil by Ronald. Among the signatures discernible are those of the writers Arthur Calder-Marshall, J. D. Scott and Christopher Fry, the Labour MP and journalist Tom Driberg, the cartoonists Leslie Illingworth and Nicolas Bentley, the *Punch* drama critic Eric Keown, the actors Hermione Gingold, Yolande Donlan, Denholm Elliott and Claire Bloom, the critics J. C. and Wendy Trewin, the artist Edward Ardizzone and his wife Catherine, the architect Denys Lasdun, Clement and Jill Freud, and the theatre and film director and choreographer Wendy Toye.

Tucked into this ledger was a verse from J. C. Trewin, including this stanza:

He said, 'My head is in a whirl –
I am the goofiest guest:
Now tell me, who's the golden girl
Upon the left of Godfrey Tearle?'
I told him it was Mrs Searle
And he was much impressed.

One youthful visitor to Newton Road was Quentin Blake, who at twenty had just had his first drawing accepted by *Punch*. The BBC brought him to meet Ronald, for a programme that introduced young hopefuls to seasoned practitioners. The conversation with Ronald, as 'Q' recalled, was not about approaches to illustration but about the fountain pen Ronald used, and his distinctive brown ink, made from a free-running furniture stain.

Thanks to both Searles' theatre connections, there were as many actors as artists in their circle. John Mills wrote after one party, inviting the Searles' au pair, Anna Romersa, who had found his treasured cufflinks, to be his guest at *Charley's Aunt*, in which he was starring. Alec Guinness, 'all set to be thoroughly bored' in a hit play, implored the Searles to come any night, and dine afterwards. James Mason regarded Kaye as one of his 'belles of lettres': he needed to know what books could be turned into films, so 'now is your time to speak, for I am a market'. He was seeking a story about an English gent arriving home from abroad, to find his family's Palladian mansion 'encroached upon by slag heaps' – but with a heart-warming twist that would leave the audience 'fearfully pleased with everything'. ('Nothing downbeat, get it?') Kaye sent him *Who Goes Home?* by Maurice Edelman, adding, 'Claire Bloom came round the other evening and is all agog at the prospect of playing with you.' She sent Mason several more ideas over the years, including an Arthur Calder-Marshall novel about Mexico that roused the Masonic enthusiasm. In turn he kept the Searles informed on films the children should see, and in due course warned them about *Lolita* (in which he played Humbert Humbert) and its brush with the Legion of Decency.

In Newton Road the Searles started their own publishing house, Perpetua Books (named after Eric Gill's serif typeface), to produce illustrated volumes, elegant and finely designed, with Ronald's colophon in eighteenth-century cameo style.

Their first product (printed for 2s 4d, sold at 7s 6d) was *An Experience of Critics*, Christopher Fry's address to the Critics' Circle. It contained a symposium of leading critics' approaches to dramatic criticism, illustrated with Ronald's caricatures. The critics gratefully accepted the original drawings of themselves in lieu of a fee. 'So we are all set to break the bank,' Kaye told her father. To the launch party came several of the critics, and the book sold out its 3,000 print run in two days. It was followed by volumes of André François and Sempé. Soon they could afford a car: a scruffy little 1936 Morris 8.

Domestic life in the 1950s was simple. Entertaining was rarely lavish, decor was unexciting. So the Searles' distinctive home was much written about. ('Their marriage is a model of domestic happiness enriched by professional collaboration,' wrote the *Sunday Times*'s Atticus.) Unusual *objets trouvés* were displayed everywhere – a Webb toy theatre, a model of an old steam engine, a rocking-horse, a row of marionettes, a ladder painted with stars and diamonds, an American wall-clock with an enormous winking eye painted by Ronald on its pendulum. The curved fireplace wall was hung with Japanese masks, costumed dolls, prints and drawings, and plastered with invitation cards. There was imaginative use of vivid colour, even on radiators. Their bedroom was in lime-green and maroon. The back door was candy-striped in pale blue and white, with sunbursts of yellow and black. The bathroom had curtains of striped towelling. Such ideas were the *dernier cri* in pre-Conran, pre-Habitat 1952.

Ronald had even painted the light-switches: one was disguised as an eye with heavily fringed lashes and an arched eyebrow; another had a cow's head with switches in eye and nostril; another had a bird perched on it. Any corner or door panel was embellished with a mural – a simpering mermaid brandishing a frying pan and a fork; a tricorn-hatted military figure with twirling moustache, on a bicycle. Ronald's sprawling studio on the top floor had a sky-blue ceiling, its white walls covered in drawings and posters, shelves of art books, with concealed lighting, and a Berber rug on the parquet floor. The crimson and white striped curtains were of deckchair canvas. The playroom had one wall coated in blackboard paint, and a glass-topped table displayed the children's paintings.

One of the living room's adornments was the barrel-organ, brilliantly painted in fairground reds and yellows: a good ice-breaker at parties, and useful for musical bumps. Ronald had found it in a storage yard in Covent Garden. To get it home, he was yoked to the barrow, with its huge wooden wheels, with Kaye tripping alongside. They had never before noticed the gradients between the Strand and Paddington: uphill was tiring and downhill was terrifying. 'There were no brakes . . . he had to run like a rickshaw boy to avoid getting squashed.' Before installing it they tried it out in the street, Kaye bursting into song, and made 1s 9d within minutes. Two years later, Canon A. O. Wintle of Bury St Edmunds, aged seventy-six, wrote ('Dear Fellow-Enthusiasts') offering to renovate their organ for them, free: 'I do some lovely tunes which give me lots of thrills.' The dear old boy was house-bound, but 'I am happy, and devotedly cared for by two Maids, Sisters, with us 41 and 36 years. Bless you.'

Kaye had been asked by the BBC to scout out interesting American visitors for a new television programme, so she asked her father for suggestions. Arthur was enjoying a newsman's scoop in the presidential election of November 1952: the *Daily Herald* was first to announce Eisenhower's victory over Adlai Stevenson. He was a whiz at modern communications, and had organized a Western Union cable link from the cellar of his home/office in Cleveland Avenue, Washington, plus AP and UP tape machines and a radio and TV set – 'which I bought for cash, although the storekeeper tried vainly to get me to sign an HP contract!' He was still an inveterate newshound and his triumph won him 'an Oscar from the office. Enthusiastic eulogies from Percy Cudlipp and others.' On Arthur's retirement two years later, Malcolm Muggeridge described how Arthur lived 'in amity and bliss' with his ticker-tapes. 'His last act at night was to tear off the latest, his first act in the morning was to see what the night had brought forth.' Arthur's name was honoured and loved, Muggeridge wrote, 'wherever two or more journalists are gathered together. He represents the best qualities in our profession – honesty, understanding, political and professional loyalties . . . above all a rich sense of humour and the dear companionship that goes with it. I have never heard anyone speak other than warmly of him.' Ronald's cartoon of his father-in-law appeared alongside this encomium.

Looking at London and *People Worth Meeting* were published in one volume in 1953. In his foreword, the *News Chronicle* editor Robert J. Cruikshank noted, correctly, that most Londoners are insular, sticking to their own patch: 'Ealingites seldom seek out the sunset splendours of Wapping Old Stairs.' But the Searles were true London-lovers, 'sympathetic venturers in a city which is the most mysterious, bashful, withdrawn and misunderstood of all the world's capitals'. Ronald's endpaper drawing was the view from the roof terrace of Newton Road: his left hand, wielding his pen, is poised over a drawing-board, and there is a Remington typewriter on the table alongside, with Kaye's hands holding a sheaf of typescript. Cups of coffee, bottles of ink and potted plants frame a vista of mansard roofs, chimneypots and distant church spire.

Ronald soon became the highest-paid *Punch* artist, getting £75 per drawing for 'The Rake's Progress'. When this was published in book form, Kaye asked Max Beerbohm to write an introductory essay. But Max said he could never produce an essay worthy of Ronald's 'wondrous' work. Nor could he dictate it, as she suggested. 'I could as easily *sing* it to a packed audience in the Albert Hall on the spur of the moment this afternoon.' He urged them to come back to Italy, but it was Ronald who travelled there alone that summer, painting and looking at Renaissance art from Milan to Taormina in Sicily. He also designed costumes and sets for Wendy Toye's *On the Twelfth Day*: a delightful and witty twenty-four-minute film based on *The Twelve Days of Christmas*, shown in the US that December.

The radio producer Janet Quigley had liked Kaye's earlier 'How We Met' broadcast, about her first encounter with Ronald, and invited Kaye to become a monthly diarist on *Woman's Hour*. 'I think we may expect a crowded diary from Kaye Webb,' said the announcer. Kaye's voice and accent were ineffably stamped with the 1930s, high and brightly inflected, like Annette Mills talking to Muffin the Mule on children's television. She said she hoped listeners would not respond like the woman who, sharing a railway carriage ('kerridge') with Kaye when she met an old friend, listened to their 'long catch-up of gossip', and 'suddenly put down her book, made a horrible face, said, "Yap-yap-yap-yap-yap!" and flounced out of the carriage'.

But she must introduce herself to listeners. 'About what I look like,' she said. 'Well, when my friends want to be kind they say, "D'you know, Kaye, I believe you're a little thinner."'

She lived, she said, in 'Peddington' – 'that sooty, busy area near the station, where you hear every foreign tongue because there are so many small hotels and student lodgings'. Their modern house was 'like something left over from the Festival of Britain . . . We're often visited by architectural students and sometimes by mothers with children who have mistaken us for the chest clinic down the road.' Local cats had polished off the goldfish in the garden pond, and boys threw bottles at the conkers in their chestnut tree, but the house had 'a nice big studio where my husband works all day (and half the night sometimes!)'. She told listeners, 'I expect some of you are wondering why I work at all, considering that a successful husband and two children ought to be a full-time job. The chief reason is – well, I can't help it! I've got the habit. I like housekeeping but I'm happier writing than cleaning or ironing.' She had been a full-time journalist until Kate and John were born, but stayed at home 'once they reached the crawling-into-the-fire stage', and helped her husband run their publishing firm. Now the twins were at school and 'I am going to edit a children's monthly magazine, but . . . I shall get home when they do in the afternoons.'

The magazine was the *Young Elizabethan*, owned by John Grigg. Grigg, Eton and Oxford, was a Tory, but decidedly more liberal than his father, Lord Altrincham of Churchill's wartime government. John Grigg already edited the *National Review*, and had acquired the *Young Elizabethan*, 'the magazine to grow up with', an admirable if slightly stuffy publication for ten-to-sixteen-year-olds. Originally founded in 1948 by Billy Collins as *Collins Magazine*, it had been renamed after the coronation of Elizabeth II. Its previous editor, Laura Fergusson, wife of Sir Bernard, the wartime general, suggested Kaye to take over from September 1954.

Meanwhile, what a lovely life she had. She was going to the opening of Ronald's new exhibition and would have to wear a 'het'. Another excitement had been the premiere of *The Belles of St Trinian's*. Ronald's schoolgirls were now an entrenched feature of British life, but his only involvement in the films was allowing them. However, they couldn't resist visiting Shepperton Studios, and seeing how make-up artists rumpled the girls' shirts, frizzed their hair, pulled holes in their stockings. (Their daughter, Kate, who was an extra, kept tidying her hair and pulling up her socks.) The Searles joined a crowd playing parents berating Alastair Sim, the headmistress. It was 'jolly hard work' being extras, Kaye discovered. 'We dripped with perspiration . . . but I was very thrilled because I always wanted to be an actress.'

She usually ended her diary with an amusing children's saying. Kate had just come back from a visit to her Searle grandparents in Cambridge. Ronald suggested that she wrote down the names of all the stations the train stopped at. Her list read: 'Cambridge. Audley End. Bishops Stortford. Gentlemen. Liverpool Street.'

When Kaye's American friends, the film star Gloria Stuart and her husband Arthur Sheekman, the Marx Brothers' scriptwriter, visited, Kaye passed on her favourite line from *A Night at the Opera*, when 'Groucho is signing a contract and going through clauses one by one and someone says, "What about the sanity clause?" And he says, "There ain't no Sanity Claus."'

One month, Kaye recounted how she met a woman who had just walked out on her family and was taking a train to Brighton for the day. Kaye decided she would do the same. She walked along Brighton pier, had her picture taken for sixpence, and hired a fishing-rod; visited a palmist and a hand-impressionist machine which told her she had a powerful fate-line, was influenced by affairs of the heart, had a magnetic personality, led a full and interesting life ('True'), and had a happy marriage ('True'). She found in the Lanes an old town crier's bell for Ronald. It was not possible, she decided, to forget one's children and husband, even for a day. And it had given her confidence, she said, talking to strangers without seeming like a sad friendless person, or a pickup.

But Kaye was never abashed by the vox pop: talking to strangers was second nature, and she switched on her tape-recorder everywhere. For another *Woman's Hour* broadcast, from Paddington public library, she waylaid people to inquire what books they were borrowing. One of her accostees was a six-year-old named Judy. Kaye asked her, 'Did you like that book? Why?' It was a question she was to ask children hundreds of times, a decade later.

Talking to children and interacting with them was to prove her special genius. Editing the *Young Elizabethan*, she established an uncanny rapport with readers. It had been a rather serious magazine. 'But it got more jokey once I was editor, because Ronald really styled the magazine,' she recalled. (She also enlisted André François, Sprod and E. H. Shepard to draw for it.) 'We had a club which provided a model for the Puffin Club, and the magazine itself was a model for *Puffin Post*.' One reader remembered it as 'a cross between a civilized *Boy's Own Paper* and the *Illustrated London News*, for grammar-school children given to browsing in bookshops'.

Children of the 1950s regarded heroic, adventurous and distinguished people as their models and beacons. The *Young Elizabethan*'s patrons included the violinist Yehudi Menuhin as president, the composer Benjamin Britten, the scientist Julian Huxley, the leader of the 1953 Everest expedition Brigadier Sir John Hunt, the showjumper Pat Smythe, the Oxford don Lord David Cecil, the author Noel Streatfeild, the Chief Scout Lord Rowallan, and the heroic World War II fighter pilot Squadron-Leader Neville Duke. The poet Stephen Spender and the cricketer Colin Cowdrey wrote articles. Readers were invited to study the colophons (from the Greek for 'summit') of different publishers – Rupert Hart-Davis's fox, Allen Lane's penguin – and to read David Cecil's biography of Lord Melbourne, or Rosemary Sutcliff's historical novels.

Kaye got J. C. Trewin to write a play, which readers acted at their Christmas party in 1954. *A Sword for a Prince* was an Arthurian tale set in Trewin's native Cornwall. In the cast were Trewin's eleven-year-old son Ion (later the author and publisher), and Hugh Gaitskell's daughter Julia. Kaye's barrel-organ went to the party

– 'a great success', John Grigg said, 'owing to your imagination and vigour'.

In September 1954 Kaye had gone away alone: she spent a week in Rome for *Woman's Hour*. Her notebook is inscribed by Ronald, 'Kaye Webb's Roman Diary'. 'Darling, I can't write a diary,' she wrote on the train to Milan. 'I keep thinking about posterity and being embarrassed, but I love writing to you . . . so it shall be A Letter To My Husband.' When it came to her broadcast, she read from her letters to Ronald, describing her hot little hotel room, the noisy Romans yelling all night, the Vespas spluttering by till dawn. 'Really, holidays without you are a rotten idea,' she wrote. 'I feel only half here.' But despite its noise and her loneliness, Rome seduced her with its ancient beauty, its sparkling air, its parks, the kiosks selling peaches and grapes and ice-cream, Roman men murmuring ego-boosting 'Ciao, bella', dark-eyed girls in snowy white blouses, teeming cats, the Trevi fountain. She began to appreciate the timelessness and peace of old buildings ('I've never been much of a one for places, I've always preferred to look at people') and saw the film actress Anna Magnani and the American playwright Tennessee Williams on the Via Veneto.

The Searles had lent out their house for a young people's dance, with Strip the Willow and the Eightsome Reel and the Paul Jones, and champagne cider cup. The lesson she learned was that instead of grown-up fare the young like 'piles of buttered bread, sliced meat, hot sausages and spreads', to 'make up their own enormous sandwiches'. Next time she would write their names on paper tags and twist them round the stems of their glasses, so they could discover each other's names. 'I suddenly realized what bliss it is to be grown up . . . I used to be so tongue-tied and gauche . . . now I know young men are shy too. What a lot we suffer unnecessarily, and how useless it is to tell our daughters so.'

★

Ronald had now replaced Vicky (Victor Weisz, an intense, quarrelsome, Berlin-born Hungarian refugee) as weekly cartoonist of the *News Chronicle*. He began illustrating the subversive Nigel Molesworth stories written by Geoffrey Willans, who had been introduced to him by Kaye. He also drew for *Le Canard Enchaîné*, set and judged competitions for *Time & Tide*, and designed the decor for the Chelsea Arts Ball on New Year's Eve of 1954/5. The Searles took John Grigg, who had 'never enjoyed a party more . . . Everything about it was fun – the company, the decorations, the music, the balloons, the dresses, the dinner, the champagne, the atmosphere of abandon.' He hoped Ronald did not begrudge his seeing in the New Year with Kaye. 'Quite apart from the exciting venture in which we are partners,' he wrote, 'I feel we shall always be great friends.'

Early on the day after the ball, Kaye had departed, with the twins (but not Ronald), for Austria, and a skiing holiday. 'How did the children stand up to it?' Grigg wondered. (They loved it.) Grigg's admiration for Kaye was boundless. 'With you as Editor,' he told her, 'the magazine could never be dull.'

8: Social Whirl

1955–8

'All the birthday mornings I've had for the last five years have been the nicest since my childhood. It's the one day that your husband and children really go all out to make you feel precious and important. The day starts with a scuffling outside the bedroom door, and an outbreak of Happy Birthday Dear Mummy. Then they burst in with arms full of interesting, homemade parcels, including their own toys wrapped up to make it look more. My bath salts this year were called Heart of a Rose, and a parcel from my husband was done up so beautifully that I would like to keep it unopened for days . . .'

Filling a newspaper column, or broadcasting a diary, colours a writer's life, and the tint is rose. Everything is grist, any event becomes material. So when Ronald went with Eric Keown to cover the Dublin theatre scene, Kaye went too, for her February diary. 'You'll begin to wonder if I really have a job and a family and a home,' she apologized to listeners. But it was her birthday weekend. And she was curious to see the city where her father had once worked.

The Searles were interviewed and photographed like celebrities. Dublin was 'a darlin' place, because of its inhabitants'. In her view, the river Liffey was as romantic as the Seine – and 'somehow more comfortable'. There were masses of cake shops and everyone was friendly. 'I suppose it is their soft voices and the Irish lilt . . . When we asked the way, the reply was, "Ah sure it isn't far at all, you may go there on your own two feet if you wish."'

Micheál MacLiammoir drove them into the mountains, because Kaye wanted to see some countryside. And Kaye now owned a model gown by the Irish designer Sybil Connolly, a gymslip-style black pleated linen dress with a white waistcoat; Sybil named it St Trinian's, and asked Ronald to sign it. 'He thought it was pretty and would suit me, and the next thing I knew, I was having a fitting. The awful thing is that I shan't look anything like that gorgeous slim tall model in it, and I'm dreading to see Ronald's face when I put it on . . . thank goodness the summer is far away and I may have found a miracle diet.'

One wonders how listeners felt, 'wearing the same shabby dress'* in their humdrum homes, hearing about the bright busyness of Kaye's metropolitan life. She had been to the birthday party of Kenneth More's daughter. She had met Gene Kelly. She had sold flags in Regent Street, and would never again pass a rattling box without stopping. At the Royal Academy summer show, she 'bumped into so many distinguished people and brushed past so many undistinguished paintings I realized what a purely social as against artistic occasion it was'. She went with Christopher Fry to see his play *The Lark*, adapted from Jean Anouilh, with Dorothy Tutin, a gamine twenty-five, 'like a radiant child' as Joan of Arc. When she read John Verney's new book, it 'made me prouder than ever that he is a friend of ours'.

All that spring she had 'the doubtful pleasure' of watching her husband design dresses for, and attend the fittings of, actresses 'with much better measurements than mine'. Ronald was doing the costumes and decor for Donald Swann's new musical, *Wild Thyme*. Next Monday they would be sitting in the Theatre Royal Bath, 'clutching hands, our hearts in our mouths as the curtain goes up for the first time'.

* As in 'Try a Little Tenderness', the 1930s song by Irving King, recorded by Bing Crosby among many others.

Life was a social whirl: they dined with the Muggeridges at the
Garrick, attended the *Spectator* party, gave supper at home for
the formidable American publisher Blanche Knopf. Ronald was
off to Paris, Kaye was doing a pilot for a TV programme called *Kaye
Webb's Scrapbook*. Arthur Sheekman had told her she should 'play
herself up as a personality' and she did just that. 'I have now made
my maiden appearance on television,' she told James Mason. 'It
wasn't as frightening as I thought.' But she found rehearsals time-
consuming, and although she loved looking stylish, maintaining a
telegenic appearance – beauty treatments, manicures, coiffure by
Alexander, waxings at Cyclax, dress fittings at Roth – was expensive.
When her six-month contract was up she did not renew it.

Kaye had managed to drag Ronald up to Birmingham for the
Young Elizabethan readers' Easter party on 15 April 1955. But they
were too busy to take up Robert Graves's invitation to his house
at Deya, Majorca. 'Don't work too hard,' Graves told her. 'I do,
and like it, but it's a vice.' Kaye told him Ronald was working
non-stop on *Wild Thyme*. 'There is wild thyme on these
mountains,' replied Graves. 'It is used, infused like tea, to cure
insomnia.' They did get away, to join Wendy Toye at Le Lavandou
in the South of France that summer, and before they left, Ronald
wrote his wife a charming note from Paris: 'Darling love: Nah
– this 'ere cheque. I order you – I insist – as your husband I
demand – that you spend it on clows – stuff for the holiday tra-
la-la – and nothing serious. I have enough in my deposit and this
is SPARE' (underlined eighteen times). 'Wendy says she has found
that Lavondoo has a lovely beach – huts and pedalos. Don't
overwork – leave as much as you can for me . . . xxx I love you
xxx. Ronald husband.' He drew a squawking fledgling. They
had acquired two fantail pigeons, after Ronald remarked that
he'd like to have some flying about outside his studio window
– actually he meant doves – and now there were several pigeon
eggs on the terrace. 'PS: Let me know if the eggs hatch.'

They were still, it seemed, compatible and happy. When first married, Ronald had encouraged her to remain Kaye Webb, as the name 'meant something'. Five years later, she regarded 'Kaye Webb' as a separate entity; her real name was Kaye Searle. 'Too late now,' she wrote in a piece on 'Partnership', 'but I honestly think having two names is a bit silly.' She did confess to a twinge of resentment when introduced as Mrs Ronald Searle and people said 'Is he here?' or 'Oh how marvellous for you.' Ronald hated the telephone, letter-writing, and arguing; 'I rather enjoy them,' said Kaye. Packing for their holidays was a clichéd cause of marital discord. All Ronald needed was 'the same old sandals, re-stitched six times, clammy and oily to handle'; she took so many clothes she could never shut her case. 'R says what do you want to take all that stuff for, we can always get things there.' Her travel tip, to the girls of an Ilford school where she gave a speech, was practical: never wear a tight girdle on a flight.

After France that summer, when they saw the work of Le Corbusier in Marseilles, Ronald went on to Geneva, to draw the Four Powers conference for *Life* magazine. 'There is no doubt I've married a very clever man,' Kaye told her father. 'But can you imagine a more difficult assignment?' Just to draw the empty conference room required endless protocol. He had tiptoed along the hotel corridor to be shown the suite John Foster Dulles would occupy – only to find someone asleep in its bed. Arthur himself was off on a lecture tour of the Midwest, and Kaye urged him not to squander his fees by treating everyone he met. 'You and Ronnie are a great pair for picking up the check.'

In an era of proliferating female columnists, we are used to women writing intimately about their family lives. Such columns are hostages to fortune, especially if the prevailing tone has a snug smugness, despite injections of self-deprecation. In Kaye's jaunty broadcast accounts, the picture of their family suggested contentment. At Christmas 1955, Kaye had taken the children carol singing, feeling like 'The Listeners' in de la Mare's poem. She and Ronald had both managed to finish work by Christmas Eve, and Ronald had again covered the wrapping paper with drawings, which made his presents 'unbearable to tear open'.

The children's cousin Nick Webb, arriving at Christmas with his father Bill, mother Eva and sister Anna from their council flat in Kew Gardens, remembered feeling like poor relations on Newton Road's highly polished parquet floors. The housekeeper, Elvira (who stayed with Kaye for ever), would cook, and Ronald would carve 'a turkey the size of an ostrich'. 'Kaye wanted us all to be fantastically jolly and play games. Ronnie would sit aloof and shy, and disappear as soon as he could.' But Nick was 'a po-faced little oik' in those days. (He grew up to be the publisher of Douglas Adams's *The Hitchhiker's Guide to the Galaxy*, and Adams's biographer.)

Elvira Martín Alvarez had arrived in England from Galicia in northern Spain, after being jilted by her fiancé. 'The house would echo to the sound of her singing Spanish folk songs as she worked,' John Searle recalls. 'She had arrived in a tolerant and liberal world, in which her sunny personality blossomed. We taught her the pidgin English she adopted – "I no likey this" and "Why you no . . . ?" – and her shocked cry of "Ayeeee" greeted almost any bit of news. She could not read or write but never hesitated to express her passionate opinions and convictions. When Elvira said someone was a bad man, there was no room for doubt.

'Elvira was the first truly uninhibited person we met in our childhood, warm and grounded and never ill at ease. She cooked us glutinous fry-ups, unfazed by our requests for fried bananas and pineapples, and her paellas were legendary. She would join in our parents' New Year's Eve parties among the great and good, the pompous and massive egos, and dance flamenco style, with her head tossed back, to general admiration. She was the beating heart of our life at Newton Road.'

Kaye, 'having persuaded Ronald to allow the children some pets', reported that they had 'a menagerie': a sweet intelligent dachshund called Rusty, and the pigeons, which now numbered five. 'They never stop quarrelling and acknowledge us only by vicious peckings.' One newborn was found frozen on the lawn. 'Ronald kept it by the fire, clearing up after it, feeding it, but the moment it was better, it lashed out at us with its beak.' But at their New Year's Eve party, when everyone went out on the balcony to hear the bells at midnight, and all five pigeons flew in the air, 'it was breathtaking. The bells ringing, the clock chiming, the hooters on the river boats going and the beating of these white wings over our heads.'

There is no mistaking the flavour of a charmed life.

Soon Kaye was relating a domestic milestone. After clearing away Sunday tea, she had sat down with a book – and realized the room was silent. Not only was her husband reading but 'both our children were sitting quietly reading'. 'And I realized that what I'd waited for for eight years had suddenly come true. Ever since they began their first baby bangings and squallings, and as they grew up all that wrestling, acrobatics, and the game where they had to get round the room without touching the floor, well, you know! All that time I'd thought, "*one day they'll start reading* . . . " And now it's happened! It's marvellous. And has cured me once and for all of wishing they were small and helpless again.'

We should always be careful of what we wish for, Kaye added. When she was ten, her father took her and her brother to visit an American millionaire (Dr Emmanuel de Marney Baruch was the name, she recalled) in a grand hotel. Dr Baruch promised the children all the ice-cream they could eat. It came in a soup tureen. Eagerly they started spooning it into their mouths, but soon realized that all they could eat was not very much. It ended in tears.

★

It was up to Kaye to organize visits from the ageing Searle parents, or her mother; to find a new char; to view schools for the children (Miss Kynaston at Queen's College, Harley Street, for advice about Kate, and Mr Trevor-Roberts in Hampstead for John; Ronald 'never knew the names of their teachers or where they were in class'), and to arrange dentists and polio shots, and riding lessons and the pantomime. Ronald had 'got into a habit of working which I simply couldn't dissuade him from'. But the society photographer Baron's portrait of the artist, taken on 15 December 1955, perched at his drawing-board under a red lamp matching the red-striped studio curtains, is a happy one.

At thirty-five Ronald was increasingly in demand, in Britain and America. *Punch* invited him to carve his initials on the hallowed Table, and offered him £100 a week for his exclusive services 'in this country' apart from his Lemon Hart Rum adverts (displayed, thirty-seven feet high, above the Monument in the City; he was paid 250–500 guineas for these). He was drawing London characters for a *Punch* series called 'The Big City', or 'The New Mayhew'; and colour caricatures for 'Heroes of Our Time' (among them Somerset Maugham, Picasso, Samuel Beckett). The *Young Elizabethan* now used Molesworth, published in book form as *Down with Skool!* (50,000 copies sold in months), *How to Be Topp*, *Whizz for Atomms* and *Back in the Jug Agane*. Children who had never been near a public school got to know the St Custard's types – headmaster Grimes, 'Peason with face like squished tomato', Sigismund the Mad Maths Master, Basil Fotherington-Tomas, who trilled 'Hullo clouds, hullo sky', and sundry 'oiks, snekes, cads, oafs and dirty roters', summoned by the sound of 'Clang-pip, Clang-pip' (the skool bell, which – as eny fule kno – 'hav been cracked on one side'.)

He was made a life member of the Garrick Club. He was swept up unwillingly into the Suez crisis, persuaded by Bernard Fergusson (who said it would 'prevent bloodshed') to produce propaganda fliers – which were never dropped. He returned from

Cyprus with acute peritonitis. In 1957, for *Life* magazine, he attended one of the murder trials of the century – of John Bodkin Adams, the Eastbourne doctor, 160 of whose patients had died under suspicious circumstances, leaving Adams the beneficiary of their wills. (Adams was acquitted, and lived to be eighty-four.) Such was Ronald's life in the mid-1950s. As his biographer later noted, three of Ronald's collaborators – Eric Keown, Alex Atkinson, Geoffrey Willans – died young, of heart attacks.

On the first day of spring in 1956, Kaye regaled *Woman's Hour* listeners with her euphoria, a 'light-hearted headiness which makes everything seem possible'. Instead of doing mundane things like spring-cleaning, she said, we should all 'look a little longer at the sky and achieve a refreshment of the spirit'.

What filled her with the joys of spring was that she had at last met 'the most loved of living poets'. She told listeners about Walter de la Mare's praise of her schoolgirl poem. 'My nursery days were made joyful by Messrs Wynken, Blynken and Nod. And Miss T, do you remember? "It's a very odd thing, / as odd as can be, / that whatever Miss T eats / turns into Miss T."'

John Grigg had taken Kaye to tea at de la Mare's house in Montpelier Row, Twickenham, overlooking Marble Hill Park. The dates got muddled, they were not expected, and de la Mare was in bed. Miss Saxton, who looked after him, said it would take an hour to get him dressed. Nearly eighty-three, and not long for this world, he lay in his gothic room, in his high bed, his blue cardigan matching the blue counterpane, looking out on the green sweep of park, daffodils, and a plane tree said to be the tallest in England, which had survived lightning damage that removed twelve barrowloads of bark. His gramophone was a gift from Joyce Grenfell. If wheeled to the window he had a glimpse of the Thames. Inscribed with a diamond on one of the window panes was a verse from one of his poems:

'Look thy last on all things lovely, every hour. Let no night / Seal thy sense in deathly slumber / Till to delight / Thou hast paid thy utmost blessing . . .'

They had tea with three kinds of cake and two kinds of jam.

Why had Kaye never sought him out before? 'Perhaps I was afraid he wouldn't live up to my image. Well, he does – he exceeds it. He is courteous, gentle, witty and modest and a great man . . . He also has a lovely voice. To me it's always been extraordinary how close he managed to get to a child's mind.' They chatted about his earliest memories, and about the shock one gets, seeing one's reflection in a shop window, 'because no matter how earthbound and dreary one's body, one's mental conception of oneself is still young and eager'. On 23 March, de la Mare wrote in a shaky hand, sending three new poems for *Young Elizabethan*, to be illustrated by Ardizzone, and Kaye continued to go to tea with the old man every Wednesday afternoon until his death later that year. 'I'd drive along the road to meet him with my heart beating, as though to meet a lover,' she once told me. He telephoned her one day to say: 'Do you realize, Kindness also begins with a K?'

On 20 April he let her record him as he lay in bed, seeing in the faded mirror the reflection of tree, sky and birds. On the precious tape, she asked him why, in so many of his stories, the protagonist is 'a bit of a clot? I mean, the reader feels like saying to the chap who's telling the story, "Well, you silly fool, can't you see what's happening?"' He asked her, did her husband really hate people so much as his drawings suggested? He sent Kate, aged eight, a copy of *Peacock Pie*, signed 'with love at pre-sight'. Kaye said she too had loved him at pre-sight.

He died three months later, on 22 June 1956. Kaye went to his memorial at St Paul's Cathedral, and Joanna Scott-Moncrieff, editor of *Woman's Hour*, found Kaye's enthusiasm 'wildly infectious' in a rare programme about a literary figure which never sounded in the worst sense 'literary'. From Inverness-shire, John Grigg said de la Mare's last letter to him had paid tribute to Kaye. She had given the old man 'much comfort and happiness in his last days', Grigg said. 'He responded at once to your vitality and affection.'

Grigg was a steadfast ally, even when they disagreed about Suez, on which she held strongly anti-Tory views. 'I am quite ready to give way in argument,' he wrote. 'I merely claim . . . to have a better case.' He offered the Searles 500 shares each in *Young Elizabethan*, 'which might prove a substantial asset to you and the twins'. The circulation had risen by 5,000, so he would raise her salary by one shilling for each new reader: an increase of £250 per year. (He would not operate the scale backwards, should there be a setback.) Later, Kaye took John and Kate to Grigg's Scottish fastness – a magical holiday, John recalled, when he hunted deer, fly-fished, rode around in the Land Rover, went out in glass-bottomed boats and dined at a baronial table with trophies gazing down from panelled walls. And Kaye took Grigg to see Flanders and Swann's hit revue *At the Drop of a Hat*, where Grigg's immoderate laughter filled the house. Afterwards they went backstage, and Kaye offered 'helpful hints' to Michael Flanders: the set was too monochrome – two chaps in evening dress, and the black piano – and needed an injection of colour. Flanders wrote back equably, 'Perhaps I might wear a cummerbund?'

The *Young Elizabethan* office consisted of two attic rooms at 2 Breams Buildings, off Chancery Lane, a Dickensian ambience. Writers came puffing up the winding staircase to deliver their copy. Photographs of the office showed readers 'How your magazine is made'. 'We have always felt that *Young Elizabethan* is closer to its readers than magazines usually are,' wrote Kaye. 'All Your Own work' featured among others the future historian Ben Pimlott and, in a poem, fifteen-year-old Alan Ayckbourn. The

Young Elizabethans' Club had a badge, ran competitions and published readers' drawings, from 'Timothy, my dormouse' to sophisticated portraits. The Jills and Jennifers who won prizes were the sort who also read *Pony* magazine, which advertised in *YE*. Articles like 'Making your own marionettes', 'Who was the Pied Piper?', 'The bravest man I knew' by Sir John Hunt, 'Great escapes' by Geoffrey Trease, and 'An introduction to P. G. Wodehouse' by Richard Usborne, were edifying. Arthur Webb ('our American correspondent') reported 'The strange case of the talking horse'. This was a small mare with white fetlocks leading a placid life on a farm in Virginia, which had uncanny powers, spelling out answers on a typewriter with a keyboard the size of a piano. A schoolboy wrote in about tracking down the places in Arthur Ransome's books, from Beckfoot in the Lake District (from *Swallows and Amazons*) to Potter Heigham on the Norfolk Broads. Phillida Gili, daughter of the engraver Reynolds Stone, and now an illustrator herself, won a prize for drawing an ant's-eye view of a human foot, among daisies and celandines. Nobody will be surprised to learn that Nigel Rees, the omniscient presenter of *Quote . . . Unquote* on Radio 4, was an enthusiastic Young Elizabethan. *YE* readers, now aged sixty-plus, remember how educational the magazine was, covering science, history, current events, book reviews. The competitions were pitched at the brainy child: 'Draw a plan for a science lab, or an open-air theatre'; 'Invent a way of keeping flies off a horse with a docked tail'; 'Write a sonnet to a hippo' (obviously inspired by Flanders and Swann). The prizes included a week at the Edinburgh Festival – won by Kaye's godson, Jonathan Fenby, son of Charles. 'I had no hand in the judging,' wrote Kaye, 'but it was a bit embarrassing that my conscientious godson won so often.' Fenby, who grew up to be editor of the *Observer*, recalls enjoying the Edinburgh Tattoo, but not (at fourteen) the ballets.

Whenever Kaye appealed for extra pages, Grigg insisted that

'the determining factor must always be advertising'. He could not agree to forty pages, even if (as Kaye pointed out) the Duke of Edinburgh was contributing. But he approved of Kaye's Christmas parties for readers, when she got Joyce Grenfell, Larry Adler and Hattie Jacques to do cabarets. Rolf Harris entertained at the piano at the *YE* Christmas party in 1956. One reader, Mary Lowerson, recalled: 'The festivities included apple-bobbing, after which Kaye came round in such a jolly fashion drying our hair and complimenting the girls on our wonderfully scented shampoos. She was an enthusiastic force, genuinely enjoying herself.' Kaye's husband, Mary decided, 'looked rather bored and sat aloof from the jollity'.

Days later there was a *YE* New Year party for northern readers, in the grand restaurant of Kendal Milne's, the Manchester department store, with cabaret by Tommy Cooper. Gwynn Pritchard, then aged nine and at primary school in Chorley, Lancashire, was a typical boy reader: a bright and curious only child, encouraged to read the magazine by his father, a left-wing Unitarian minister. Molesworth, baffling at first with its public-school references, made him laugh until the tears rolled down his cheeks, and he remembers enviously reading about James Mason's party-going daughter Portland. Having longed to meet fellow readers, he was dismayed to find girls at the party outnumbered boys by three to one. Kaye 'looked like one of my mum's friends, but very London, perfumed and smart – slightly intimidating, but she talked to us in a friendly, grown-up, spontaneous way. Just like her editorial letter, which seemed to place her readers on an equal footing with herself.'

When she organized a poetry competition she roped in Christopher Fry, who broke off from his new play, *Curtmantel*, to judge it. Of a poem by Clare Laurel Harris, from Cardiff, Fry wrote: 'There is no fault to be found with it, because it is simple, direct, exact, and deeply sincere. The pattern of the poem makes itself, complete and perfect, and the images have a quiet, telling inevitability.' He would go up to Hampstead and recite it to the author Eleanor Farjeon, who had missed the judging.

Fry was one of many friends to whom Kaye would send thoughtful presents. He was enraptured by the 'Rexel Home Office' stationery set. 'The black and red of it. The self-sharpening of it. The refillability of it. And not just a namby-pamby stapler – but a BAMBI stapler.' J. C. Trewin was equally grateful for a book, 'a work of perverted genius' which 'shall go into my most precious Stuffed Owl collection'. Rebecca West wrote from Ibstone House, thanking Kaye for the bottle of brandy 'which was, by God it was, badly needed'. She had just endured an experience that 'might afford material for your husband's genius', if that did not make Kaye wince. She and her husband had returned from America to find that their secretary, 'a lady of fifty', had *rearranged the contents of their house*. 'We can't find anything, including the typescripts and copies of a complete novel, of which mercifully I still have the original.' They found a bowler hat perched on a lamp-stand, and in the gardeners' cellar, an eighteenth-century cradle, a family heirloom, had been 'hit with something hard and left among the stored potatoes', draped with a 'quite valuable Bosnian carpet'. The soon-to-be Dame Rebecca was prostrate with indignation: 'I went to Switzerland in a state of collapse to recuperate.'

Kaye drove the children every weekend to Westgate to see their 'Nan', who had recently reported to Arthur that the twins were 'frightfully spoilt – I cannot stand their ways'. (She added: 'But I like them – and hope they will soon be improved.') In April 1957, en route to Westgate, they crashed into a coach. Despite fractured ribs, Kaye flagged down some sailors and got them to drive them all, with luggage and dog Rusty, to Westgate. Grigg, 'horrified' to hear of the accident ('My hatred of charabancs, already very considerable, is now deep and permanent.

No doubt your 3 jolly sailor men will support you up to the hilt. If they don't, then it certainly is time we abolished the Navy!'), urged her to take a rest.

'You must now <u>absolutely</u> and without cavil have a holiday. Please make your plans regardless of the Duke of Edinburgh or anything else!' He was in Spain, and could book her into the local hotel for 160 pesetas a day, but he knew Kaye liked night-life and his village, though charming, was not sophisticated. Instead, another possibility arrived. Standard Oil of New Jersey commissioned an animated film from Ronald. He had never been to America, and could do a New York sketchbook for *Punch*. They sailed on the SS *Mauretania* on 8 May 1957 and were away three months, based at the Beekman Tower with its fantastic views over Manhattan. They saw Count Basie in Brooklyn, and *My Fair Lady* on Broadway, visiting Stanley Holloway backstage. When they got to California Kaye sent breathless bulletins to the *Young Elizabethan*. 'Well, here we are, in Hollywood . . . our aeroplane, a Jet Stream Constellation, flew over Oklahoma City and the Rocky Mountains.' They bumped into John Wayne in a corridor, shared a lift with Norma Shearer, dined at a table between Jane Wyman and James Stewart, had a swimming race with James and Portland Mason (and lost), and went to MGM to watch Danny Kaye making a film called *Merry Andrew*. 'We've also got a date with a wonderful place called Disney Land.' Walt himself showed them round. Ronald got on well with the animators, and eventually his film, *Energetically Yours*, won eleven awards, and its techniques were later copied in *The Hundred and One Dalmatians*.

The children, whose tenth birthday they had missed, were taken by Kaye for a 'healthy, primitive' holiday at La Baule in Brittany that August. She also took her godson Jonathan Fenby, who (in John Searle's view) was Kaye's ideal son. The children hired a boat and went out to sea in a fierce current. It was raining,

Fenby recalls, and the boat was ancient and the skipper shouted instructions in bad-tempered French. They were all relieved to get safely back to shore.

John Grigg told Kaye that if she should run into Picasso in Brittany, he sent homage 'as one subversive to another!' Grigg, now reluctantly titled Lord Altrincham, had just attacked the royal family in the *National Review*, saying that the Queen's utterances were those of 'a priggish schoolgirl'. 'Like her mother, she appears to be unable to string even a few sentences together without a written text.' His article caused a furore. He was attacked in the *Daily Mail* for 'daring to pit his infinitely tiny and temporary mind against the accumulated experience of centuries'. Kaye too was horrified that he had written such things.

They were back in time for a sneak preview of *Blue Murder at St Trinian's* that September. But Kaye's life was 'literally a nonstop rush', she told Arthur. She had to get her magazine out, buy and mark the children's uniforms, get their hair cut – and visit her mother every day in Brentford Hospital. Ann's memory and concentration were waning, 'poor darling'. She would detest a nursing home, so Kaye rang Mrs Brophy's employment bureau in Dublin and found a nurse-companion, Mrs Keevil, to live at Ann's Brighton flat. Arthur must send postcards, or paperbacks, or magazines, 'so that she knows you are thinking of her'. John was 'in a fearful state emotionally poor love' – anxious about his Nan, and reluctant to go back to school.

Such were Kaye's concerns, while Ronald went on 'producing like a machine'. After the Edinburgh Festival that year he returned to New York, to be paid $1,000 a minute to say the words: 'But artists, like children, should be seen and not heard,' an addendum to his film. He met the *New Yorker* artists, and was made a member of the Cartoonists' Club of America. Before leaving for Paris again he took part in *Who's Next?*, a television chain of interviews: Siân Phillips interviewed him, he interviewed Cleo Laine. In order to give him more peace at weekends, Kaye found a country bolthole, Little Pines, at the edge of a forest on the South Downs, for £1,700, with five acres of garden, ideal for growing organic vegetables and for teaching the twins about country life. She encouraged John to learn to shoot, and installed Arthur's eccentric sister, Aunt Elsie, who spoke Esperanto, kept bees and milked her two goats.

At Newton Road there were more urban concerns. The council were replacing the Victorian street-lamps with concrete gibbets, offending the residents of 'this snug and attractive backwater', as the *Manchester Guardian* called it, 'tucked away behind the dingy commercial highway of Westbourne Grove'. A meeting was convened on 5 November 1957 at the home of Mr and Mrs Ronald Searle. Neighbours – including a novelist, a TV actor and an LSE professor – ranged themselves before the impressive window of the Searles' sitting room, to protest against this municipal vandalism. The irony of the concrete modernity of the Searles' house, in a street of Victorian stucco façades, was not lost on anyone. The council turned down their offer to pay £150 for imitation period gas lamps, because everyone would want the same. Ronald illustrated this news story with three drawings: of a pretty ornamental gas lamp, a gently curved modern one, and finally the offending gibbet, with a householder hanging from it. But it was a lost cause. When the old gas lamps went, the Searles bought one for a fiver.

Two weeks later, Kaye decided her life was all too much. She would have to give up editing the *Elizabethan*. John Grigg was on a flight to New Delhi when he wrote to tell her what a marvellous job she had done. 'You have turned this mag from an incipient wreck into a highly successful paper on the up and up, in the short space of three years – and despite having to deal with a thoroughly tiresome proprietor!' He totally understood her reasons, recognized the burdens and difficulties of the past year, agreed that she had no choice 'but to lift some of the weight off yourself, and *YE* was the only thing you really could shed'.

He enclosed a cheque for a Ronald drawing which he knew would 'cause great joy' at Tormarton (his country house) at Christmas, and urged her to return with redoubled vigour one day, perhaps to edit a magazine for adults. The *Elizabethan* would now be edited by Pat Campbell (Mrs John Grigg) and Tom Pocock (already known to readers as 'Guy Allcot'). The January 1958 magazine was its tenth birthday edition, but it could never hope to flourish in the 1960s. Its flavour was already dated. In the birthday issue, Eleanor Farjeon wrote about the varieties of pasta, describing spaghetti, macaroni, vermicelli, 'and the little stars and letters which, if you are lucky, the cook sometimes puts in your soup'.

But it looks, from Kaye's 1958 'Agenda', a diary bought in Paris, as if Kaye's workload was not much reduced. Christopher Fry had urged the Searles to leave foggy London and join him in Rome, where he was filming *Ben-Hur*. But she was busily writing theatre reviews for Grigg's *National Review*: *My Fair Lady*, *Expresso Bongo*, *The Cherry Orchard* in Russian by the Moscow Art Theatre, Pinter's *The Birthday Party*. She presented another television programme, *Swap Shop*. She wrote long and demanding pieces, involving multiple interviews, for various magazines – on London's famous old hotels, for instance. But in one respect life would be simplified. The Searles had decided to send John to board at Wells House at Malvern Wells, Worcestershire. Kaye saw him off (after the statutory treat, *Robinson Crusoe* at the Palladium) from Paddington on the 1.45 p.m. train on Friday 17 January.

John never forgave his parents for sending him away. Kaye had always wanted him to be self-reliant and independent, and on his second day at his prep school, the Hall in Hampstead, she had sent him to catch the 31 bus with 'Off you go, darling.' 'I couldn't even open our front gate,' John remembered. 'I'd never been on a bus on my own.' That term she told James Mason that his godson was 'at camp, on a three-day hike, carrying a tent on his back and blissfully happy'. But Wells House meant leaving home, and John hated it from day one. 'I begged her, every term, not to send me back. Even now it haunts me.' The school had a 'brutalizing' regime of cold baths each morning, naked swimming, cross-country runs 'to keep you hungry' and beatings. Each bed in the icy dorm had a single blanket. 'To make a man of you. Muscular Christianity, preparing you to be a district officer in Swaziland.'

To escape, John read his way through the school library. A favourite book was a tale of smugglers of 1898, *Moonfleet* by J. Meade Falkner. Kaye – who went without Ronald to visit John at exeat weekends – suggested that, for his birthday, she should drive him to Chesil Bank in Dorset, where *Moonfleet* was set. 'Kaye would make outings into adventures. She filled me with Allan Quartermain and was all for me having a go at anything adventurous. She drove an old Wolseley, and when I asked if I could ride on the bumper, she agreed – typically – and drove off down the country lanes and of course I went flying into the road.' Chesil Bank and its Fleet lagoon are notorious for treacherous currents, shipwrecks and drownings. 'Mum suggested, why don't you see if the undertow is as bad as Meade Falkner says it is? So I dived in – and sure enough there was a fierce undertow. It was a very positive thing, gave me the sense that I was immortal. And it made me value authenticity in experience.'

At Easter that year Ronald and Kaye took the twins to Robert Graves's house on Majorca. Kate recalls that there was an outside loo, guarded by a donkey which had to be given a carrot to gain entry. Graves read aloud to them the more amusing bits of the *Iliad*, which he was translating and Ronald was illustrating. John developed acute appendicitis and was rushed home, writhing in pain, to a London hospital, from which he emerged wraithlike.

Kaye took him to convalesce in Brighton with Ann, then to the
Fergussons' at Dover, where she addressed the Wives' Guild
(while tea-ladies clanked away with trays and cups) about
appearing on television. 'We're very simple souls, here in Dover,'
Laura Fergusson (her predecessor at *Young Elizabethan*) had told
her, adding that the castle was 'a goldmine of inspiration for an
artist's eye'. But Ronald would not join them, Kaye said. 'I never
really know what Ronnie will be up to.'

When the great James Thurber came to the *Punch* Table that
summer, Ronald invited him to dine at Newton Road with the
Fenbys. (Thurber was by now quite blind and Ronald had not
only to help him into the lavatory but also, unforgettably, to
direct his aim.) The rest of the year followed a now familiar
pattern: Kaye took the twins to St Austell with the Trewins
(J. C. Trewin, his wife Wendy and their sons), for a buckets-and-
spades holiday; Ronald went to Edinburgh; his mother came to
stay at Newton Road; Kaye's mother was in and out of clinics.
There were residents' meetings, Ronald's exhibitions, and
deadlines. Kaye's diary for 27 October 1958 says, in Ronald's
hand, 'Publication Day The Big City'. But Ronald wasn't there.
Three days before, on 24 October, are the words 'R to Paris until
Nov 3'. In fact he did not return till 7 November, and he came
back a changed man.

9: Which Way Did He Go?

In Paris, on 1 November 1958, just before the election of President de Gaulle, Ronald met Monica Stirling. He and Eric Keown were on their regular tour of French theatres, and were meeting a man from French radio at the Café de la Régence, Place du Théâtre Français. The radio man was late, and sent along the chic, dark-haired Monica to keep the two Englishmen amused. She was born in Surrey. Her father, Charles Koenig, seriously injured in the Royal Flying Corps in the Great War, sold Bohemian crystal in the City of London, which gave Monica, from childhood, 'a passion for anything that glitters'. At eight she was sent to Berlin, where her maternal grandparents lived, and went to school there, where she was made to write in Sütterlin script with her right hand, although as a left-hander (like Ronald, and Kaye too) she drew and painted with her left. In 1934 her mother died. Monica and her sister returned to England, but in 1940 their father's showrooms were destroyed in an air raid, and he too died in 1943. Monica was conscripted at eighteen for war work; invalided out of a factory, she went to the Ministry of War Transport. In 1947 she married Kit Stirling, a Cambridge graduate who had served in Intelligence, and was able to study art at St Martin's and Kingston. When her marriage broke up, she moved to Paris.

She was designing for the theatre on both sides of the Channel when she met Ronald. That evening of 1 November 1958, she sat waiting under a portrait of Napoleon. 'It was

Waterloo (English side fortunately) for both,' Monica later wrote.[*]

Ronald returned home six days later for the launch of a new Perpetua book, *The Lover's Keepsake*, by Raymond Peynet, the French cartoonist, and life carried on as before. Kaye met the Queen Mother at a Women's Press Club cocktail party. There was the Lord's Taverners' Ball, and the Press Ball, a *Punch* supper for members of the Table and their wives, and Alec Guinness was reminding them of their date 'next Wednesday at 146 Piccadilly at 7.30. Film sharp at 8.0. Supper La Reserve at 10.0. As ever, Alec.' When Guinness later excused himself from dinner at Newton Road, he invited them instead for a weekend at his country home, Kettlebrook Meadows, sending a hand-drawn map, his house indicated by an arrow marked 'This way madness lies.' Ronald too had decided his life had become a madness. Apart from the punishing deadline chart, he was recording his first, but not last, *Desert Island Discs* (indicated by his drawing of a palm tree in Kaye's diary) and a book programme. Then there was their lavish New Year party, now a fixture. Some said these parties were Kaye's thing, with Ronald a withdrawn presence. Kaye said he seemed to enjoy them. He certainly did the personalized invitations, which were treasured as souvenirs by the guests. On the invitation list were their friends Wendy Toye, the Day-Lewises and the Dankworths, actors such as Peter Finch, cartoonists such as Vicky, Franta Belsky and Nicolas Bentley, the artist and designer of the Festival of Britain Hugh Casson, critics including Penelope Gilliatt and Philip Hope-Wallace, Ronald's journalist colleague from *The Granta* days Charles Wintour, the Searles' *Paris Sketchbook* publisher, Tony Godwin, the comic actor and early star of *The Goon Show*, Michael Bentine, and Kaye's godson Jonathan Fenby, who was about to go up to Oxford.

[*] In *Searle & Searle*, Hirmer Verlag, Munich, 2001.

'Ronald began to see his life as a series of imprisonments,' in the words of his biographer, Russell Davies. He was living 'in a family structure he had not sought, with a lively social life he did not desire, and an involvement with publicity he frequently resented, while playing along with it in his dutiful way'. Davies called this chapter of Searle's life 'Back in the Jug Agane', echoing the title of the fourth Molesworth volume, implying that the years 1951–61 were a prison sentence. Certainly, the temperamental gap between him and Kaye had widened. In Ronald's view they were two egotistical personalities who could not go on working happily in tandem.

But there was no sign that anything was amiss that spring, in 1959. Ronald went to the US for *Punch*, and to Germany for the Suddeutsche Fernsehen, and to Edinburgh. They were involved in an exciting joint enterprise – an animated *A Christmas Carol*, drawn by Ronald, scripted by Christopher Fry, cast by Kaye. Months of negotiation followed, in which Kaye approached top actors to do the voices: Charles Laughton (Mr Fezziwig), Alec Guinness (Scrooge), John Gielgud (Christmas Past), Stanley Holloway (Christmas Present), and, among others, Hermione Gingold and Edith Evans. Yip Harburg and Burton Lane were keen to do the music: Harburg was 'more excited by this than by *The Wizard of Oz*'. Peter Brook was approached to direct. Kaye adored plotting with the American producers Jerome Hellman and David Hilberman (at the Waldorf), fixing finance, pinning down peripatetic stars in Hollywood or Stratford-upon-Avon. With Arnold Goodman's help she drew up contracts (£200 a day for Laughton, 200 guineas for Gielgud, £100 for Robert Morley) and noted whether the stars wanted a piece of the action. John Gielgud 'would like even the tiniest slice'. Peter Finch said 'slip me whatever you can afford on the side'. Julie Andrews 'would do it for £100; she would make money on the record'. Alec Guinness 'insists on a percentage'. John Mills 'is a smart businessman and will want as much as he can get'. The Americans were vastly impressed by Kaye's powers of persuasion. 'When Ronnie said "She's good at that sort of thing" he was guilty of the grossest British understatement,' wrote Hilberman. She even snaffled James Mason at the last minute, as Marley's Ghost, and found rooms in Hereford Road, a stone's throw from her home, where the producers could set up an office.

(Ronald sent her a spoof letter when she was in the Scilly Isles that spring, on 'Perpetua Films' writing paper, allegedly from a producer named William W. Wordsworth, about the production of 'A Saga of the Scillies, provisionally entitled Around the Daffs in Eighty Bees'. It would be filmed 'in Cinemaskimp, a technique only recently made possible by the development of a remarkable new perpendicular lens, which enables us to project a film three times as tall as it is wide'. It would be possible to present on screen a daffodil 183 feet high. Would she therefore place under contractual obligation a suitable daffodil?)

Then the problems began: agents' fees, Equity deals, storyboard changes, stars' availability. They needed a fine musical voice 'and singers, as you know, eat up money'. *A Christmas Carol*, sadly, fizzled out – until Ronald's animated title-sequence resurfaced in 1970 in the film *Scrooge – The Musical*, starring Albert Finney, with Alec Guinness as Marley's Ghost.

Kaye was broadcasting talks – 'London is a Writers' Club' was about authors' fondness for enclaves like Hampstead – and writing for the *Bookman* about the recent book launches for William Golding, John Steinbeck, John O'Hara, Jules Feiffer, Keith Waterhouse: *Billy Liar* was her favourite novel that year. Her own book, *The St Trinian's Story*, came out, 'the whole ghastly dossier' Ronald called it. Apart from Alastair Sim's performances, he found the St Trinian's films 'crass and witless'. *The Penguin Ronald Searle*, published the following year, said in its introduction: 'Nobody hasn't heard of Ronald Searle; mid-century Britain is a Searle-haunted land.'

The market for line drawings in magazines and newspapers had dwindled. The *Leader* had folded in 1950, *Our Time* and *The Strand* in 1955, *Picture Post* in 1957, *Lilliput* in 1959 and the *News Chronicle* in November 1960. But one last collaboration was offered to the Searles in late 1959. It was the United Nations' World Refugee Year, and its young PR, Roland Huntford, who admired Ronald, invited him to tour the displaced persons' camps in Austria, Italy and Greece. The UN would cover expenses, and *Punch* and *Life* would run Ronald's drawings. So the Searles arrived in Salzburg, where the Austrian authorities selected deserving subjects. Kaye took down the inmates' often harrowing stories, Ronald sketched their tragic faces, and the result was a fascinating and moving book, published by Penguin, called simply *Refugees*.

Huntford got on well with both Searles. But in the various hotels where they stayed, Ronald seemed to him to be much alone despite Kaye's presence. He never saw them talking together. 'Kaye would not leave his side, constantly praising him to the skies. He seemed taciturn, detached. In my memory he is all but invisible, yet his unseen presence made the deeper impression. One afternoon we were in a hotel lounge when Kaye appeared, having obviously been to the hairdresser, sitting up with a very straight back as if wanting to be noticed. Ronald avoided looking at her at all. I felt there was something rather odd there. Is this being wise after the event? I don't know. Hindsight is 20/20 isn't it?'

Huntford felt that Ronald intuitively found the *Refugees* enterprise spurious – and was right. 'It was organized to drum up a problem that didn't really exist. The refugees were the aftermath of the Hungarian revolution, and the displaced persons of World War II. The good ones had been snapped up, and these left-behinds were the poor devils with nowhere to go. But UNHCR needed to justify its existence and persuade the world that there was still a problem.' However, there were many offers of help for the refugees afterwards, and the Searles' book was widely considered a noble enterprise.

When their New Year party for 1960 rolled round, Ronald did jolly drawings on pink dusters, suspended on the ceiling like a washing-line, which were let down on the stroke of midnight. Guests scrambled for them so everyone took home a signed original Searle. One recipient was Alison Blair of *Lilliput*, who had come back from the US and was about to depart, 'to get away from a tiresome love affair', for the Algarve, where she became the doyenne of the expatriate community. John Grigg wrote apologizing for bringing extra guests, and for staying so long. 'A tribute to your hospitality . . . If it's any comfort you gave great pleasure and made the prospect of a new decade seem almost welcome.'

That summer, having turned forty, Ronald was plotting his departure. In fact, he had been plotting his departure for about three years – long before he met Monica. While in Europe, he met their friend from the UN, Roland Huntford, at his hotel in Montreux, and asked him how one opened a Swiss bank account. 'I said you just went into a bank and put money in. He asked, would they accept travellers' cheques? I was surprised that he knew so little of wordly affairs. I told him travellers' cheques were as good as cash. And which bank would I recommend? I told him I banked at UBS.' Ronald added, 'Don't mention this to Kaye.' He presented Huntford with one of his original *Refugees* drawings, and signed it 'A souvenir of our trip, 12 August 1960.'

All that summer, Kaye was broadcasting – covering first nights, an authors' cricket match, a Miss Soho beauty contest. In September she took the twins, aged thirteen, for their first visit to Paris, to a hotel overlooking the Palais Royal gardens. They went to the top of the Eiffel Tower, and with *Woman's Hour* in mind, she recorded tourists everywhere, including a woman standing in front of the *Mona Lisa* in the Louvre, asking, 'Who is it by?' In November, Ronald went back to the US for Kennedy's election victory, and returned seven weeks later to a pile-up of work. When Sir Bernard Miles of the Mermaid Theatre invited the Searles to supper, Ronald postponed the date, 'as between now and January I have to illustrate two volumes of Dickens . . .'

Then Kaye was offered a new job. She had met the publisher Allen Lane years before at El Vino's (when he was demonstrating a bullfight to fellow denizens) and later interviewed him at Champneys, the health farm at Tring in Hertfordshire. He suggested she stay too, so she did. She arrived on Lane's third day, by which time starving inmates were quivering jellies of emotion, she said; Lane sat in his white dressing-gown and she found him 'beguiling'. He had immediately suggested she should come and work at Penguin, an offer he often repeated. Now, the Searles' old friend Tony Godwin, the publishing dynamo who had joined Penguin that year, telephoned. Eleanor Graham, founder-editor of Puffin Books, was retiring. He offered Kaye the role of 'Outside Editor' of Puffin, and she said yes.

The ensuing year proved to be the worst of Kaye's life, but it was also the making of her.

As 1961 dawned the Searles appeared to be their usual sociable selves, giving what was to be their last New Year's Eve party. Ronald again spent days doing drawings on dusters – producing extra ones at the last minute as more invitees replied. Guests regarded these as heirlooms. (In 2009, a Searle duster dated 1 January 1961 hung in a London gallery priced at £2,250.)

Kaye was buoyant about her new job. Godwin had vaguely said that she would be 'choosing and advising on titles'. Production would be left to the 'Internal Editor', Margaret Clark, Eleanor Graham's long-serving deputy. Kaye would be paid £500 a year in quarterly instalments, plus £50 for every title that appeared under her editorship. Kaye pointed out that this £50 was a muddy area. Some forthcoming books would have been edited already by Eleanor and Margaret. They could pay her a percentage of the year's turnover instead. And Godwin must confirm that she need not go into Harmondsworth, that she would have a secretary on tap, and that he would cover such expenses as postage, periodicals and books, and travelling to see authors and entertaining them.

Clearly a dynamic force had arrived at Penguin. Lane's choice of Kaye seemed, in the book trade, capricious. Everyone had assumed that the quiet, self-effacing Margaret (who knew the business backwards) was Eleanor Graham's heiress-apparent.

Before Kaye's arrival, 'children's departments usually meant one woman in a cardigan, in a cubby hole under the stairs', as Shirley Hughes puts it. 'They were patronized, exploited, pathetically paid and not expected to make money, or to export. There was no hoop-la, no Bologna Children's Book Fair.' The business was still dominated by male grandees. When Margaret Clark got her first job, and queried the meagre wage, Stanley Unwin, accustomed to employing girls of private means, retorted, 'But what about your father's allowance?' In fact, Margaret, an Oxford graduate (who had been Louis MacNeice's secretary, and Allen Lane's, before becoming plenipotentiary to Eleanor), later devoted years to looking after her ageing father, often working from home.

Judy Taylor, children's editor at the Bodley Head, heard about Kaye's appointment in advance from her boss, Max Reinhardt, who had been gossiping over lunch with Allen Lane. She rang Margaret and assured her – without divulging what she knew – that if she ever wanted a job at the Bodley Head, she would be welcome there. So when Godwin told Margaret that she 'hadn't a hope in hell' of getting the Puffin editorship (Lane generally left it to Godwin to impart bad news) she departed at once, to spend many years at the Bodley Head, building up a formidable

"Wandering about large corridors in the nood!"

What! No Crumbs?

"Did you ever run around like this - looking hearty?
(Hurrah for St Trinian's!")

1. Ronald Searle's letters to Kaye, when he was released from Changi in 1945, were illustrated with his enchanting little drawings. Even before they met, his letters were a chaste form of courtship

2. Ann Stevens, née Fahy, Kaye's mother: red-haired, glamorous and theatrical, with a penchant for stylish clothes

3. Arthur Webb, Kaye's journalist father: 'He represents the best qualities in our profession . . . I have never heard anyone speak other than warmly of him,' wrote Malcolm Muggeridge

4. The toddler Kaye, 'Princess Sunshine', at the seaside

5. John Webb, Kaye's younger brother, journalist turned soldier: he was killed in Burma in 1944

6. Bill Webb, Kaye's elder half-brother, sporting journalist and avid reader, in his wartime airman's greatcoat

7. Miss Webb of *Lilliput*, everyone's favourite wartime magazine.
Her early journalistic career introduced her to the best writers, poets and
photographers of the day. 'Oh yes,' she would say. 'I was a war profiteer.'

8. Wing-Commander Keith Hunter, cheerful and amiable,
had been at school with Kaye, and became the second of
her three husbands in 1942

9. A jobless single mother: Kaye sailed home from the US on the *Queen Elizabeth* in October 1947 with her twin babies, born in Washington on 17 July

10. The twins, Kate and John Searle

11. Ronald Searle and Kaye Webb, recently married, in Ronald's studio in Bedford Gardens, Notting Hill Gate

12. The happy Searle family at Westgate-on-Sea, *c*.1950

13. Kaye and Ronald on holiday at Le Lavandou, in the South of France, 1955

14. Kaye makes her TV debut, 1955

15. The Searles dance at the Chelsea Arts Ball, New Year's Eve 1954

16. The Searles dine out with their New York friends, the Marx Brothers' screenwriter Arthur Sheekman and his actress wife Gloria Stuart, 1954

17. 'Handsome goat assists': Kaye leads the goat towards the Young Vic theatre for the Joan Aiken play performed by the Puffin Players in January 1968

18. Kaye insisted that Puffin Club members must have watery adventures – and would invariably join in herself

19. Even when Kaye was frequently in hospital, the Puffin Club had to go on: 'Kaye's girls' at a bedside editorial meeting, c.1977

20. The great violinist Yehudi Menuhin had been one of Kaye's distinguished patrons at the *Young Elizabethan* magazine in the 1950s, and remained a lifelong friend

21. Kaye and her brother Bill at St James's Palace in November 1974 when Kaye was awarded her MBE

22. Kaye always blossomed in the Mediterranean sun, and when arthritis struck, sought sunshine whenever possible

23. Kaye's favourite occasions were parties with authors: here with the poet Roy Fuller, Oxford Poetry Professor (who contributed to *Puffin Post*), and the perenially popular Noel Streatfeild

children's list. But her departure meant Kaye was completely on her own; she had to learn about children's books from scratch, fast. 'I came to it quite fresh,' she said later, 'because although I'd edited a children's magazine, I hadn't read many children's books.' Informed that a child could read 600 books during childhood, she resolved that every single one must count. This became a cause.

She knew she would get 'fearfully involved' in the job, as she told her father, but the workload was daunting. 'Have somehow to come up with a concrete plan of campaign as quickly as possible because they produce so far ahead . . . you've got to read every one of them first . . . and with quite a different eye.' She said her deputy had quit, 'so there's no-one but me running the show', adding, 'Only hope I live up to their expectations.'

That letter, written on a Sunday in February, reflects the complications of her life at this juncture. Ronald and his secretary had both been away, so Kaye had to deal with all the Perpetua admin. Both twins had been in bed for a week with flu. 'You can have no idea of the pace I'm going at,' she told Arthur. She'd been to get an exercise regime from 'an old dame', who told her she was too exhausted 'and all I needed was relaxation and massage'.

John had just started at Westminster, a school only twenty minutes away, yet he was to remain a boarder. Kaye hoped he was settling in, 'except that he pops back every day for tea (which is out of bounds), and has not yet palled up with anyone'. One subject John did not do at Westminster was art; he claimed that the art master hated him, just for being Ronald Searle's son.

In addition, Arthur was returning to the UK, to live with his girlfriend Ethel, Herbert Morrison's former secretary. Kaye hoped he would be staying in Newton Road, because in May Puffin would pay her fare to accompany Ronald to the US, provided she did some work there. ('So that settles a little cash problem we had.') If Arthur did not come, Kate would be left to the tender mercies of Elvira, who hated being alone and was 'worked off her feet'; and Jacqueline the au pair was going home. 'You could still see Ethel every evening . . . and do the shopping for Elvira when I'm away – yes?'

Meanwhile Ronald was off to Paris for *Punch*, and would be away most of April, so she would take the kids to Scotland. In Brighton, her mother now required the full-time caring services of the saintly Mrs Keevil, her nurse-companion. At Little Pines, Elsie 'seems to hate doing anything for me, except send in the bills and light the fire occasionally'. There were other problems. The Searles were 'in the soup' financially, with a £4,000 surtax demand, and 'Edwards says we are overspending by £600 a year and something must go'. Kaye's brother Bill feared that *Sporting Life* (where he was senior sub-editor and a racing tipster, 'Man on the Spot', 'Augur' or 'Solon') was about to fold. 'But maybe there will be a war and we'll all be engaged in making munitions, I mean atom bombs,' she wrote, striving to be jocular.

Since Arthur was sorting out his papers, she urged him to save whatever he could find for her 'Birthday Books' idea for Puffins, which would need 'facts figures ideas and stories about each age' from eight to fourteen, especially stuff about the children of the great. 'Sorry this is a scrappy letter,' she added, 'interrupted by the arrival of James Mason and his cousin for supper (unexpectedly)'. She threw a party for Mason, inviting Michael Redgrave and Laurie Lee, whose childhood memoir *Cider with Rosie* was a bestseller for Penguin that year.

She still had no office at Harmondsworth. Help came when Doreen Scott arrived to become 'Puffin editorial manager', eventually the linchpin of the entire operation. By April, Godwin realized Kaye was doing far more than had been bargained for, and suggested putting her on the staff, at £1,500 p.a. But the Searles' accountant warned of 'tremendous complications' if she were taxed at source. 'My income would be added to Ronald's

and in spite of my nice fat salary he'd almost be out of pocket.'
So Kaye must remain a self-employed freelance.

She needed an assistant, but told Godwin most bright girls
would find the salary a drawback. 'Could I say they would get
£1,000, or would the starting money be lower?' (It was lower.)
Linda Villiers, a graduate of St Andrews, arrived in April. Linda
had been working at Macmillan for two retired army officers,
and wanted desperately to get into children's books: Macmillan
had Rumer Godden, Lewis Carroll and Enid Blyton. At twenty-
two, 'young enough for my childhood reading to be fresh in my
mind', she was engaged at a salary of £750, to work part-time as
a Penguin proofreader and part-time for Kaye, either at Linda's
own flat (a grand address – 1 Pont Street SW1, above United
Dairies) or at Newton Road.

During the first session at Newton Road, dusk fell, and Linda
watched as Kaye switched on at least half a dozen low lamps.
The house appeared well-organized, with Kaye and Ronald each
employing a secretary, and Elvira giving the twins their tea. But
in the ensuing months, Linda became conscious that there was
'an atmosphere' at Newton Road. 'Kaye would often ring Ronald
on the intercom, to remind him about something he had to do
– but he never rang her.' (The twins did not notice this atmosphere.
Their parents still shared a bedroom, with separate single beds,
as was more common in the 1950s; they saw their father mainly
at Sunday lunchtime, and as John says, Kaye would often tell
him, 'Your father is very detached,' as if it were a commendable
trait. He took it to imply that Ronald's PoW experiences had
given him an emotional detachment.)

Linda was swept up in Kaye's exciting schemes as she 'took
the job by the throat, buying up everything she considered good.
I was like a bridesmaid who picked up what she dropped behind
her.' Feeling very grown-up, Linda went to her old firm,
Macmillan, aiming for the Rumer Godden titles which, for the

moment, were denied them. Kaye also sent her to see the pioneering Grace Hogarth, the influential American who ran Constable Young Books, to go through her list, targeting the 'Auntie Robbo' books. (Grace Hogarth and her fellow American Marni Hodgkin had come to Britain from the already exciting and energetic children's book publishing scene in America, where they and other redoubtable women had collaborated with librarians to make children's books brighter and better. The *Dr Seuss* books were typical of their commercial success. Now they had transferred their energy and expertise to British children's publishing.)

Hardback publishers remained obdurate about letting their best stuff go to Puffin, lowering their income by splitting the royalty, unless Kaye could convince them that higher sales at a low price would benefit everyone. Oxford University Press books were out; Mabel George would not let Kaye near Philippa Pearce or Rosemary Sutcliff. Dent, Hutchinson, Methuen, all had to be persuaded to release rights. From Collins, Kaye targeted Michael Bond's *Paddington*, and from Cape, Hugh Lofting's *Dr Dolittle*. Curiously, she shied away from pony fiction, favourite of so many small girls. (Nor did she attempt, it seems, to acquire Richmal Crompton's William books, adored by adults and children alike, including her twins.) She tried to persuade writer friends to do original stuff for Puffin. Robert Graves, congratulating Kaye on joining Penguin – 'Nice people' – demurred: 'I'm snowed under with work & daren't attempt any new job: already behind schedule. Have refused fifteen at least since we last met. And these plaguey poems always have preference and priority; and I am still beset. Love, Robert.'

While Kaye wooed publishers, Ronald departed for Paris, and then for Jerusalem, commissioned by *Life* magazine to draw the Eichmann trial. Eichmann, the former SS commandant captured in the Argentine, sat inside a bulletproof glass booth as more than

100 prosecution witnesses testified to his crimes. He did not deny that he had condemned thousands to death: he was only following orders – the Nuremberg defence. Ronald filled his portfolio with drawings of concentration camp survivors 'to give the trial the aspect of horror', wrote Paul Hogarth, 'that lay behind the cold recounting of the court'.*

He was home for just ten days before returning to America for *Holiday* magazine, an eight-week assignment. Kaye went too for part of the time, and made recordings in Atlantic City, Provincetown and Paris, Texas. They were both at *Punch*'s 120th birthday in July. Then it was Ronald's last summer of theatre first nights. Meanwhile Kaye accompanied Godwin to see the publisher Billy Collins. They talked of *Mary Poppins*, but P. L. Travers ('essential in any deal') wasn't keen on paperbacks. 'Noel Streatfeild? We have two already. Could take another,' says Kaye's note. 'Durrell's *Island Zoo*? Masses of photographs, would be too expensive.' Collins was huffy about Puffin taking his bestsellers, but Godwin persuaded him to release fifteen, over three years, with a special 'Puffins group' royalty.

Kaye was rapidly mastering the intricacies of the trade. Godwin had told her firmly, 'It isn't enough to say "This is a nice book which we ought to do", we have to be sure it will also sell.' She took advice from Ian Norrie of the independent High Hill Bookshop, whose Hampstead location guaranteed avid readers and buyers. Kaye had once interviewed him for a *Woman's Hour* series on shops, during which she had a go at serving behind the bar in the King of Bohemia pub next door – a role, said Norrie, for which her outgoing personality was well suited. He described Kaye as 'a jolly, large earth mother of a woman'. 'Her face and head were beautiful, and she was delightfully funny and outrageous. Charisma is an overworked word, but

* Paul Hogarth, *The Artist as Reporter*, Gordon Fraser, 1986.

she had it.' Kaye noted Norrie's suggestions: Kipling's *Kim* or
Just So stories, *The Midnight Folk* by John Masefield, *Farmer Giles
of Ham* by Tolkien. 'Confirmed continued popularity of Dr
Dolittle. And Arthur Ransome, beating all others. He suggested
"heirloom" titles: *Little Women, What Katy Did, Children of the
New Forest, Heidi, Swiss Family Robinson*. Murray do Conan
Doyle, is it worth doing?'

She asked Peter Hebden of Michael Joseph for Paul Gallico's
The Snow Goose, prompting 'much laughter'. He told her that
with children's books, you can't expect bestsellers, only 'a slow
building up of confidence in a title'. Kaye's idea for a series on
'Kings and Queens' had been done in their 'Reign by Reign'. But
Hebden hinted that Mary Norton was restless with Dent's – and
Kaye later got her, and also Philippa Pearce from OUP, offering
what Philippa called 'a colossal advance of £1,000' for *Tom's
Midnight Garden*: 'She communicated very directly, almost
volcanically, by phone – "Darling!"'

She dined with Richard Hough of Hamish Hamilton and his
wife Charlotte, 'an illustrator, delicate but rather good', and their
four pretty daughters (including the future novelist Deborah
Moggach and the future children's author-artist Sarah Garland).
Hough told Kaye it was simple to get authors for his Antelopes
and Reindeers, by writing to them c/o their publishers. 'They
were all delighted to earn quick lump sums.' Two days later,
Grace Hogarth, Judy Taylor and Kaye together came up with
the idea of a Children's Book Circle – a creative, collaborative
and sociable alliance of children's editors. Judy agreed to let Kaye
take six or eight Bodley Head titles a year. Eventually Maurice
Sendak's *Where the Wild Things Are* was one of these. Sendak's
wild things, who 'roar their terrible roars and gnash their terrible
teeth', were expected to terrify children, and it had taken Sendak
years to find a publisher before Judy Taylor championed him.

So Kaye packed her days with meetings: Noel Streatfeild,

Edward Ardizzone, Roger Lancelyn Green, Laurent de Brunhoff, creator of *Babar*. She was still doing talks for *Woman's Hour* on things like 'swimming in the Serpentine in winter: should women be allowed to join in?' She lunched with Arnold Goodman, the arch negotiator, about Perpetua deals. She took control of Puffin covers – she thought the old Puffin covers were 'awful' – and of blurbs and publicity. She planned an 'October Puffin Push', featuring Oscar Wilde, *Moonfleet* and *The Hobbit*. (Margaret Clark had secured a one-year lease, from Allen & Unwin, in *The Hobbit* – a book Eleanor Graham had greeted with 'a grimace of distaste'.) She would start a series of books for older children, Peacocks, for 14–16s, with Puffin seniors for 11–14s, Puffins for 8–11s, and large-format Picture Puffins for under-8s. 'Important to be clear about age groups in planning, although overlapping will occur,' she noted.

Shirley Hughes, who had drawn for the *Elizabethan* and was about to have her third child, saw Kaye as a breath of fresh air, ready to seize opportunies and think big. 'Everyone was thrilled, because she got out there, talked up the list. Tremendously admirable.' Also manipulative. 'She would say, "Darling, I've got this wonderful idea, come straight round, you have to do this, it's just YOU, it's your big chance" and then you found you were on board, with a <u>fantastic</u> amount of work.' One such book was *Something to Do*, a Young Puffin Original of 1961. Seven women ('under the frightful collective pen-name of Septima – overtones of septic tank') produced a calendar of children's activities for each month of the year: puppets and papier mâché, how to make a toy theatre or shop, what birds to look out for. Shirley had to produce hundreds of line drawings, 'for a pittance'.

To complicate life that summer, she was driving to and from Brighton to be with her dying mother. Her car was stolen from outside the house, the phone was out of order, and Ronald was still away when the school holidays began, so she sent the children to stay with friends in Northern Ireland. Arthur, currently on holiday with Ethel in Ischia ('Look out for a nice little place for me to come and get rid of my rheumatics one day,' wrote Kaye), was returning soon, so she offered him Ann's flat in Arundel Terrace. It would need about £80 spent to make it draughtproof ('when the wind comes off the sea it can beat away like anything').

She confided her anxieties about her mother to Eleanor Farjeon, who 'flowed with sympathy'. 'I've had it all, more than once, in my life – the aching heart . . . the spinning head in the desperate battle against time – the leap of joy, not for myself, when the end came. God bless you. Lovingly, Eleanor.'

Kaye's next letter to her father announced the peaceful death of 'our darling', in Kaye's arms: 'She looked her dear self once it was finished.' Kaye got there in time to talk to her before she lapsed into a coma. Ann understood that Kaye was there, and Bill too, and tried to smile. There were 'no moments of fear or fright': 'Bless her darling heart she had timed it all beautifully.' Ann left Bill a letter saying that she was to be cremated quickly, 'without ceremony, grave or headstone, and without any relatives present'. Kaye put notices in *The Times* and the *Telegraph*, and Ronald sent flowers on Arthur's behalf. They did not wire Arthur, not wishing to spoil his holiday: 'Mummy wouldn't have wanted that.' Only Bill and Kaye were present at the cremation in Brighton.

Kaye told her father: 'You know she so often said to me that she wished you could find someone else who would make you happy. I mean not once but often and often. She would have been so pleased about dear Ethel.

'So please please don't be unhappy. And please take what she has given you. The chance to be happy with someone else.' She hoped that Arthur would marry Ethel, and 'have not the faintest doubt or regret in your hearts for what's past . . . I'm your daughter and nearest relative and what I say goes!'

Linda Villiers was greeted by Kaye in the office on the day after Ann's death. 'Tell me that there is life after death. I must know.' Eleanor Farjeon wrote: 'Kaye my darling, do come if you can and if only by putting my arms round you I can help these hardest of all the days.'

'Several times in his life,' as biographer Russell Davies put it, 'Ronald Searle has made a new start. He has seldom revisited those parts of his existence he left behind.'

It was, Kaye said with hindsight in 1993, obvious that Ronald wanted a different life. He was hardly ever with the family, and was glad to have the house to himself at weekends, or to leave immediately after she did. 'The last two years before he left were not happy. I believed, absolutely stupidly and wrongly, that it was because he was having trouble with his sex life. I had consulted our doctor who thought it was very likely a result of lack of nourishment in the prison camp. I also thought he was preoccupied and cross because my mother was very ill. I had to spend a great deal of time, and Ronald a fair amount of money, keeping her happy and looked after.'

'All these mistakes I made are ridiculous,' Kaye reflected, 'but we got to the point where we weren't talking to each other and I was so convinced it was my mother he was worried about that I didn't look further.'

She had confided in her friend Gloria Sheekman that she and Ronnie weren't getting on, weren't even talking. Gloria told her she must talk. 'So I summoned sufficient courage to ask him what was the matter and if there was someone else and I remember clearly he came straight across the room and put his arms around me and said, "No, it's nothing like that. I'm just so worried about work." I suggested that he take a year off and go wandering round Europe and when he said how can I, I pointed out that we had the house and that I had a job and we could go on much more carefully if he wasn't there. And he said, "Well I just might do that." If only then he had said to me, "I want more than that" – but the chance had passed and he never did.'

When Ann died, Ronald came down to Brighton. 'And I realize now that the moment when he decided not to stay with me was when, as he put his arm round me for the first time in many years, I said, "As long as I've got you," and I felt him tense. He must have decided that he had better go then, because I should certainly have become aware of his many disappearances, once I had stopped having to spend weekends with my mother.'

On Friday 8 September, Linda Villiers left Harmondsworth and went to her hairdresser in Knightsbridge. But first she went into a phone-box to make a call. While in the hairdresser, she realized she had left a precious envelope in the phone-box. Kaye had been wooing Arthur Ransome to let her do *Swallows and Amazons* in Puffin, and had commissioned a new cover. This artwork had been sent for Ransome's approval, which he had grudgingly given; the drawing was in the envelope left in the phone-box. In a panic, with wet hair, Linda rushed out to the box, to find the envelope gone. She went straight to the police to report the loss, and in despair took a taxi to Newton Road. There she found only Ronald and his secretary, Jean Ellsmoor. 'I've done something terrible, I must tell Kaye,' said Linda. They told her Kaye had left for the country with the children; she could see her on Monday. Linda explained what had happened: couldn't they let Kaye know, somehow? But Ronald said, 'No, no, tell her on Monday, and don't worry, you've done all you can – and artwork can always be reproduced. The artist will probably have a tracing of it.' So Linda went home to face an anxious weekend.

On Monday, she arrived at Newton Road. Kaye's secretary answered the door and said Kaye was not well. Linda told her, 'Ronnie said I was to come back and tell her on Monday . . .'

'You saw Ronnie? When?' 'On Friday at about 4.30.' 'Just wait there.' Kaye came down, and so Linda learned that Ronald had left home. 'And Kaye was terribly cross with me for several weeks, understandably but also unreasonably, for having been the last person to see Ronnie at Newton Road.'

That weekend, Ronald had packed his suitcases, and had written his wife a letter before leaving for the airport. 'By the time you read this, I shall have gone for good.' When Kaye read these words, Kate was leaning over her shoulder asking, 'Why has Daddy written you such a long letter?' Kaye took the letter up to her bedroom to read it for herself, 'convinced that I would wake up at any moment and find it was one of my nightmares'. Francis Long, a French teacher from John's prep school, was staying at the cottage to tutor John when Kaye received Ronald's letter. She knocked on his door and woke him, in tears, that Monday morning, so he was the first person to hear the news, and witnessed her shock and distress.

Oddly enough she had had a dream two nights before. 'The children and I were going to meet Ronald, and we came to a cottage and stepped through the front garden and knocked at the door and a small woman in a bright green dress with straight black hair stood at the door, and we said, "Oh, Ronald Searle" and she shook her head and said, "I'm sorry", and I woke up with tears all over my face, thinking something bad must have happened to him.' Sleepless, she waited until 8 a.m. and rang home, ostensibly to remind Ronald that she would be on *Woman's Hour* that day. Elvira told her, 'Mr Searle's gone out,' not mentioning when. Kaye thought he'd perhaps gone to see Wendy Toye, or might even be coming down to the cottage. 'I spent the day saying to my children, "I wonder where your father is?" I'd decided not to ring in the evening because I thought it would look as if I was chasing him too much.'

★

Ronald had gone to Paris. He went to Monica's flat at 2 rue Antoine Dubois, and never came home to live in England again. Friends told Kaye that in Edinburgh the week before, he had seemed excitable, constantly on the telephone. She could not avoid telling the children that their father had left her, and she implored them to write to their father and make him come home. She wrote to Francis Long, John's French teacher, a few days later. 'Please don't tell anyone,' she begged him. 'I have a wild hope that if I leave every door open, and he doesn't think anyone knows, he might come back.' By a ghastly irony, *Woman & Home* magazine the next month featured a six-page article on Ronald, showing the Searles as a happy smiling couple in their ideal home. His new Perpetua collection that November was called *Which Way Did He Go?*

There was much retrospective speculation in their circle. Ronald's behaviour was, to some, baffling – but to others explicable, even understandable. He had shared his plans with no one. Publicly he always said he felt manacled, engulfed by demands on his time, 'in the theatre almost every night until 10 o'clock – drawing until two or three in the morning, in the office by nine'. He felt he had been totally unprepared for life as a husband and father, with social demands as well. 'Suddenly I stopped; I was dead. I thought, this is absolutely ridiculous.'

Kaye told Russell Davies: 'What he did was brutal, and I think it was worse to do it just after my mother died.' But she knew he had seized 'his last chance before he was enveloped in domesticity for ever'.

'I wrote immediately saying that I understood, especially as he'd found someone else, but would he just please come back for the children's holidays, because that's all they really saw of him – so if he came back for Christmas and summer they wouldn't feel so deserted. He replied that he wasn't able to do that.' (As his biographer writes, 'Searle has never left any loose sentimentalities lying around the world.')

In a state of shock, Kaye got through the next week with the help of pills. Linda saw her gulp down tranquillizers and pep pills in alarming quantities. She spent hours on the telephone, trying to persuade Ronald to return. 'I didn't tell anyone else for quite a time. I kept thinking he'd change his mind and come back, and in fact that's what our doctor who gave me the pills thought too. He said, "Don't chase him, he'll make up his own mind and come back, I promise you."'

Elvira had known all along about Ronald's absences. Kaye would leave instructions for 'Mr Searle's meals' when going away for the weekend, and on her return she would inquire crossly why the food had not been eaten. The fact was, he had usually left the house soon after Kaye did.

'He took nothing but himself,' as Kaye told Russell Davies. 'He carried on paying household bills; and I sold some of his pictures. But he had been told by a clairvoyant that his life would change at forty . . . How much are you affected by that? It might have tipped the scales.'

The twins had never witnessed an angry scene between their parents, but were adult enough at fourteen to be aware of the loss for themselves and their mother. 'Basically, neither of my parents should have had children,' says Kate. 'They were career people. Dad was always working. And he was manic about noise.' In Newton Road, sound carried, 'so if you switched on a light in the basement, you could hear it in the studio', as Kaye admitted – and the twins' playroom was directly below Ronald's studio. 'We were always slightly fearful of our father,' John said. 'Especially in his glasses and beard. It's a mask. As a child you don't access people with beards.' (One of Ronald's full-page cartoons in *Punch* in 1954 was called 'The Child-Hater'.) The worst thing for John in the long run was that Kaye leant on him 'to the point that I took the whole brunt of her emotional pain and her demands, which I resented deeply. I gave her a hard time.'

It was said that the enormous wall-clock with the decorated pendulum stopped on the day Ronald left. George Konig, who had recently photographed the Searles at home, remarked how possessive, even smothering, Kaye was. (Konig was himself a former PoW in Germany, who had married the nurse who pulled him through, but later left her. Many vulnerable PoWs, Konig said, regretted their impulsive post-war liaisons.)

For Roland Huntford, their UN friend, there was an embarrassing aftermath. The Searles had told him to call if he was ever in London. So he rang in the autumn of 1961. Kaye answered, and asked him to come at once. He arrived to find Kaye 'a broken person, but keeping up appearances'. She said she had seen a photograph of the press gallery of the Eichmann trial, 'including the woman she was sure Ronald was having an affair with'. Huntford recalls feeling curiously unmoved. 'Why, I wonder? I enjoyed her company, and she went out of her way to be kind to me.' She begged Huntford to stop in Paris on his way back to Geneva, and ask Ronald to come home. 'Of course I could not do anything of the sort, but hadn't the heart to say so outright. I'm afraid I temporized.' He said he would let her know, but that if she didn't hear from him, there was no hope. 'I travelled on the Simplon-Orient Express, and changed trains in Paris for Lausanne. There would have been enough time to make a phone call to Ronald. But I shrank from even trying.' Years later he was told that Kaye had waited by the telephone for his call. 'It is not an edifying tale,' he says sadly.

Wendy Toye, the friend closest to both Searles, went to see Ronald in Paris soon afterwards. She recalls thinking the break-up was probably inevitable. 'Kaye was so overpowering: almost anyone might have wanted to get away a bit.' Jill Balcon felt the same: 'Ronnie was so retiring, and had suffered all that horror, and Kaye was likeable and genial and jolly, but a bit overwhelming.' Jill Freud said, 'She went on loving him, and expected him to come back. The cruelty of it: one minute you're married and the next, he's gone. It came as a bombshell to everyone. But Ronald told Cle [Clement Freud] that his deadlines had him in a straitjacket, he was trapped, and the only way out was to go. I think Gauguin did the same.' Linda Villiers reflected: 'She was a warm-hearted woman, a bit of a mother-goddess, and felt him slipping away from her. She carried the pain of it with her for ever, there's no doubt about that.'

Jean Ellsmoor, who was slightly in love with Ronald herself, sent to Paris the things he requested. Doreen Scott typed 'businesslike' letters to him at Kaye's dictation. Letters from friends addressed to 'Dear Searles' became 'Dearest Kaye'. Elvira kept the children fed, and brother Bill was a rock.

Kaye's instinct was to reproach herself, even for encouraging Ronald to do the hated St Trinian's drawings. It was a heavy blow to her pride that having been a famously perfect family unit with her successful husband and twins, she was suddenly a single mother. Two bereavements – death of mother, departure of husband – had struck just as she was coping with a demanding job. 'The only thing to do was be busy.' Editing Puffins, and meeting authors, at least got her out of the house.

Within a month, Kaye wrote a résumé of her financial deal with Penguin. She had agreed to the £1,500 salary, but felt she could not suggest more Puffin titles without appearing to be trying to increase her fee. And she had to chivvy them even for the £1,500. Her broadcasts for *Woman's Hour* – she was presenting a programme about twins on 12 October – hardly constituted a living. Also, Puffin work consumed far more than two days a week: 'the job is a big one and should be paid accordingly'. Godwin knew she had been 'mucked about', with no personal office space. He had suggested that she should use his Harmondsworth desk on Tuesdays, as he was always in London that day; they could meet 'on an ad hoc basis, arranged by phone'. It was deeply unsatisfactory. Addressing her accountant, Kaye declared that she had been used rather badly. But should she protest? 'I need the job and they are notoriously mean. Also with my mother's death and other difficulties I have not perhaps been around quite as much as I will be in future. So you may feel it will be better to hold our horses for a month or two.'

Pauline Baynes had been Kaye's lunch date on the day she discovered Ronald's letter. Pauline, illustrator of the Narnia books, also became Tolkien's favourite artist. Having studied at the Slade, she led a solitary life, dedicated to her drawing, with two pet Rottweilers, in her hideaway cottage in Surrey. One day in 1961 there came a knock on the door from the local dog-meat man, a German ex-PoW named Fritz Otto Gasch. They were married within weeks, so Pauline (aged forty) was a new bride when she and Kaye met, and they confided in one another as women do. Next day Pauline thanked Kaye for lunch 'despite the worrying news'. She was sure it would all come right in the end.

She was full of enthusiastic suggestions for Puffins. De la Mare's *Peacock Pie*, Aesop, Christina Rossetti's 'Goblin Market', Browning's 'The Pied Piper' 'and other Jackdaw of Rheims type poems' would be 'gorgeous to illustrate'. Kaye had told her she was determined to go to Paris. 'Be terrifically extravagant and buy lots of clothes,' Pauline advised. When Kaye got back Pauline said she was glad it hadn't worked out too disastrously. 'You couldn't have been nicer all along – and Ronald (if I may call him this) couldn't have been naughtier! . . . If you are ever reunited, you will certainly be in a very strong position!' And Pauline added, 'It was a relief to know you hadn't jumped into the Seine!'

10: Nuffin' Like a Puffin

1962–6

Kaye's stroke of good fortune was arriving at Puffin just as children's books were entering a second 'golden age'. She always acknowledged this when asked the secret of her success. 'The climate was right, suddenly everyone was interested in children's books, and Allen Lane had made a nice lot of money from Penguins and was prepared to take risks. And people were writing amazing children's stories.'

Kaye had stated her credo in an early Puffin catalogue. She liked stories with pace and a strong moral sense, without being prim. 'We spread a wide net, insisting on genuine invention, integrity, quality of writing and an ability to communicate with the young.' These elements were already to be found in the writing of Rosemary Sutcliff, Penelope Farmer, Gillian Avery, Philippa Pearce, Mary Norton, Lucy M. Boston and William Mayne. The 1960s saw a flowering of work of modern classic status, from Leon Garfield, Joan Aiken, Alan Garner, Maurice Sendak, Nina Bawden, Penelope Lively, Margaret Mahy, Peter Dickinson, Mary Lavin, Helen Cresswell, Jill Paton Walsh, John Rowe Townsend and Barbara Willard. A generation of prolific writers seemed to have some magic key to exciting young readers: they dwelt in ancient lands of myth, using mystery, fantasy, history, time-travelling, and a hot-line to hobgoblins.

Specialist magazines sprang up, guiding bewildered parents: Margery Fisher's *Growing Point* magazine, Naomi Lewis's annual list of best children's books, and Anne Wood's *Books for Your*

Children from 1964, the year the Bologna Children's Book Fair was launched. From 1968, the serious broadsheet newspapers devoted whole pages to children's book reviews by discerning experts like Brian Alderson, Naomi Lewis, Elaine Moss and John Rowe Townsend. The 1944 Butler Education Act had proposed libraries in state schools, and from 1964 Harold Wilson's Labour government provided hard cash. The impact on the children's book trade was exponential: publishers could make money from a genre they had formerly disregarded, and well-funded libraries no longer resisted paperbacks.

Illustration assumed greater importance, thanks partly to technological advances in colour reproduction. Artwork could now be electronically separated into the four colour printing plates, and Brian Wildsmith's *Mother Goose* in 1961 was a positive kaleidoscope of inventive colour. Kaye's experience at *Lilliput* and the *Elizabethan*, and as Ronald's wife, made her a keen judge of illustrators. She knew that certain matches of illustrator to author, like Searle and Willans, are made in heaven: Ernest Shepard and A. A. Milne, Thomas Henry and Richmal Crompton, Pauline Baynes with Tolkien and C. S. Lewis, Margaret Tempest with Alison Uttley. (Ardizzone was his own illustrator, but Ardizzone and James Reeves were another match.) Some pairings proved interchangeable: *Paddington* was first illustrated by Peggy Fortnum, who really established the little bear's distinctive character, but after 1974 others took over. Roald Dahl was first illustrated by Faith Jaques, and Kaye's choice for Dahl was none other than Ronald Searle; but Tom Maschler had the inspiration to link him with the brilliant Quentin Blake, whose antic drawings made him Dahl's perfect partner, injecting charm and humanity even into horrid characters. (Ronald did illustrate one Puffin, in 1962: Thurber's *The Thirteen Clocks and the Wonderful O*.) Shirley Hughes, who had done classic Puffin covers in the 1950s, when these still involved skilled and intensive lithography, produced warm, scratchy drawings for Dorothy Edwards's *My Naughty Little Sister*: another ideal pairing.

It hardly mattered that Kaye was inexperienced. Hardback publishers did the commissioning and she chose from the best. The tough bit was cajoling them into leasing her the rights. She did her homework: she said she had discovered Barbara Willard just by asking a library which books were most borrowed. Within her first year Kaye doubled the number of Puffins, but she was keen to develop Puffin Originals. *Stig of the Dump* arrived as a scruffy manuscript which had clearly been the rounds of several slush piles. It lay on Kaye's desk for the entire year of 1961. All she knew was that the author, Clive King, lived abroad. King was a Cambridge graduate who had served in the war and then worked in foreign parts as a language teacher. His book was inspired by the ancient chalkpit near his childhood home, Ash in Kent, where his teacher, formerly governess to Christopher Robin Milne, would read aloud stories about Stone Age man. Years later, King lit on the notion of writing about a caveman reappearing in Ash. His agent, Murray Pollinger, sent it to half a dozen publishers on both sides of the Atlantic. All rejected it. Then, in Beirut, King heard that Kaye was taking a chance on *Stig*. In three years it was one of Puffin's top sellers, a modern classic, read on *Blue Peter*, and was later filmed. This encouraged King to carry on writing; and, never going out of print, *Stig* provided him with a pension 'on which I subsist very comfortably', he told Kaye thirty years later. *Stig* was one of the books Kaye said she was proudest of publishing. *The Wizard of Earthsea* by Ursula K. Le Guin was another. Ursula, a science fiction writer, told Kaye that she'd done one children's book, published in America, about Ged, a boy at a college of wizardry. Kaye loved the fact that it treated wizardry logically, implying that you have to be trained properly, and use the gift with restraint. (We shall never know how she would have reacted to Harry Potter.)

Kaye reckoned she read twenty books a week, usually in bed: 'I felt more like a child there.' She knew children would read what is easiest, and would often tell a salutary tale of two boys taking out Enid Blyton's *Famous Five*, then getting sick of 'the same story', and looking for more variety. 'They just need a bit of help. You have to make children want to make the effort for themselves.'

Kaye's 1962 diary, under 'in the event of accident please notify', gave Ronald's name, and his Paris address. In public Kaye disguised her misery, but privately she was full of self-reproach, and anxious about the twins. She sought reassurance from the cartoonist 'Haro' Hodson, a friend from *Lilliput*. He wrote after a lunch at Newton Road, having quaffed too many glasses of vin rosé ('continually conscious of your heart'), urging her not to blame herself for Ronald's defection. 'It doesn't make one any less miserable or dumbfounded inside – to be left rather than leave. But how could you continue to please <u>against</u> your inward spirit?' She had done nothing wrong. Ronald's denial of all hope was 'wilfully naughty'. 'So no regrets (however many thrash at you), you do know what is true & kind, & what is not.' She was not to worry about what people thought. 'You have to be true to your best self.'

He told her not to forget that the twins 'are compounded of you as much as Ronald'. John 'under the unsure carapace' would be resilient. 'And Kate who is so profoundly kind is – as well as you – probably Ronald translated into a woman & thus far more able to stomach life than he.'

The family story is that when the twins met the cheerful and dependable Keith Hunter that year, they turned on Kaye and asked how she could have left such a nice man. They had just seen their father again. Kaye's diary simply says 'Kids Paris'. They stayed in the Hotel Madison, and the sensitive Kate, now fifteen, remembered trying to make herself presentable for her dad, so he would be proud of her; but she got hairspray in her eyes, and arrived red-eyed and miserable. They were introduced to Monica, and when Kaye afterwards asked Kate, 'Was there a woman there?' it was the start of a life fraught with the need for diplomacy. The twins' sporadic meetings with their father after that were mostly in Cambridge, when Ronald visited his parents.

In her first summer alone, Kaye took the twins to the seaside. On Pevensey beach they met a man, Arthur Cooksey, who was planning to cross the Channel in the smallest boat ever. 'We'll come along too,' said Kaye, typically. Two weeks later, they were aboard, with dog: the skipper in the wheelhouse, Kaye drinking rum with Cooksey, John throwing up over the side of the boat, and Kate ashen-faced, clutching their dachshund Rusty. 'We got over to France,' John recalled, 'and Kaye told me, "Take Rusty for a run around Calais," as we moored alongside *The Girl Pat*, a gun-running boat. Then we got back on the boat and headed back to England. At Dover, customs officers appeared and Kaye realized that Rusty, if spotted, would have to go into quarantine for six months. "Quick, quick, hide in the heads and keep very quiet," she said, and then, "Quick – run down the dock and throw him in the car."' Amazingly, he did, and they escaped detection. 'It illustrates her ability to solve any situation,' John says, 'and her total disregard for authority. Kaye was always cavalier about the law. She taught me to drive at eleven. At sixteen I was driving her Mini when we went into a ditch. When the police arrived she told them she'd been driving.'

On the first anniversary of her mother's death, Christopher Fry took Kaye to tea at Perrins Walk, Hampstead, where Eleanor Farjeon produced cucumber sandwiches and cakes and her best china. Afterwards Eleanor thanked Kaye for her strawberries, and the 'enchanting' de la Mare volume. In a wise and consoling letter, she told Kaye to come back whenever she needed to talk.

'We have to clear, ultimately, our most deeply painful experiences within ourselves.' She could help, 'if only by being a listener who cares. As I do, truly, for you Kaye.' Kaye had asked Eleanor to contribute to her 'Birthday Books', but Eleanor declined, setting out her objections to this 'cute' idea. She was convinced that 'there is no such thing as the mass-produced Child of Eight – or Nine – or Ten or God help them, of above all ages, Eleven'. The eleven-plus exam stamped and graded them for years to come, said Eleanor, but all children developed differently. 'Don't impose on them an artificial adult notion of the thrill of becoming curly-figured 8 after being straight-limbed 7,' she pleaded. 'Don't be twee with children, Kaye, respect them. We adults have forgotten too much to be able to tell children what to think or feel or be at any age.'

She followed up with a letter which Kaye cherished: 'Kaye, dear Kaye, I do <u>like</u> you so much, I could say with equal truth that I love you, but that isn't the object of this letter. I like your kindness, your integrity, your inability to hate, your lack of bitterness in great suffering. I like your looks and I like your company. I like your sweetcorn (my best cob of the year) and I like your cabbage, I like your beautiful tolerance of my disgraceful letter, and I shall not be tolerant of myself if anything in it checks your pleasure and interest in producing your Birthday Series which I'm certain will be delightful, and delighting, especially if the contents are ageless as well as age-ful – I wish I could find something to give you for each of the three books, and I know I can for the Elevens if you come so far – because, in short, Kaye, in three Words in a Nutshell, I like <u>You</u>. Eleanor.'

'This letter,' Kaye said, 'overflowing with her lovingness and perception, came out of the blue when I was deeply unhappy and out of conceit with myself . . . I remember how it helped.' It demonstrated Eleanor's 'gift for doing the right thing', and her praise for Kaye's qualities was 'most sustaining and confidence-restoring'.

(Eleanor's modesty about her own excellent qualities was famous. Her charming story collection *The Little Bookroom*, illustrated by Ardizzone, became a Puffin and won several prizes including the Carnegie Medal. Resisting publicity, Eleanor refused even to be photographed; when a hapless reporter rang and asked what she looked like, Eleanor replied, 'Like a cheerful suet pudding.' And was her hair now silver? 'No dear, it's <u>gunmetal</u>.' She turned down a damehood: she did not wish to be 'any different from the milkman'.)

When Eleanor became ill, Kaye took gifts and grapes. Eleanor wrote: 'When my Joaney was about three, & not well, Mother went to see her, and brought her a bunch of grapes. Joaney said delightedly, "I like you to come and see me, granny." Mother laughed. "With grapes, Joan?" Joaney looked at her with surprise and said seriously: "Without grapes." I love you without grapes, Kaye.' Eleanor died, aged eighty-three, on 5 June 1965, and the Children's Book Circle established its annual award in her name, for services to children's books. Kaye won the Eleanor Farjeon Award herself in 1970.

Kate had been at the fee-paying Queen's College, Harley Street, but Kaye arranged for her to switch in September 1962 to the excellent state school in Kentish Town, Camden School for Girls. It gave Kate a new perspective on her home: she had come to hate Newton Road, and was embarrassed by it. At Queen's College she had friends who lived grandly in Kensington; her new schoolfriend Penny lived in a Tufnell Park flat – 'a nice happy normal family with mum and dad and gran and brother and everyone mucking in'. John too says he found Newton Road a cold house, 'a big antique showroom for the strange things he and mum collected, the barrel organ, a human skull, musical instruments, the death mask of Victor Hugo'.

Gradually Kaye picked up her spirits and resumed a social life.

In October 1962, 'Haro' wrote again, glad that Kate was happy at school, glad that Kaye was at long last 'so to speak, beginning'. She was about to launch Peacock books with a party. 'I hope,' wrote Haro, 'that someone on Wednesday taps a glass at a table & says "Ladies – ah, and – ah gentlemen, I'm sure we would all like to raise our glasses to the little lady in the corner without whom etceterah etceterah" . . .' He appended a cartoon: a bird carrying a placard reading 'JEAN MUST GO!' (Ronald's secretary had become a somewhat irritating presence at Newton Road.)

Linda Villiers left Puffin after one year, because the profligate Godwin had overspent his budget, and was cutting back. Kaye's vociferous defence of Linda was audible throughout the open-plan office. At least Linda departed with a bonus: Penguin shares went on the open market that year, and everybody on the staff gathered in the warehouse to receive their moiety. (Linda was pursued by her father's stockbroker friends to sell them her shares, and eventually gave in.)

Early in January 1963 another young woman arrived at Penguin who was to be a good friend. Dorothea Duncan was twenty-six, and caught the Penguin bus which took staff from Notting Hill to Harmondsworth (as the tube didn't go that far out), but because of the snow that had fallen on New Year's Eve in that famous winter, she didn't arrive till noon. Kaye and Dorothea immediately took to one another. Kaye invited Dorothea to her parties, where 'everyone was famous' and – daunting moment – guests were invited to perform, among them Joyce Grenfell and Michael Flanders. She liked to orchestrate her guests, Dorothea found. 'She would grab you just when you were getting on with someone and introduce you to someone else. Once she said, "James darling, I would like you to meet a very good friend of mine" – and I was dumbfounded to find it was James Mason, who turned his back on me at once.'

Puffin writers became vital to Kaye's social life. She went to the theatre with Clive King, Naomi Lewis and the illustrator Richard Kennedy, whose account of his life with the Woolfs, *A Boy at the Hogarth Press*, was later a big success. In 1964 he sent her John Lennon's *In His Own Write*, urging her to grab it for Peacocks. Kaye needed devotees like Kennedy. But she began to value women writers, who were frank and confiding about their own predicaments, emotional, familial and financial. They belonged to a fine breed of British woman of a certain era: robustly overcoming disasters and 'getting on with it'. One was Noel Streatfeild, author of the perennial Puffin seller, *Ballet Shoes*. She was a bishop's daughter whose chin-up approach to life was always a tonic.

In 1963 a letter from Noel arrived, postmarked Gibraltar. She had left London precipitately, without calling anyone, when she was getting no response from her agents. To eke out her dwindling capital she'd gone abroad. 'I went into the P&O on a Monday and asked when the next ship was going south. They said "Tomorrow".' She immediately bought a ticket, rushed home, packed, and the next morning was on the boat train to Tilbury. 'I found a very pretty and cheap town on the Atlantic coast of Spain, Tarifa. It is on the straits of Gibraltar and the surrounding country is wild and beautiful.' The magnificent six-mile Hurricane Beach was aptly named: 'a dream when the weather is good . . . untenable in the wind. But it all suits me. I go to Gib once a week for mail and to see a film, and I am satisfied.' Kaye at once bought Noel's childhood memoir, *A Vicarage Family*, for Puffin, and in distant future years made it a priority to promote and cherish Noel, eventually seeing that she got an honour, the OBE.

Kaye was determined that children's authors deserved the kind of rewards enjoyed by bestselling writers for adults. She gave a dinner at L'Écu de France, attended by Sir Allen Lane and other Penguin grandees, to launch Iona and Peter Opie's collection of nursery rhymes into Puffins. Peter wrote afterwards, quite overwhelmed ('we are not over-much party people as you know'). 'I have frequently passed L'Écu de France on the way to the London Library . . . I never thought it would have anything to do with us, one day.' Kaye gave the Opies some sweetmeats to deliver to Pauline Baynes, who had missed the party: also a pearl-studded bag, and a copy of the menu, which had included 'Pineapple Pauline'. 'To have one's name printed on a menu is fame indeed,' wrote Pauline. 'It was just about the biggest miss of my life . . . Oh dear – I gloomed for 2 days . . . I hope that there may yet be other Rewards and Surprises for me in life!'

Later, when Michael Flanders gave the Opies' book an enthusiastic review on radio, Kaye sent him some Puffins for his six-year-old daughter Laura. She asked Flanders to edit an anthology of humorous verse, but he replied that apart from bits of Lear, Carroll and Hood, and possibly Belloc, he didn't really enjoy humorous verse: 'Don't like my own all that much!' Kaye also suggested herself as a panellist on *Call My Bluff*, the TV word game in which Flanders chaired a team. Why did they invite only 'glammy actresses and models' as their token women? Kaye was still doing radio, however, including a long interview with Rosemary Sutcliff about how she managed to 'breathe life into the old bones of history' without a forsooth or a gadzooks.

The 'Birthday Books' project consumed swathes of Kaye's time. She commissioned dozens of writers to contribute stories, poems, games, quizzes; permissions were sought for extracts from Thurber, Alison Uttley and Noel Streatfeild. She collected the writings of children at each age, including, for *The Birthday Book of Ten*, her own schoolday essay on Waterfalls. But after three years Tony Godwin called a halt to the project on the grounds of economy.

The world at large did not yet know that Ronald was absent from Kaye's life, and she maintained the illusion. In March 1964, on a Puffin mission to Australia, where she addressed the Adelaide

Arts Festival, and New Zealand, where she stayed at Government House with Sir Bernard and Lady (Laura) Fergusson, the papers still described her as 'wife of the celebrated British humorous artist Ronald Searle'. She spoke to reporters as if he were still around; so they would write, 'Her husband is now concentrating on social comment rather than jokes' and 'Her husband is at present in New York doing drawings of the World's Fair.' The Searle children were 'hoping to follow in their parents' footsteps, Kate as an artist and John as a journalist'. (John was a prolific young poet, and Kate was artistically promising.) Of her collaborations with Ronald, Kaye was quoted as saying she might as well never have written the books: 'Everyone speaks of them as "by Ronald Searle".'

In 1965 James Mason returned to London. The acerbic Pamela had divorced him (her grounds being 'habitual adultery', changed to 'mental cruelty'), after which Mason swore he would never marry again – though of course he did, ten years later. He was depressed and bitter about having to work continually, bestowing his distinguished services on inferior films, to pay millions in alimony. He and Kaye could console one another. Kaye later told Mason's biographer, Sheridan Morley, that she could probably have married James. 'For quite a long while,' she said, 'I think I was the best woman friend he ever had.' 'I loved him very much,' she added, 'and I think if I'd fought my way through all that reticence, as some other women did, then we might have ended up together.'

Kaye was promoted to the board of Penguin, becoming the only woman director, on the retirement of Eunice Frost, Allen Lane's first editor, in 1966. It was what she wanted, she said, because 'although they were all frightfully glad about the sales figures' (a 300 per cent increase) 'there was nobody else on the board speaking up for Puffin'. Her promotion meant a public acknowledgement that she was a power in publishing. Her salary increased: a three-year contract signed in 1965 gave her £2,500 for the first year, £2,750 the second, £3,000 the third. When she addressed the Women's Employment Federation about women in publishing, she sent a questionnaire asking fellow women publishers how they had got there. Livia Gollancz, a former musician, and Sir Victor's daughter, said she had blatantly got in by the back door. Livia's only gripe was that she found 'the social part of publishing very much harder than anything I have to do inside the office'. One respondent said girl applicants, often graduates, were rarely interviewed; if they were, they might get offered £600 a year. Marni Hodgkin said it was down to pulling strings and using contacts: 'The insoluble problem is always "no experience, no job. No job, no experience".' This dictum never bothered Kaye, as we shall see.

A new concern began to bedevil children's publishers. There was no escaping the fact that the previous 'golden age' of children's literature, the worlds of Milne, Kenneth Grahame, E. Nesbit and Frances Hodgson Burnett, had been firmly upper- and middle-class. Stories of children with cooks and nannies, and mothers who wafted into the nursery in tea-gowns, ignored the sensitivities of children who had none of these things. Until the 1960s books had been blithely published for white middle-class children with parents who took them to the library on Saturday mornings. A social view of children's literature arrived, based on the capacity of books to enlarge the lives of the disadvantaged young. Labour boroughs of inner cities were especially committed to equipping children's libraries, but librarians were uncomfortably aware of the gulf between the golden-age books and their increasingly multi-ethnic readership. 'Celebrating working-class lifestyles for their own sakes soon came to seem a legitimate aim of children's literature.'* Elaine Moss, librarian at Fleet Primary

---

* Kimberley Reynolds and Nicholas Tucker, *Children's Book Publishing since 1945*, Scolar Press, 1997.

School in Hampstead, wrote of the scarcity of black and Asian faces in picture-books. There was a similar imperative to show girls in other than passive, domestic roles. Fierce argument developed between teachers and librarians (who knew children's reactions to books), and the specialist critics who gave awards to books deemed to possess literary and artistic excellence. None of this academic argy-bargy interested Kaye much: the words authors wrote were their own, and writers like Hugh Lofting were writing at a time when the terms racism, sexism and elitism did not yet exist. She was not inclined to alter her criteria just to widen Puffin's appeal to a multicultural readership. Her evangelism was reserved for books that were written with imagination and subtle characterization, and she stuck to that. She cared only that the Puffin name should be 'impeccable, synonymous with good books', as she said twenty-five years later. 'To be in Puffin was an accolade. Parents could see the name Puffin, and know it was OK.'

Eleanor Graham had told her, if you nurse a book for five years it will have a life of another twenty. By the end of the 1960s even authors who had resisted being in paperback learned to enjoy wider availability and high sales. 'Everybody wanted to be Puffins,' Kaye recalled. 'I didn't have to look for new authors. I could have almost all the authors I wanted.'

Allen Lane took an equable 'swings and roundabouts' approach to sales. The important thing for him was 'making readers'. By the mid-1960s Kaye's winners included Tolkien, *Mary Poppins*, *Paddington*, William Mayne's *A Parcel of Trees* (commissioned by Kaye), Clive King's *Stig of the Dump*, and Dodie Smith's *The Hundred and One Dalmatians*. Dodie, who now rarely came to London except 'for dentistry', invited Kaye to her thatched cottage in Essex, to meet 'our Dalmatian, Disney, and our recently acquired donkeys, Sugar and Spice', but Kaye's schedule allowed scant time for leisurely excursions.

Her next Penguin 'mission' was to Israel and the Lebanon, where along with Puffin-promoting she prepared a *Woman's Hour* broadcast (as she did wherever she went). In Beirut she stayed with Clive King and they worked on his new book, *The Twenty-Two Letters*. 'I particularly recall [Kaye] striding through the haunt of sin, Le Casino du Liban at Djounie,' King wrote, 'recording on her portable tape machine the rattle of betting-chips and clang of one-armed bandits. She had dragged me there, and we were both disappointed by its atmosphere of an English seaside bingo hall.'

At home Kaye began taking carloads of books to primary schools, which were keen to stock their libraries. School libraries in north London bought £60,000 worth of books a year from the High Hill Bookshop alone. Ian Norrie devoted a third of his floor and shelf-space to children (providing one sixth of the turnover). 'I took the view, as Kaye did, that children were the readers of the future. And as you can imagine, there wasn't a child in Hampstead who wasn't brilliant, or gifted: I know because all their parents told me so.' (Norrie allegedly pinned up a notice: 'Children of progressive parents admitted only on leads.')

On 6 June 1966, the High Hill hosted a Puffin event, a story-writing contest, won by nine-year-old Lalage Everest-Phillips, from Mill Hill. 'Lalage, 9, writes sad story' said the headline in the *Ham & High*, the local paper. Catherine Storr presented the prize, a Dansette record player. Meeting Kaye on that memorable date, 6.6.66, proved significant to the future novelist and artist Charlotte Cory, as Lalage became. And for Kaye this was the forerunner of many such events. Her mind teemed with marketing ideas, one of which was the Puffin Song (suggested by the sales director of W. H. Smith, who said he would play it in the shops), written at speed, with some help from Laurie Lee:

There is nuffin', nuffin', nuffin' like a Puffin,
Nuffin' like a Puffin book to read, yes indeed.
A Puffin's so exciting, the finest kind of writing,
Yes there's nuffin' like a Puffin book to read.

There's so much in a Puffin, it's full of super stuffin',
Enuff to keep you happy all day long, all day long,
So for boys and girls who're needing some extra special reading,
All you've got to do is sing this Puffin song.

There is nuffin', nuffin', nuffin' like a Puffin,
Nuffin' like a Puffin book to read, yes indeed,
A Puffin's so exciting, the finest kind of writing.
Yes a Puffin book's the kind of read you need, yes indeed.

11: Sniffup Spotera!

1967–70

'British cartoonist Ronald Searle of *Punch* and his mate Kaye are asunder,' announced the American columnist Walter Winchell in December 1966. Kaye had finally accepted that her marriage was over and consented to the divorce she had hitherto refused Ronald. After many months of legal wrangling between them, her petition appeared in the list of undefended suits in the High Court. The report appeared in *The Times* in February 1967.

'Mr Ronald William Fordham Searle, the cartoonist, offered no defence in the Divorce Court yesterday when a decree nisi was granted his wife, Kathleen, a director of Penguin Books, of Newton Road, Bayswater, W., because of his desertion . . . The court's discretion was exercised in respect of adultery admitted by Mrs Searle.' Mr Searle, who was ordered to pay costs, would 'transfer his share of their jointly owned home, said to be worth about £20,000, to his wife in lieu of maintenance'.

Ronald and Monica – who had travelled constantly since 1961, Ronald producing some fine satirical reportage from North America – had been absolutely certain, when they first met, that neither would ever marry again. But on 16 June 1967, at the British Embassy in Paris, they became man and wife.

So ended Kaye's third stab at matrimony, but not the hurt that cut so deeply it never went away. For ever more, any new person she met was told, wistfully, about 'Ronnie', as if he had gone yesterday. But at fifty-three she was as vivacious and compelling as ever, and men continued to be intrigued by her. The 'admitted adultery', which hardly justified the term since she'd been alone for nearly six years, referred to Jim Cecil, who rented a cottage from his friend Lord Gage at Alceston, a pretty village on the Sussex Downs. Jim was an old Etonian, grandson of Eustace Cecil, younger brother of the Victorian prime minister Lord Salisbury; so he was a second cousin to Kaye's old friend Lord David Cecil. An affable, bohemian, buccaneering chap, who looked like Jack Hawkins, Jim was large, rotund, kindly, good company and of independent means. He owned a hotel in Amsterdam, cooked with lashings of garlic, and introduced Kaye to the opera. So she had an amiable escort of her own age, whom everyone liked. Her friends were pleased and relieved.

She sought Allen Lane's advice about whether to marry Jim or 'live in sin', as it was still known. In August 1968 Lane told her to come and talk to him about her 'marriage problems'. 'If Jim is satisfied with the status quo there's a lot to be said for it. If the government policy tax-wise is to make cohabitation outside the blessed state so much more attractive, who are we to oppose it?' 'Jim was obviously a physical thing,' said a Puffin staffer. 'Kaye once came into the office and gave a sigh. "Oh!" she said. "Jim's so *heavy*".'

But her marital status was insignificant compared with the plot Kaye was hatching in 1966–7. The cute jingle 'Nuffin' Like a Puffin' had paved the way. 'The sales boys at the conference asked me, what are you going to do next year, Kaye? and I said I'd like to start a Puffin Club . . . I was going to add "if the directors will let me", but after "if", they started to clap. So one of the reps stood up and said, it looks as if Kaye has got her club.' Kaye had to start a magazine, she said, to answer requests from children for information about authors. 'I liked doing magazines and the only way to sell magazines for children is by subscription. So I suggested a club.' She said Allen Lane doubted it would be profitable. But Lane's biographer Jeremy Lewis asserts: 'He had always liked to think of Penguin readers as members of a club, waiting for the monthly list of new publications, and Kaye's initiative appealed to this side of his character.'

The template for Puffin readers as authors' groupies had been her twins: John's curiosity about the scene of *Moonfleet*, and Kate's unprompted fan letter to Arthur Calder-Marshall, starting 'Dear author', after she'd read *The Fair to Middling*. *Moonfleet* and *The Fair to Middling* were among Kaye's first Puffin titles. And Kaye had earlier found *Young Elizabethan* readers intensely curious about authors. Many children of the 1950s, myself included, read the much less intellectual *Enid Blyton Magazine*, which carried the absurd strapline 'The only magazine I write!' Miss Blyton's letter to readers from her home at Green Hedges, Beaconsfield, Bucks, made us feel we knew her and her daughters, Gillian and Imogen, and their pets. When I was ten, my sister Alison and I, and our friend Rosalind, started our own Pony Club (though we had no ponies) and I wrote to Enid Blyton inviting Gillian and Imogen to join. Miss Blyton's polite reply explained that actually 'Gillian now has children of her own, and Imogen is at university!' I was thrilled to get the letter from Green Hedges, all the same. And perhaps the fact that Kaye wished she had written to Walter de la Mare when he praised her poem, instead of waiting twenty-five years, was a factor. The Puffin Club would provide every child with a link to favourite authors.

What Kaye needed was some helpful girls. Rosemary Sandberg was twenty-seven, a languages graduate working for 'an old bat on *Woman's Journal*' who told her Kaye Webb needed an assistant for a new club. Rosemary was summoned to Newton Road, and greeted with 'Come in, darling, I'm just sorting out John's sock drawer.' Kaye's ebullience, glamour and style were a surprise. She had known everyone, it seemed, and travelled everywhere, and seemed confident that Allen Lane would back whatever she did. Rosemary had once worked at J. Walter Thompson, and asked Kaye, 'Have you got marketing reports on children's book sales?' 'Darling, what are you talking about?' was Kaye's reply. So Rosemary set up a mailing list and a distribution centre, and was gathered into Kaye's social life, meeting authors at Sunday lunches at Newton Road, seated next to the flirtatious Laurie Lee, and meeting 'silent, solemn' William Mayne. One night, the Sandbergs dined with Noel Streatfeild. Rosemary's husband moaned that he was missing Chelsea in the Cup Final replay; but when they climbed the stairs to the Elizabeth Street flat, they found Noel watching a huge TV screen, drinking a Bloody Mary: 'Come in, sit down,' she cried, waving her cigarette-holder, shaped like a lorgnette. 'I'm watching Chelsea.'

Rosemary was dispatched to the East End to find cheap competition prizes, and got used to Kaye's random commands: 'Ring Vanessa Redgrave and Stirling Moss, and ask what books they read as a child,' or 'Find out the times of trains from Hampstead to Godalming,' when there is no such train. 'Kaye was on a different planet from the rest of us.'

Kaye's great stroke of luck was finding Jill McDonald, an illustrator lately arrived from New Zealand with her two children. Jill's middle name was Masefield; her father was a cousin of John Masefield and kin to Christopher Fry. She had an anarchic, subversive, often surreal sense of humour and Kaye gave her free rein to mastermind the Puffin Club logo and badge. 'I love doing Puffin stuff. I feel like a round peg in a round hole,' she told Kaye. Engagingly modest, she agreed to come in from Greenwich to the Puffin office one day a week ('tell those mingy pigs I can't do it for less than £10 a day') and put her distinctive stamp, including her lucid handwriting, on *Puffin Post's* zany 'thinksbubbles'. She invented the philosophizing dog Odway, who spoke in Olde Englishe and suggested strange themes for readers to write about, such as 'A dichotomy: Ephemeral Delights vs Everlasting Joy'.

Puffin Post was launched on 23 March 1967. On Jill McDonald's cover, two Puffins were chatting: 'I say old boy, shall we join this new club?' 'Good idea. I hear they have some p'super prizes.' 'The membership forms landed like an avalanche,' Rosemary wrote. Within weeks there were 7,500 members; after two months, 20,000. Tony Godwin wrote in April, not surprised that Kaye had 'retired for a few days' rest': it all looked 'bloody good' from where he sat. Clearly the Puffin Club was a stroke of genius. It was a shot in the dark, a kind of *folie*. But it worked.

Readers immediately saw Kaye as a kind of friendly aunt. 'We feel as if we know each of you personally,' she told them. In fact, she was already Aunt Kaye to several of them, the offspring of her famous friends. They included Tessa Dahl, daughter of Roald; Ian Norrie's daughters Amanda and Jessica; Emily Thwaite, daughter of the poet and literary editor Anthony Thwaite; Rupert Christiansen, now opera critic of the *Daily Telegraph*, whose grandfather was the legendary 'Chris', editor of the *Daily Express*, and whose mother had worked with Kaye at the *News Chronicle*; Julia Eccleshare, daughter of Colin, who ran Cambridge University Press; Hannah Cole, the children's author, niece of the writer Catherine Storr; and Ellen, Adam and Katharine Garner, the children of author Alan Garner .

The membership list is stuffed with the writers, artists and publishers of the future. The political journalist Matthew d'Ancona says the Puffin badge was the only badge allowed at his school. The children's book critic Nicolette Jones (daughter of an artist) and Profile Books managing director Andrew Franklin, son of Routledge publisher Norman Franklin, were both pioneer Puffineers. So were the author Virginia Nicholson, great-niece of Virginia Woolf; the *Observer* theatre critic Kate

Kellaway, daughter of gardening writer Deborah Kellaway; the cookery writer Sophie Grigson, daughter of the cooking guru Jane and the poet and critic Geoffrey; Condé Nast's managing director and author Nicholas Coleridge; *The Week* magazine's arts editor Lucinda Bredin; the journalist and broadcaster Mary Ann Sieghart; and Kate McFarlan, who now prints every Puffin and Penguin book, as she is managing director of Clay's.

The novelist and artist Charlotte Cory, the erstwhile Miss Everest-Phillips, became member 359, 'and that number has dogged me ever since,' she says. 'If I'm catching a plane, it turns out to be flight 359 . . .'

Puffin Post is studded with names, because Kaye published the names of 'all the entrants who were any good'. When I first met Kaye, she gave me some old *Puffin Posts* to look at and my eye was caught by the name of Emma Thompson aged twelve, on a clever two-line verse, 'Lines written by an Aphid landing on a Rose':

Too pink,
I think.

'Is that *the* Emma Thompson?' I asked Kaye.

'OF COURSE it's *the* Emma Thompson!' Kaye replied. Of course. Emma's father, Eric Thompson of *The Magic Roundabout*, was an old friend of Kaye.

Puffin Post's prime purpose was to introduce authors, in all their quirky eccentricity, to readers. The first 'Meet Your Author' featured P. L. Travers, who lived off the King's Road at World's End ('What a suitable address for the author of *Mary Poppins!*'). She was born in Australia. 'Like William Blake's Black Boy – you know the poem? "My mother bore me in the southern wild".' Her mother, she said, had the eye of a snake. A hunchbacked old Irishman once told her, 'The only education you need is spitting.'

And when asked about writing for children, she replied, 'Oh no, I don't write for *children*.'

Kaye's friends Joyce Grenfell, Malcolm Muggeridge, Yehudi Menuhin, Harry Secombe, Christopher Fry and James Mason listed their favourite childhood books in the first issue. There was a poem by Spike Milligan and a letter from Worzel Gummidge. Readers were encouraged to start collecting 'precious junk': 'A stone or a bone or a leaf or a shell, or the innards of an old clock or a piece of Japanese writing . . . an Easter egg wrapper, a bottle top, or a ticket or a marble or an old door knob.' There was soon a Puffin code, encrypting the alphabet, and a Puffin password: 'Sniffup!' to which the response was 'Spotera!' ('Puffins are tops' backwards). It was quintessentially Puffinesque to ask children to produce a collage on the theme 'The Thinginess of Things', or to 'List seven smells you like best, and say why. Seven Suitable Sweet Smelling Surprises to the Seven Best entries.'

The critic Nicolette Jones was just seven when she won a prize for her poem about 'Someone I Like', selecting 'Ken Ford, our laundry man'. Later, with her sister Rachel, she walked fifteen miles to raise money for a puffin sanctuary, and won two tiny books Catherine Storr had made in childhood. The children's author Hannah Cole was thirteen when she wrote to tell Kaye she liked *Puffin Post* – 'but I can't do the crossword, what shame and ignominy'. The artist Charlotte Voake, who has now illustrated many Puffins, won a paintbox, at ten. The journalist Jessamy Calkin was twelve when she won a prize for a cartoon in which an adult ghost says to a trembling baby ghost: 'Don't be silly, Solomon, I've told you before, there's no such thing as humans.' Kate Kellaway of the *Observer* was 'an ardent Puffineer'. (The word 'Puffineer' wasn't adopted until the fourth issue; Kaye first referred to 'Puffinites' and then asked readers' views.) For Kate aged ten, the Puffin Club was 'heaven'. 'It was permission to do what I loved most – to write whatever came into my head.' Her story about a hen named William Shakespeare was judged by Noel Streatfeild to be 'absolutely delightful'. She won many prizes: from a packet of sunflower seeds (a desperate measure when Kaye had promised a prize to every entrant, and got hundreds) to a five-year diary emblazoned 'My Secret Life', with a little key attached. But her best prize was tea at the Ritz with Kaye and Alan Garner. Garner, author of *The Owl Service*, appeared somewhat morose and 'unreadable' – 'but Kaye was charm itself, and took me under her wing. I felt safe, flattered and cherished, as if I'd been admitted to a writerly fairyland, which involved tea at the Ritz! The Puffin Club did that for many children. All my friends read *Puffin Post* avidly. And the magic came from Kaye, the sense that good things would grow out of it, like sunflowers.'

Virginia Bell, aged twelve, daughter of Virginia Woolf's nephew Quentin Bell – now the author Virginia Nicholson – resembled Tenniel's Alice, with her long fair hair, high brow and Pre-Raphaelite mouth. She spent hours writing illustrated volumes entitled 'The Collected Works of Virginia Bell', and was taken with her sister Cressida every week to the bookshop in Leeds (where her father taught art) to choose a Puffin. She entered the very first *Puffin Post* contest, asking for favourite words: hers was 'nourish'. 'It sounds deep and exotic and cosy.' Virginia won a Penguin encyclopedia and dictionary in a boxed set, kept to this day. She never went on Puffin sprees ('The idea of meeting other children filled me with dread') but Kaye declared, just as she had on the *Elizabethan*, that there must be treats and parties, in the provinces as well as in London. 'Kaye arrived in Liverpool,' Rosemary Sandberg remembered, 'and greeted the kids like a whirlwind – "Come over here" – clasping them to her great bosom in a cloud of her favourite scent, Youth Dew.'

And Kaye urged the children to have adventures. Puffins, readers were told, were 'merry, lazy, inquisitive, shy, comical and elusive' creatures. Founder members could go and see real live puffins for themselves, by entering a draw to win a trip to Lundy Island, off the Devon coast, in 1967. That trip was never forgotten by any of the participants. Everything that could go wrong went wrong.

Allen Lane told her they couldn't possibly travel to Lundy in a day, so Kaye must bring the children to stay the night at his farm, and he'd put on a barbecue. (He loved what he called 'Kaye's junketings'.) But it rained on Lane's barbecue, so they had lamb chops and sausages indoors. Next day it was still raining when they set off: one of their cars skidded off the road and hit the bank. ('Luckily no one was really hurt,' said the children's diary.) Stonehenge, their next port of call, was closed. At Taunton, they stopped for a poached egg, 'but some of us didn't have anything because we were feeling car sick'. At Ilfracombe, they hit 'the biggest traffic jam ever' and reached the quayside just in time to see the Lundy steamer sail away out of sight. Kaye managed to get them into the Manor Hotel, arranged for them to be ferried across to the island next day by a Mr Jackson in his crabber, the *Elizabeth*, and took everyone to a comedy thriller called *Busybody* at Ilfracombe's Summer Playhouse.

Next day it was raining in torrents. The sea was grey and extremely choppy. Mr Jackson tried to warn Kaye that it was unsafe to set out, but she misheard him. The *Elizabeth* plunged and rocked on the waves and seemed about to capsize in the Force 4 gale. 'Water was coming over, the children were thrown about, we tied them all up with rope,' Kaye said later. She covered the younger ones in her huge mac, and prayed that none would be flung overboard. She felt sick herself: 'I thought, oh God, if you let me get them there I shall never do anything silly again.' But in the diary the children compiled, they said, 'Kaye tried to be as merry as her usual self.' The child who wrote, 'And we were SO COLD' was excised from the diary printed in *Puffin Post*.

Of course they had a good time, thanks to the island's friendly warden, Cliff Waller, at the Old Lighthouse, who took them to see the puffins, flying and gliding about. 'Without you the whole expedition would have flopped disastrously,' Kaye wrote to Waller, sending him *Bird Watching for Beginners*, a 1952 Puffin (would he correct and update it, quickly please, for 10 guineas?). She also thanked the long-suffering Mr Gade at the hotel. 'Lundy itself in spite of the rain will remain a most delightful memory and so will Mrs Gade's lovely cakes.'

Kaye really was lucky that none of the children drowned, said Rosemary, and 'as for Health and Safety, none of us gave it a second thought'.

The next holiday was on calmer inland water in September, at the Severn Sailing Club, near Cheltenham, where they sailed, camped, had late-night suppers by candlelight and sang songs. The Puffineers were divided into Fulmars, Guillemots, Auks and Razorbills. They built a Puffin boat, a four-seater sailing dinghy of unsinkable buoyancy, designed by Barry Bucknell. They acted a play called *The Pirate's Tale*, and went to tea with Ursula Moray Williams at her farm near Tewkesbury. Her book *Gobbolino the Witch's Cat*, published in 1942, had been a steady-selling Young Puffin since 1965, and she was one of those rare creatures with a natural gift for amusing children. She showed them the real Gobbolino, which had arrived one Hallowe'en as a stray, and let them drive a mini-tractor, and ride ponies, and gave a splendid tea with home-made chocolate éclairs and wild-strawberry tarts. She also performed her party piece, 'the egg trick'. To add to their amusement, the egg broke.

Kaye's cavalier approach to safety did not concern the unwitting parents who left their precious charges with her. What the Puffineers' mothers were fearful about was their little darlings' sociability. Kaye gave a *Woman's Hour* talk in 1968 about taking thirty-six children aged eight to fourteen, all strangers to one

another, on holiday. Several arrived with warnings from mothers
– 'Arabella has always found it hard to make friends' or 'Thomas
is a lone wolf' – and from teachers – 'He is a withdrawn child,
not much good at communal activities.' They would add hopefully,
'We think it will be good for him.' But Kaye resisted all such 'tags
and labels'. She wanted no preconceptions or expectations about
behaviour. The shy might become clowns, the apprehensive could
shine at charades. 'They flower because they are away from home,'
said Kaye. 'I do think we can over-understand them, and I think
we slow up our children's development by deciding for them what
they are like. "Jack isn't much good with his hands." "You can't
rely on Tim."' She spoke with feeling, as she knew she had done
the same herself, about her own two. Books broke the ice. On the
first evening, the children would be rather silent. But after a treasure
hunt, they would find books lying round the common room, 'and
conversation simply sprouted – about books . . . I never stop
hearing mothers say their children are "shy". You jolly well don't
know!'

Kaye had bought a small Victorian house at Chiswick close by
the River Thames – 3 Montrose Villas, Hammersmith Terrace.
Newton Road was rented out, though Kate still inhabited the
studio at the top. Kaye had planned a farewell party on Bonfire
Night, 1967 – but cancelled it for a Penguin mission to Canada.
'It's disappointing, because my new little house is so small that I
don't think I shall ever be able to have a big party again,' she told
the cancelled guests. Her new home was in the pretty enclave of
Chiswick Mall, containing several famous artists and writers
including Mary Fedden and A. P. Herbert. Montrose Villas,
though conveniently close to where Kate worked (for the theatre
designer Peter Rice), lacked the accessibility of Bayswater, and
Kaye almost pleaded with friends to call. 'Do you ever come to
Chiswick – my house is in Hammersmith Terrace on the river

side of the A4 . . . I'd love you to come and see me here.' She rented out a ground-floor room, with french doors into the garden, to Dorothea Duncan; the front parlour was Kaye's office, strewn with paper, piles of poems and competition entries.

One day in 1968 Kaye knocked at the door of Swan House, one of the handsome eighteenth-century houses nearby, facing the river. When Jane Nissen, an American aged thirty-three, opened the door, Kaye (in a bright red anorak) asked could she leave a boat in Jane's front garden until it was ready to be launched and sailed away? She was just back from a Puffin Club holiday and they had built a boat. Jane, who knew all about Kaye, having worked in publishing and at Hatchards, agreed – 'if you'll let me do some reading for you'. So Jane began writing reader-reports from home, and her four children (Dinah, Rosanna, Timothy and Edmund) became Puffineers. The boat was eventually launched on the river by A. P. Herbert himself.

Kaye's brazen habit of enlisting others' help and goodwill was legendary. When she wanted advice on recording the Puffin song, she called on John Dankworth ('Johnny dear . . .'). Doreen Scott's engineer husband, Scotty, who had built a new kitchen at Newton Road, found himself dealing with a cascade of water down the stairs at Montrose Villas. The Scotts' boat, the *Albadine*, was commandeered to ferry children to Chiswick; and they had Rusty the dachshund dumped on them when Kaye went abroad. (Rusty was taken to the office every day, and would howl for Kaye, disrupting board meetings.) Quentin Blake painted a caravan for her. Nicholas Fisk, prolific Puffin author, searched for a sketch of Greenwich in Nelson's day. 'I'd never ask this of anyone but you, Nick,' ran Kaye's typical appeal. Everyone agreed: Kaye inveigled you into dropping whatever you were doing to fulfil her requests. Naomi Lewis would be telephoned if a particularly impressive poem arrived at *Puffin Post*. She could tell from the first line whether the child had copied it out (as a few did). In return, Kaye invited Naomi Lewis as the family's 'honorary aunt' every Christmas. 'Kaye was a great user,' as Charlotte Cory says, 'but also a great giver. So one forgave her.' The standard of the children's poems and drawings was remarkably high. Invited to write a 'concrete poem' drawn in the shape of the subject (which brought forth a cello, a leaf, a mouse, an octopus, a Catherine wheel, a worm), one young reader, Deborah Findlay, aged thirteen, anticipated the moon landing, and wrote in the shape of the moon:

> Poor moon, will you really shine so well
> When men step upon you and break your spell?

So impressed was Kaye by the children's creativity, she invented an annual Puffin exhibition to display their work. Rosemary Sandberg's husband Robin was an industrial designer: 'Oh darling, what's that?' said Kaye, sensing a man with useful skills. Robin was roped in to design the first exhibition in March 1968, beneath the National Union of Teachers' HQ in Grays Inn Road. In years to come, children flocked to her exhibitions in droves; there was not much else for them in the Easter holidays. Noel Streatfeild, and later Roald Dahl and Quentin Blake, caused queues of children to line the street outside. Spike Milligan would stand at the door with a stick of chalk, making a white squiggle on every child who came in. Other publishers were astonished and impressed. 'We began to wonder whether we should set up clubs too,' said Judy Taylor.

For the next decade, anyone's child embarking on a gap year would be urged to 'Come and help out at the Puffin exhibition!' Miranda Birch, daughter of Lionel, Kaye's old *Picture Post* colleague, was recruited; Lizza Brown, daughter of Joan Aiken, and Sally Fenby, daughter of Kaye's friend Charles, were also among the conscripts. Annabel Bartlett, daughter of the TV announcer Mary Malcolm, was running the Children's Book Centre before she became 'jokes editor' of *Puffin Post*: she revealed a flair for finding inventive prizes for almost nothing, and for dealing with Kaye's sudden commands – she must have flame-throwers, or a hot-air balloon, or would say, 'Oh, but darling, I wanted it all in silver!' 'You felt it was a privilege to work for Puffin, and help children,' Lizza says. 'In fact, whenever Kaye exercised this ability to get people to do things for nothing, they ended up thanking *her*. She operated the rest of her life by Puffin Club rules, really.'

These included under-paying authors for *Puffin Post* work. Most didn't mind, but she obviously had a fight with Alan Garner, who wrote in September 1967, soothing her. 'You are a <u>frantic</u> kind of lady,' he began. 'Lulla-lulla-lullaby, it's all <u>right</u>. Shhhhhhhhhhh. There. Oh, what a raw lady, too. We love you. All of us.' She was one of the most important people in books, he assured her. 'So I will do most things for Kaye Webb, even if Sir Allen Lane collects kudos of one sort or another from my labours. But I do know that there are those who say, "Why should I turn myself into a sweat-shop of free copy and prestige for Allen Lane?" And to hell with the goodwill engendered by *Puffin Post*.' It would have a 'snowballing, bad effect on the magazine', he said, if she did not pay professional rates. She would run out of people willing to write for it. He rehearsed the arguments: time is money, authors would get bloody-minded, only the same old names would appear. 'You see, writers are obsessed by money, mainly because they have to be.' Word had got round that she expected authors to be filmed, with no fee. Kaye had told him she had to fight for money. 'But so do authors, and you, out in front at Puffin, will look as though you are in the Lane camp.'

Mammon was crucial, too, in securing Roald Dahl. Dahl, a wartime bomber pilot, had been writing his 'Tales of the Unexpected' for adults since 1946: unexpected being a mild word for his '*contes cruels*'. Cruelty, he decided as a father of five, was what children not only relished but found funny. *James and the Giant Peach* had been published in America in 1961, but British publishers were repelled by the 'heartlessness' of his characters, and not until 1967 did readers meet Charlie Bucket and Willy Wonka, and James and his aunts Spiker and Sponge. Lady librarians were said to disapprove of Dahl profoundly, but Elaine Moss, a lady librarian herself, reviewed *Charlie and the Chocolate Factory* in *The Times* and judged it 'the funniest children's book for years'. Not just funny, she wrote, but 'shot through with a zany pathos, which touches the young heart'. Interviewing Dahl, Elaine asked about the aggression and violence of his stories, and Dahl heartily agreed, there was cruelty in all of them. 'Children like things to happen 100 per cent,' he said. 'If you do away with someone, then have his head off, crunch him up, run him over, and they'll roar with laughter.' In writing for children, 'you have to exaggerate a million times in order to ram the point home'.

This was not Kaye's view, but Dahl soon bestrode the children's book scene like a colossus. He was one of the six top favourites of *Young Observer* readers, and Linda Villiers, now its editor, interviewed him for the magazine. He invited her to bring her children for lunch at Gipsy House, Great Missenden. It was the Easter holidays, and he was looking after his handicapped son, Theo, while his actress wife, Patricia Neal, was away filming. Over lunch Dahl told Linda: 'I want to be published by Puffins!' She said his agent simply had to pick up the phone to Kaye. But he warned that the usual royalty – Kaye never went above 9 per cent – would be inadequate. Dahl wanted 17½, 'because they'll sell a lot'. At the Puffin exhibition, Linda passed on his message to Kaye. So Kaye was emboldened, she said, to sign him up: Dahl got the royalty he wanted, and more. But he repaid their investment in astronomical sales. Kaye had her doubts about some of his books – she hated *The Twits* – but she was too canny to moralize about him. He sold in millions, and his six foot six presence became a fixture at Puffin exhibitions.

The twins turned twenty-one in July 1968, and celebrated with a riverboat trip. Before that, in May, Kate went to see her father in Paris. The Searles' flat was right in the heart of *les événements de mai*, and she arrived on the night the barricades went up, and tear-gas was unleashed on the students in revolt. The Searles managed to sneak Kate out to dine at Maxim's, her choice of a birthday treat. But all Paris airports were closed, and to get her back to London they had to take her to Brussels in a taxi.

Kaye had a new anxiety that summer. Penguin director Edward Boyle broke the news at an editorial meeting that Allen Lane was suffering from bowel cancer. 'You must try to be the best, fastest-healing miracle patient they've ever had,' Kaye told Lane. In August, he was convalescing at his Berkshire farm after radium treatment, and wrote a fond letter, 'staggered' by her energy. 'I don't know how you can crowd so much into your day,' he ended. 'No wonder Puffins are so dynamic.'

By Boxing Day 1968 he was writing from his sybaritic hideaway El Fenice at Carvajal, near Málaga – a house Kaye was hoping to borrow for a holiday with Jim Cecil – to say he'd read *Puffin Post* and 'my mind boggles at all that is going on'. He was pleased that she had taken up Norman Hunter, author of *Professor Branestawm* (first published by his father in 1933), and said Noel Carrington, Eleanor Graham and 'Frostie' (Eunice Frost) must be invited to the *Branestawm* party. Norman Hunter flew in from South Africa and Kaye went with Doreen Scott to welcome him at Heathrow. 'Kaye grabbed a trolley and fastened to it an enormous yellow dahlia – "so he'll know it's us"!' Hunter became a *Puffin Post* regular, and competition winners were taken by boat to his home on the Thames near Staines. Kaye's authors were not allowed to be shrinking violets.

Whenever Kaye wanted advice on books she turned to the remarkably well-read Joan Aiken. Joan had been schooled at home by her mother, a Radcliffe graduate, until she was twelve, so she read through the vast library of her father, the American poet Conrad Aiken. She had been widowed young, at thirty, and like Kaye was the lone mother of a 'pigeon pair' of children: John Sebastian and Elizabeth (Lizza), who were sent to a boarding school, which they hated, so that Joan could work at *Argosy* magazine. *The Wolves of Willoughby Chase* took her a decade to finish and publish: an agent left her manuscript mouldering on an office windowsill for years, then one publisher asked her to 'take out the wolves'. After Cape published it in 1962, its film rights sold and re-sold until it was filmed in 1988.

Unlike Kaye, Joan was tiny in stature, and unassuming by nature – until Kaye hauled her out of her shell. Having always had a horror of the public eye, Joan was persuaded to meet her readers. She agreed to be filmed, at Kaye's behest, by John Phillips, an amusing young television director who lived nearby in Chiswick and shot several Puffin authors with a borrowed camera and a budget of £100. Joan hated her 'stiff and affected' recorded voice, and said Kaye was 'a wretch' to quote Joan's first childhood poem in *Puffin Post*: 'I ought to demand a bushel of sunflower seeds for first British serial rights.' But she appreciated Puffin's superlative production of her books – 'makes the Gutenberg bible look like a Sears Roebuck catalogue' – and entered thoroughly into the spirit of the Puffin Club, complying with Kaye's requests ('Could you send a little personal souvenir to give to a child who has raised money for the Puffin coastline?') and filling in her Puffin Passport: ('Special virtue: good temper; Special vice: bad temper; Personal motto: 'Before crossing the river, do not sneer at the crocodile's granny'). She was good at slogans, having worked at J. Walter Thompson, and sent two pages of ideas such as:

Off in a car, a train or a ship?
Stuff in a Puffin to brighten the trip . . .

Arthur Webb, now settled with Ethel in Brighton, was swanning off to the winter sun when his 'ludicrously overworked and underpaid daughter' wrote telling him she would pop in, while at Jim's Sussex cottage, and pick up her big waterproof coat. She would need it, as she would soon be 'with my 50 kids in Northumberland brrrh . . .' This was the first Puffin/Colony holiday, the 'Winter Whoopee' at Featherstone Castle near Hadrian's Wall just after Christmas 1969. 'Spend New Year's Eve with us in this castle!' said the notice in *Puffin Post*. The cost per child for a ten-day holiday (27 December – 5 January) was just £17, including accompanied travel 'from London, Birmingham or your nearest big station'.

This was the first of many collaborative jamborees with Colony Holidays, copied from the French Colonies des Vacances and superbly run by a schoolmaster, Chris Green, who believed children needed a chance to mix with others from different backgrounds, run about in green fields, sample life without television. Colony's slogan was 'Give your children back some real childhood', and they saved the sanity of many mothers in the 1960s and 70s.

After her Lundy experience Kaye had decided she needed expert help, and with Colony the Puffin Club ran three holidays a year for the next seven years. As Kaye knew, most children's adventure stories involve absent parents, or parents being suddenly called away, the children left in the care of dotty aunts, whereupon they get stranded on mountains, trapped in caves, etc. Left to their own resources, they cope magnificently. 'Away from the "dear octopus" of family life,' Kaye later wrote in the *Observer*, 'children discover all sorts of surprising things about themselves.'

Featherstone was the last privately owned castle in

Northumberland, a former boarding school. In an icy winter (the coldest temperature for thirty years) the fifty Puffineers were met at Haltwhistle, near Hadrian's Wall, while Kaye waited at the castle. Determined that Featherstone should look like a magic castle, aglow in the twilight, Kaye switched on every light in the place. It did look magical. But half an hour later the whole castle fused, and that night they read stories by candlelight. Sally Fenby and John Phillips joined the trained Colony monitors (one to every eight to ten children) organizing games in the snow. There were treasure-hunts and a visit to Hadrian's Wall; they wrote a newspaper and performed a play. One child was a brilliant ornithologist; all were 'astonishingly good' actors. 'There was always something to occupy them, no time to get homesick,' says Phillips, 'and Kaye mother-henned the whole thing.' William Mayne and Ursula Moray Williams were the invited authors, and Ursula proved an absolute brick. She swept the stage, made up the children's faces for the play, cut sandwiches, and resuscitated a child who fainted. 'It was all such fun!' as Ursula reminded Kaye many years later. 'You meeting me on the platform and saying Chris was "so uptight" – and later he gave us sherry in toothmugs!'

A week after the Winter Whoopee, 'the Puffin Players' took over the Young Vic theatre to perform Joan Aiken's play *Winterthing*, set on a Scottish coastal croft. They constructed a complicated set with a boat on the sea, and the Northern Lights: prop-mistress, Kate Searle. John Phillips, who directed it, brought in a professional actress, Sally Mates, to play Mrs McRory, who turns into the Spirit of Winter, and a piper named Willie Cochrane, who piped from the foyer, on to the stage and into the wings. The companion play, *The King Who Declared War on the Animals*, was produced by Joan Aiken's daughter Lizza, with some good props like a flying carpet and a live goat. The *Morning Star* review bore the headline, 'Handsome Goat Assists'.

★

Puffins soon began to outsell adult Penguins. Each month, fifty Puffin books left the warehouse with lucky stickers inside, offering prizes and surprises. Penguin executives were agog at the shenanigans in the Puffin office. In March 1970 Elaine Moss dropped in, and wrote a graphic account for *Signal*, the new magazine about children's reading. She found Kaye and her team – 'Sylvia, Rachel, Dorothy, Sally, Yvonne and Glyn' – dreaming up 'fun, original, bookish' activities for Puffin's third birthday exhibition. A young man arrived carrying a small hand-printing press. 'How super, Colin!' cried Kaye. Could the kids use it at the exhibition? Could they print their own Certificate of Attendance? Might Jill McDonald draw a puffin printing his own certificate at his birthday party? There was an enormous scrapbook, full of photographs of Puffineers 'sailing, camping, singing, acting' and autographs in coloured felt-tip, labelled 'The Spree Book'. They were planning Puffin outings and events from Exeter to Dunfermline.

The four desks were swamped by the day's post, bringing new members at a rate of seventy-five to a hundred a day, plus competition entries and orders for badges, bookplates, bookworms, notepaper and diaries. There were requests ('Could I have a puffin T-shirt, do you think?') and inquiries ('I was wondering, where is the Geffrye Museum? You see, I am an American and do not know my way around quite yet'), letters of thanks ('Your firework party was fabulous') or asking for penfriends ('Please may I have a frind in astralia?') and hundreds of letters about books the Puffineers were reading (Narnia, *The Princess and the Goblin*, William Mayne's *Earthfasts*). Each letter would get an answer. Often the first reply would be a McTavish type all-purpose postcard in bright pink, with multiple-choice messages carefully selected to be appropriate.

Dear . . . . / Thank you very much for the letter / story / poem / picture / money / bomb / hippopotamus you sent us, which we received with gasps / sighs / blushes / yelps / hoots / groans

Of delight / amazement / horror / joy / despair / surprise / embarrassment / admiration / dismay / mirth.

We should like to write you a long letter, but

We are desperately busy / Our cat has had kittens / We are up to
our ears in next Puffin Post / We have been struck by lightning.

This fancy / exotic / tasteful / elegant / charming card is just to tell
you it has arrived safely and that we are

Considering it / framing it / frying it / burying it / enjoying it /
<u>going to do something about it</u>.

Love from . . . . (Kaye)

Some letters, for example 'Dear Rosemary, I have knitted
these bootees for your baby', required individual replies. Sylvia
Mogg, the colourful, bubbly Welshwoman in charge of admin,
would spend her spare evenings hand-painting individual
envelopes for those readers having birthdays. Sylvia told Elaine
Moss she felt more in touch with children now than she had in
her years as a children's bookseller.

The reward for their efforts came in effusive childish
gratitude. 'Thanks awfully for my purple bag,' wrote one prize-
winning child. 'I think it's super and a marvellous prize. Did
someone make it specially? If they did, could you thank them
terribly?'

One of the most successful Puffin sprees in the early years was
the visit to Alderley Edge in Cheshire, the setting of Alan Garner's
The Weirdstone of Brisingamen. Garner, his wife and three children
welcomed Kaye and eight prize-winners, and during the next
two days drove them 150 miles in a 'rib-rattling' Land-Rover to
the Wizard's Well, the dell of the svart-alfar, the Devil's Grave,
the Iron Gates of Fundindelve, the Goldenstone and Errwood
Hall; to Hayman's Quarry, where (in *The Moon of Gomrath*) Susan
is thrown over the cliff by the Brollachan, and to Redesmere,
where Durathror, Colin, Susan, Gowther and Fenodyree find

themselves on the floating island of Angharad Goldenhand after being chased by the Trollwomen. The children were thrilled to discover that all the scenes in Garner's novels were real, and (as Katharine Dickson wrote in *Puffin Post*) found it even more thrilling to hear the learned Garner talk about his archaeological excavations, and how he found the ideas for his books.

Kaye had undoubtedly found the key to winning readers' devotion, and her fellow publishers in the Children's Book Circle recognized this by presenting her with the Eleanor Farjeon award at Stationers' Hall in 1970. In her speech Kaye read out amusing letters and explained the importance of reaching out to children through her club. Nobody else could have thrown such energy into the pursuit of venues for Puffin sprees: any zoo, drama club, children's theatre, museum or stately home was targeted. Joan Aiken lived near Petworth Park? Acres of rolling grass for a Puffin picnic! 'House boring unless you like Turner and Grinling Gibbons,' Joan reported. 'Maybe Lord Egremont could lay on coconut shies.' John Dankworth was opening a music venue at Wavendon: could he please create an event that 'might appeal to intelligent children, with a tea laid on afterwards'? Allen Lane offered a Puffin picnic at Chapmansford, his 500-acre farm in Hampshire, 'where there will be so much going on with two or three combines & two corn-driers going full blast as well as the milking-parlour which always seems to fascinate children'.

This was one of Lane's last letters. His illness was fatal and his tone was valedictory. He mentioned friends whose children were 'madly keen about the Puffin Club and had won prizes', and added: 'As I've told you before you are really so much more than an editor, you are a great publisher.' He came home in May and said Kaye must come and celebrate her Farjeon award. But he died on 7 July 1970. The next day, the company became part of Pearson Longman. Penguin lost, temporarily, its distinctive stamp, becoming just another corporate publisher. Kaye, perhaps more than anyone, was bereft of her champion and mentor. She was, as Ian Norrie noted, 'a colleague with whom Allen Lane never quarrelled'.

But there was a contrast between Kaye's conspicuous success in her job and the 'horribly overworked' and 'disillusioned' private self she displayed in letters to her father. In spring 1970, Arthur sent a cutting about 'a career opportunity for undergraduates' with John in mind (now twenty-two, and no longer an undergraduate, since dropping out of political science courses at Trinity College, Dublin, and in London). Earlier, following a similar suggestion, Kaye had instructed Arthur not to think in terms of John's 'career' as comparable to hers or Arthur's. They had both been lucky to be committed to jobs they loved; John hadn't yet found the sort of work which satisfied him. 'His journalism wasn't our kind, and he can't "see" our kind. His aims while woolly are in a way higher . . . We could earn a living doing something we weren't ashamed of, and getting better at it all the time. He doesn't have any idea of "making a success". He thinks that's commercial. He just wants to <u>be</u> – to hurt no-one and to experience fully.'

In an unusually candid letter, Kaye now wrote again, reiterating and supporting John's distaste for conformist jobs. She didn't mind what he chose to do, as long as he had no responsibilities and 'a little money' from his father. She wished she had been able to do the same. 'Being a success isn't so much,' she said. 'It only means you carry a load and everyone wants you to help them.'

She went on: 'I haven't actually enjoyed myself properly for years and at 56 I'm just beginning to be bitterly aware of the fact. So I certainly shan't be nagging him to "get anywhere" as you put it. Because where the devil is that. Esteem in other men's eyes? Isn't it more important to have it in your own? I shall grow older and die and the only flag I'll have to wave is I did a job fairly well and wangled myself a lot of attention . . . but I shan't have read the books I wanted to, or had the thoughts I wanted to, or even really explored relationships with other people properly . . . all this in the sacred name of being successful.

'I suppose my generation was born worrying, because work was so scarce, but since our kids weren't and needn't be, why impose it on them. Frankly there's very little left to admire in my world, even the nice bits are in a way the results of manoeuvring, slightly exploiting and taking advantage of people or using one's personality for a purpose. You see what a state of disillusionment I'm in at present.

'Funny too, when you consider that I've just been awarded the Eleanor Farjeon thing for services to Children's Literature, but even that seems to me to be a bit phoney. So anyway don't worry about John because I'm not, not about that. I do in fact worry about physical things like fast driving and drug taking and not eating and him not engaging himself with other people. I don't think being solitary is such a good thing but as for "getting on" it simply doesn't matter, because it hasn't any real point.'

12: Mission Completed

1971–5

'I have taken care of New Zealand,' wrote Kaye. 'Now Australia is to receive a bashing.' This was gung-ho bravado. During her exhausting month-long Puffin mission to the Antipodes in May 1971, her recurrent arthritis suddenly 'sprang at me unawares because the pace was so hot'. She had been a 'stretcher case' and was pumped with steroids. She wrote, while resting in a mountaintop farm in New South Wales belonging to the painter Russell Drysdale, to Ian Norrie, who had invited her to address the Society of Bookmen in London on 1 July. Was the date irrevocable? Penguin had suggested she 'take a bit longer coming home', and she wanted to take a boat for part of the way.

The date was changed, but when she addressed the Bookmen that autumn, she had to be collected from St Thomas' Hospital and taken back afterwards. Over dinner, Kaye surveyed her audience and asked Norrie, 'Don't you have any women members?' The answer was no. 'I wouldn't have come if I'd known.' Norrie promised that by the time his chairmanship ended, they would admit women. The Bookmen duly changed their constitution; Kaye became one of the first women members (along with Margaret Drabble, Norah Smallwood and Judy Taylor) and remained one of this elite dining coterie until her death.

But the 'blasted arthritis' became chronic, her search for a cure unrelenting. All activities and travels from now on were tempered by bad days and good days, and the effort it sometimes took just to get up. A transatlantic flight would leave her wrecked, unable to pick up a telephone. She tried all manner of remedies: homoeopathy, osteopathy, miracle gold injections, innumerable diets, clinics, retreats and rest cures. Everyone had recommendations: copper, Vitamin C in enormous quantities, calcium, vinegar; and something called Cantopal, available from Putney Bridge Road. Roald Dahl recommended 'the great and ancient homoeopathic doctor, A. J. Milner of Penn'; someone else suggested a Devon physiotherapist, Ralph Wilderspin. Astrid Lindgren, author of *Pippi Longstocking*, recommended a Swedish treatment, so she went to Sweden. Even Ronald sent pills from Paris. Pain was exacerbated by the weather and Kaye repeatedly sought the sun. Life was punctuated by interludes in hospital (her employers were remarkably tolerant) and by apologies to friends – 'As you probably gathered, I wasn't feeling all that chipper on Sunday' or 'I can never tell from day to day whether I am going to be socially acceptable.'

In a way, her Puffin mission was already accomplished. Here is the testimony of a Puffineer, Marion Milne, who is now a BBC producer: 'Growing up in the late sixties in Northern Ireland as the child of an academic father and a social-worker mother, I was a bookish child. Our old-fashioned housekeeper, Mrs Simpson, who looked after my brother and me when we came home from school, would tell me off for retreating to my room with a Puffin, a glass of milk and a plate of Ginger Nuts, rather than "playing outside".

'I had two heroines: Biddy Baxter, editor of *Blue Peter*, and Kaye Webb, whose name was inside every Puffin book in 1968–71. I pictured them as tweedy, maternal, fun and forgiving. Mondays and Thursdays at 5.15 was a sacrosanct time, when *Blue Peter* was on BBC-1. But even more sacred was the arrival of *Puffin Post*.

'It was as if Kaye was writing to me personally, every quarter. She spoke to me, a provincial nine-year-old, from mystical London where the streets were paved with Puffins. *Puffin Post* was a doorway into a magical world that had previously only existed as fiction. Suddenly the books I owned and loved had real-life authors. The Puffin Club shed light on the magic, made it more inspiring. The characters in the books were already my friends: now I felt as if the authors were as well.

'Leon Garfield's *Smith*, Joan Aiken's *The Wolves of Willoughby Chase*, C. S. Lewis's *The Lion, the Witch and the Wardrobe*, Clive King's *Stig of the Dump*, J. R. R. Tolkien's *The Hobbit*, Arthur Ransome's *Swallows and Amazons*: I compiled lists of Puffins and waited for Christmas or my birthday, when my mother would buy them for me. They cost 3s 6d, then 5s, then, with decimalization, 25p. I still have them all. Some sport a Puffin Club bookplate: "From the library of . . . " decorated with a lion, a unicorn, a bookshelf, a pile of paperbacks and, atop it all, a puffin reading a Puffin. Underneath, painstakingly written in a wobbly fountain pen, is my name. The bookplates were a special offer from the Puffin Club and I can remember my excitement when they arrived. Only the extra-specially favourite books were allocated a sticker.

'Even more special was the badge, placed on my bookshelf alongside the trolls my father had brought back from a lecture trip to Norway. I never really liked those trolls much. I remember thinking that Kaye personally sent me my Puffin Club badge. The Puffin Club was the opposite of *Blue Peter* in that respect. We sent Biddy Baxter milk-bottle tops, but Kaye sent things to us.'

By 1972 Marion's family had moved to Southern California, where her father was on sabbatical. Her mother gave up social work and wore bikinis. 'When we came back I was a fully fledged teenager, and switched my allegiance from *Puffin Post* to *Jackie* magazine. The stuff of childhood was put away. My treasured Puffin Club badge lost amidst the sparkly eye shadow and David Bowie singles.'

Marion conformed, like many Puffineers of the 1970s, to an identifiable type of child: articulate, well-informed, untainted (as yet) by crass popular culture. Their heroes, Kaye assumed and hoped, were authors, not rock stars or footballers. The summer of 1971 was a typical one for the model Puffin reader. The Puffin holiday that August was at Oakwood School, Lavant. They left Victoria station, where William Mayne was there to wave them off, and arrived in a green bus with the numberplate PUF. There were woods to explore, ponies to feed, and a swimming-pool, and lawns for games. They were taken to the Sussex seaside (in pouring rain), to Arundel Castle, to the Roman remains at Fishbourne, and to a fishing village where King Canute's daughter was buried. They put on an exhibition, and organized games: Dr Dolittle Skittles, Puffin Hoop-la, Feeding Fat Puffin Fish and Pinning on Fat Puffin's Beak. After tea on the last day, they scampered through the house dowsing candles with water pistols. The things they had made – decorations, kites, puppets, Borrowers' furniture, 3D maps, collages, monsters, tie-dye and mobiles – were packed up for the next Puffin exhibition.

Later that summer, there was a picnic at Wallingford, the Trevelyan family's manor house in Northumberland, with a 'Hunt the Puffin' nature trail, and a local folk-singer. In London, the Finnish author of *Finn Family Moomintroll*, Tove Jansson, had tea with twenty of the best letter-writers. Kaye and Dorothy took forty readers to Whittington Court, an Elizabethan house in picturesque Cotswold country, to see a nineteenth-century hand-printing press – on which John Randle was printing Richard Kennedy's *A Boy at the Hogarth Press*. The children, 'opinionated and enthusiastic', got covered in printing ink as they printed their own souvenirs before marching in an orderly crocodile to the village hall for a picnic feast. 'They asked intelligent questions, unprompted by Kaye, and they were all obviously very fond of her,' Rose Randle recalled. 'Kaye could be slightly bombastic, but then so many organizing ladies tend to be.'

And so it went on, year after year. Summer picnics were followed by seasonal bonfires and fireworks at Harmondsworth, when Kaye conflated Hallowe'en and Guy Fawkes into 'Guyween'. At one Guyween party, she dressed as the Cat in the Hat, with moustache and whiskers and black gloves with claws, and went round hissing at everyone; at another she was a White Witch, in long flowing wig and silver gown, appearing on the canopy over the Harmondsworth warehouse door. She had borrowed the council's roadworks lamps, which melted in the heat of the bonfire.

'We had an absolutely marvellous Guyween party,' Kaye reported to Joan Aiken, 'cold as blazes, but all the villains and villainesses (including of course Miss Slighcarp) had escaped from Puffin books and had to be searched for in the pitch dark in Penguin grounds. You can imagine the excitement! Then they all came back to sausages and hot soup and a bonfire and fireworks. Our beloved Richard Carpenter was such a splendid Merlin that the children almost believed he was real. Most of the imaginative work was done by Jane Allan . . . there were some fairly frantic moments, trying to control 200 children over a mike that was constantly broken when I hadn't any idea what they were supposed to do next. But there you are – a typical Puffin party!'

Kaye's method of staff recruitment was to meet someone who impressed her, recognizing a light in their eye, and say, 'Come and join Puffins!' She was said to have met her fiction editor, Dorothy Wood, at a bus stop in New York; she met Jane Allan, aged eighteen, in Mexico; and an American named Amy Myers just 'walked in off the pavement'. Jane Allan proved to have a creative genius for devising party themes and crazy games, and bonded easily with the Puffin team. They took for granted recurrences of 'Kaye-os', Kaye's last-minute crises and panics: no money for the mini-cab, no author booked for next week's holiday. 'I once visited her in hospital,' Jane says, 'and Laurie Lee was at her bedside. "Oh Laurie," said Kaye, "Jane's going on a Puffin holiday, could you show her how to make kites?"'

Felicity Trotman's job interview ('Come and see me, darling!')

was at Newton Road, where Jim Cecil opened the door and offered her a drink. 'There was an array of bottles: but they were all empty, apart from lime juice.' Kaye came down in her dressing-gown with a Puffin badge attached – and Felicity was smitten. She was twenty-five, well-read, a *Young Elizabethan* reader in childhood, educated at Cheltenham Ladies' College followed by art college, and had worked at the publisher Dent's. Kaye was impressed by her fine italic handwriting. 'Come down and meet everyone!' she cried. And since Felicity had a car, could she give Kaye a lift? (She was to do a lot of chauffeuring for Kaye.)

The team – Doreen, Sylvia, Dorothy Wood and the new *Puffin Post* editor, Jacquie Graham – were having a party that very day: guests had to come in a decorated hat depicting a book title. Two days later there was a Grand Puffin New Year's party at New Zealand House ballroom: 'Games, authors, surprises, side shows and a grand New Zealand tea.' 'After the quiet life at Dent,' said Felicity, 'where Martin Dent would hide in a doorway rather than speak to anyone, this was a culture shock.'

Rosemary Sandberg was the first to leave Kaye's team, poached by Billy Collins. Collins had championed Kaye, but he now bridled at giving Puffin his top titles – though Kaye always made a point, in speeches, of thanking 'those publishers who allow us to publish their books'. After four years, Rosemary knew exactly which books children liked. Kaye was not best pleased at her departure but what was Rosemary to do? She was by now the mother of two daughters, grateful for her Puffin years, 'but Kaye was always going to be Queen Bee'. Running Collins's children's paperback imprints, Armada Lions and Picture Lions, she published Judith Kerr's *The Tiger Who Came to Tea* and Shirley Hughes's *Dogger*. (Shirley had long felt underpaid by Kaye, and followed Rosemary to Collins.)

Hanging on to staff was not a problem for Kaye; but hanging on to rights could be. When Joan Aiken told Kaye that she'd had an offer from Hutchinson's Unicorns for *Whispering Mountain*, and didn't want it 'to wander away from Puffins by an oversight', Kaye was furious: 'I don't know what the hell Osyth [Leeston, Joan's agent] is talking about, I've no intention of ever letting any Aikens go out of print, and the licence certainly isn't up yet.' It remained Kaye's decision to publish any title, or not. 'Darling, it doesn't feel right,' was a typical Kaye veto. Sometimes she would read a book thoroughly herself; but she was just as likely to give it to someone she'd met on a train – 'and sometimes it was the precious file-copy from the original publisher'.

Shortly after Felicity's arrival, Kaye was in hospital at Hammersmith, and Felicity would deliver her mail. One day, Doreen told Felicity that a letter had come from Jim Cecil. Somehow everyone knew it was his farewell. He had found someone else. 'It was dreadful for her, to receive the letter in her hospital bed,' says Felicity. 'There's nothing you can say.'

Kaye's relationships with her authors became increasingly important after Jim's marriage. (Not that she gave up hope of romance. On 1 December 1972 – but mis-dating it 1962 – Kaye told Joan Aiken about her weekend in Upper Bavaria 'by a lovely lake in a super house with a doctor who was a saint, and how I wish he hadn't been! But he told me he really wanted to be a monk, and now his wife has died he decided he would be – so that was that.')

In May 1972, Kaye had finally sold Newton Road, which she had come to believe was 'our undoing'. She sold it to a neighbour for £27,000, much less than it was worth. With Dick Hough, she was pitching for a radio programme on Radio 4. Hough 'couldn't imagine a more deliciously suitable radiomate' and they drafted a proposal for 'Books, Mags and Things', a miscellany of comment and chat about 'what people are reading and writing, in newspapers and magazines, in books and on the stage and screen large and small'. It would be personal, selective and prejudiced, discussing anything 'from the mannerisms of TV announcers to inaccurate book blurbs'.

Christmas 1972 was 'so hellish that I'm willy-nilly going to take a fortnight off', she told Hough. She was taking painkillers that suppressed both pain and intellect, and cortisone, which increased appetite and weight. She was judging children's television shows, 'deeply appalled' by their awfulness. Hough waved her off to Cyprus sunshine. Their radio project could wait. 'I know we'll do it well and that it would be fun.' But nothing came of it. Kaye toyed with offering it to London's new commercial radio company, LBC: she was chairing a board that monitored LBC's performance. But chairing was not her scene: she was no good at being objective. 'I had such strong opinions myself I found I was putting words into people's mouths.'

Kaye went to Nicosia with brother Bill. His son Nick now ran a department of Granada publishing, in sharp contrast to John, who was 'in Penang, Bangkok or Calcutta, running out of money'. Kaye hoped John would soon make a decent living, because 'I'm through with that lark' of supporting him, she told Joan Aiken. In fact, John had been perfectly content on his adventurous travels, and was trying to put emotional distance between himself and Kaye by living abroad, which he suspected his mother preferred. 'The one person her forceful personality wasn't going to roll over was me. Nobody else stood up to her. I challenged her, I inhibited her natural flow,' he says.

Kaye had thought of going to Spain with her father and Ethel, but changed her mind when her stocks and shares plummeted in value, and everything in Britain became 'so awful': a common view in 1973. The Penguin office was 'in turmoil', she told Arthur, under a new editor-in-chief, Peter Calvocoressi. She was organizing her sixth Puffin Exhibition, and then would be off to Bologna, and to New York. Meanwhile she had news of Ronald. The French were giving him a major retrospective at the Bibliothèque Nationale (the first living foreign artist ever accorded this privilege), and the French Mint commissioned him to design commemorative medals. 'He had a full page of *Le Monde* to himself, and it's obviously a great success,' Kaye told her father. 'But the most successful thing of all are the St Trinian's – ha ha ha! He'll hate that.'

Arthur Webb, though not well, was prompted to pour out long-harboured anger in a letter to his former son-in-law, twelve years on.

'Dear Ronald Searle,

'I wonder if you remember the taped interview in your hotel room in New York in the late 50s? You were asked the secret of your success. And answered "I married my editor." I was there & heard you. Looking back do you ever acknowledge how much you owed to Kaye? Lilliput & St Trinians; the publication of your Japanese sketches; the publicity; the articles & sketches in the *News Chronicle* etc. The Round Table of *Punch*! Etc etc. And not least, your introduction to Paris! You never seem to want to be reminded of the *Paris Sketchbook* (some of your best work) because Kaye did the captions and inspired so many of the unexpected locations . . . I guess you still have a guilty conscience about the cruel way you deserted her & the children; & betrayed her trust & love & devotion. Kate survives, but you destroyed John. He really needed a father's guidance. As for Kaye. She has made a new career for herself. She was, and is, one of the best editors in Fleet Street. She knew your work better than you knew it yourself & could have inspired you to greater things! But she seems to bear you no ill-will although today the shock of being betrayed by the cowardly way you acted has left its mark. She is being slowly crippled by arthritis – brought on by the events of 1961. I hold you responsible for that.

'If you had been more of a man & faced your problems she would have suffered less emotionally. And maybe John would have settled down to the realities of the modern world. Just think things over now you are <u>again</u> becoming a popular figure in the art world. After 12 more or less <u>wasted</u> years. You could have got there much earlier without causing so many heartaches & personal distress . . . I have waited 12 years to send this. Arthur Webb.'

(His postscript said: 'Kaye doesn't know I'm writing.')

Arthur died of a heart attack the following month, on 21 April 1973, aged eighty-three. Discovering the draft letter to Ronald among his papers, Kaye was horrified, and wrote at once to 'my dear Ronald' to tell him of her father's death, and to reassure him about the letter – if it had ever reached him, or if he had ever read it. (He never got it, in fact.)

'. . . I do want you to know that he may have written it out of misguided love for me, but I certainly had no knowledge of it and I don't share very many of its sentiments,' Kaye wrote. 'I would be sorry if you thought it was in any way instigated by me, or that I bore you these kind of grudges.'

It distressed her that her adored father had still felt so upset on her behalf. 'I knew him for nearly 60 of his 85 years,' Kaye wrote, for the vicar who officiated at Arthur's funeral, 'and in all that time I never knew him to commit a mean action or even have a mean thought. He was gay, intelligent, hardworking and he cared. All his life he was an active socialist. He would sit for hours advising young men about going into the newspaper business. As a young sub on the *Star*, he started the whole field of Diary journalism with Star Man's Diary. On the *Irish Times* he produced the paper in face of Sinn Fein bomb threats, flew from Dublin in unflyable weather to bring the first wedding pics of the Queen Mum and the late King. Douglas Jay and Tom Hopkinson were among his protégés. A man of such undemanding goodness and instinctive kindness who never looked for a return for any action . . . he truly earned the last 12 years of happiness he found with his wife Ethel.'

Arthur's death was a loss, and Kaye felt very alone. She tried to get the artist Raymond Briggs to come to New York with her, but he was teaching, and it was exam time. Briggs was one of her favourite illustrators: his wife had recently died of leukaemia, and she took him under her wing. He recalls going on a 'hare-brained' trip to a puffin sanctuary at Bempton on the Yorkshire coast, where Kaye was quite unfazed by fearless children scampering about within feet of a precipitous cliff. He also accompanied her on a 'boozy' excursion on John's boat in Suffolk, when they got locked out of their hotel at midnight (not having seen a notice 'the size of a playing-card' forewarning residents) and spent the freezing night sleeping on the floor of Briggs's Volkswagen van, wrapped in duffel coats and dog blankets, which Kaye didn't mind at all. And when Hamish Hamilton rejected a cover of his (showing Father Christmas naked in his bath) Kaye seized it from his drawing-board and put it in *Puffin Post*.

Everyone who joined Kaye at Puffin knew they would never find another workplace like it. One of her girls, Isla Evans, told her it was 'hell' to leave 'that charismatic aura . . . There is not one person in the office who is not totally dedicated to their work, which says a great deal about Puffins and a great deal about you.' The friendliness and good humour gave it a 'magical atmosphere' that she could never hope to recapture. Kaye replied that they too would miss seeing Isla 'with your long hair streaming behind you'. 'The day your father mentioned to me that you were feeling restless was a very fortunate one for me, and for the Puffin Club.'

But another new girl soon arrived, also recommended by her father, the prolific author, *Punch* man and poet Peter Dickinson. Philippa Dickinson was re-sitting her A-levels when she arrived to 'dogsbody' at the Puffin Exhibition, helping Alison Rosenberg to mount the children's artwork on to colourful cards. Would she like to stay on for a year? Kaye asked. Philippa was eighteen and was offered £1,600 a year, when her friends were subsisting on meagre grants at university. She had planned to read law, but 'I had five mad, wonderful years at Puffin instead. I'm still in my gap year really.' (Today she runs Random House children's books.) 'We were all trained as Puffin leaders, and every other weekend there was a Puffin party somewhere. We'd get up early, catch the first train, have a slap-up breakfast, and arrive at the venue in our pink tabards.' And Philippa enjoyed driving Kaye around London in Kaye's smart automatic car. 'Wherever we went, she would tell me about the lovers she had had in all these places. She had a circle of sweet elderly men who doted on her. She was a great matchmaker, and would occasionally set us up on dates. She longed for people to be in love.'

This is true: Kaye had once tried to link Jonty Fenby with Lucia Graves, daughter of Robert. Now she decided to match Dorothea Duncan with Edward Boyle, the Penguin director and MP, 'such a nice man, darling', and all three dined at the House of Commons. 'He was perfectly nice, completely asexual, and a bit solemn,' Dorothea recalls. 'No twinkle. He talked of "Teddy" (Edward Heath), and then spoke at length about Thomas Hardy. I remember thinking, I didn't know Kaye had read so much Hardy. It turned out that she thought the same of me. We discovered on the platform of Westminster tube station, with some hilarity, that neither of us had read any Hardy at all.'

Jane Nissen too joined the full-time force at Puffin, since her children were now at school. Well-read, and with tastes that chimed with Kaye's, she was installed at Harmondsworth to work on the fiction list with Felicity Trotman, dealing with piles of unsolicited manuscripts, and later taking over the Peacock list.

The intensity of the female bonding in the Puffin office had not gone unremarked at Penguin; nobody could avoid noticing the jollifications whenever one of 'Kaye's girls' had a birthday and all work stopped, for tea and cakes and shrieks. Did Kaye suspect that other executives found it slightly irritating? Some board members certainly found Kaye 'a steam-roller'. She discussed this with her friend Richard Kennedy, who wrote a frank, if convoluted, appraisal of the effect of Kaye's personality on her work. As he saw it, she was driven by the power of love, 'stronger and more primitive and atavistic' than she realized. Her love for her twins was 'colossal', he said, even if she was 'inclined to represent them in rather a bad light'.

But her network of love 'has really sucked in the whole of Penguin Books', Kennedy wrote, 'which have become, in a strange way for a business, focused round you and your group of female disciples. This sort of thing was accepted quite naturally by the Greeks in a priestess whose power was increased by the girls who served her . . . The essential female power one sees in Leonardo's drawings of spiralling clouds & vortex-like pictures of floods etc.'

Because of Kaye's 'extraordinary acute intelligence' her female power took on an 'essentially male' force. Penguin Books had become 'rather dependent on you emotionally without realizing it. I feel sure the board of directors would repudiate any such idea, in fact like your own children they are bound to show signs of rebellion, to interfere with your work & take up the same attitude as John, an average male one.' Perhaps, he said, it was time for her to 'loosen up as regards the female power'.

Even young Puffineers noticed how Kaye impelled her girls to flock around, doing her bidding. She was manipulative, enveloping, demanding, an irresistible force. Felicity Trotman says Kaye even proposed the notion of a staff house, 'where we would all live together' during the exhibition. 'We were already working all sorts of hours, and we knew if she succeeded we would be working 24/7.'

Not everyone found her personality irresistible. Harry Chambers was an English lecturer at Didsbury College, running a popular course in Children's Literature. He hosted a Puffin Club weekend, inviting authors who included 'the one who has now been airbrushed out of kiddylit, William Mayne'.★ Chambers recalls 'the saintly stoicism of John Rowe Townsend, shoving a fluffy rat down a tube for hours on end, so that children could bat it away as it came out the other end. Also, the patience and good humour of Alan Garner and his "witch" Griselda' (Griselda Greaves, Mrs Garner).

But Kaye struck him as a '*dame formidable*, a sort of cross between Lady Bracknell and Edith Evans at her most imperious'. Kaye told Chambers he hadn't ordered nearly enough ice-cream, and sent him round all the cinemas within an eight-mile radius, buying up their stocks. 'We had to offer the leftovers to our students at cut price for about a fortnight,' Chambers says. 'I felt that she needed taking down a notch or two, although I admired what she did vis-à-vis children's fiction and the Puffin Club.' A common perception. Kaye's exuberance, her evident love of the children, impressed everyone. But as Elaine Moss says, 'I don't think I would have liked to work for her.'

Indeed, her staff became wary of telling her where they were going. 'Whatever your destination, Kaye would think of some errand en route: "Oh darling, could you bring me/fetch/collect/

★ The story of what became of William Mayne, a prolific and highly prized Puffin author, was one which Kaye did not live long enough to know. Mayne attended many Puffin Club events, and would often invite little girls to tea at his home. In 2004 he admitted eleven indecent assaults, in what he called 'romps' at his home, on girls aged eight to sixteen (although he attempted to withdraw his guilty pleas, just before he was sentenced). Decades had passed, and he was now seventy-six, but he was jailed for two years and placed on the sex offenders' register for life. He has not been published since, but many critics still regard Mayne's work highly, and some new titles are appearing from print-on-demand publishers. In 2005, at a literary symposium in Oxford, the Archbishop of Canterbury, Rowan Williams, asserted that he would still recommend Mayne's *A Game of Dark*, a childhood favourite of his.

call on . . . " She couldn't help herself,' Dorothea said. There are many stories of what Kaye asked people to do for her. 'Darling, could you bring me a dustbin?' Doreen Scott was once asked. Michael Bond, author of *Paddington*, called to deliver a manuscript and Kaye asked him to bring a shovel: she wanted him to dig up the Victorian lamp-post which she and Ronnie had rescued in 1958. When Charles Fenby died, she broke off from exhibition-organizing and rushed to be with his widow, June – and later apologized for getting June to 'go and buy flowers and bath-brushes'. (In fact this was probably just the kind of diversion the grieving June needed.)

In truth Kaye was not very happy, outside the office. She had decided she disliked her Chiswick house, which was rather dark; there was 'a sort of sadness' about it that got her down. She might look for a London flat, she told her ex-husband Keith, who now lived sybaritically in southern Spain. She wondered 'why the hell' she didn't go and live by the sea in lovely Brighton 'and give it all up'. It didn't help that Keith was forever describing idyllic holidays with Barbara. 'We are in disgustingly rude health after four glorious months in our caravan in the Pyrenees,' he wrote. 'Must say you've planned your life jolly well,' Kaye replied. She marvelled that he went on so many trips in retirement, when he had always been so busy. She herself 'got edgy' on holidays. 'Doing absolutely nothing is a very engrossing and almost full-time occupation,' responded the irrepressible Keith. It was also irksome that Kaye was still 'shelling out cash' to her children, while Keith's children prospered: Angela was contracts and rights manager for Granada with 'a little empire of her own', and Andrew had married and bought a house in Oxfordshire. To be fair, John was now totally self-supporting; from being 'destroyed', as his grandfather alleged, he had gained much from working in the US, Canada and India, and later resumed his job on the *Brentford and Chiswick Times*.

Keith hoped she would get over her 'arthritic and depressed

phase smartly and get bubbling again', but it was a miserable summer. Still, she never ceased to seek further amusements for Puffineers. She went to Longleat, the Marquess of Bath's stately home, planning a re-enactment of the Mad Hatter's Tea Party there. 'I've just been collecting the costumes,' she told Joan Aiken, 'and I think it's going to be great fun.' The participants had to write a new answer to the Mad Hatter's unanswerable riddle, 'Why is a raven like a writing desk?' (The usual answers being, 'Because they both have inky quills,' or 'Because Edgar Allan Poe wrote on both.')

She could always be cheered by a party. In August she would be going to Exeter University for its annual conference of children's authors and teachers: she wanted to hear Jill Paton Walsh and Nina Bawden, 'whom I like and value'. Otherwise only the end-of-session party reconciled her to the conference, 'which I must say I was bored to death by'. One speaker, Nicholas Tucker, found Kaye surrounded by Alan Garner, Leon Garfield, William Mayne and Peter Dickinson, 'so dear old Kaye was in her element among "her writers"'. A few months later she had been 'feeling mouldy' but was thoroughly revived by Joy Whitby's party for *Jackanory*: she 'took a shot' and went along, and it was 'a marvellous party. 'There was Norman and Mrs Hunter, Richard Kennedy, Helen Cresswell, Quentin Blake, Nina Bawden . . .'

Were her authors true friends, or a substitute for them? 'As I get older,' she told Christopher Fry, 'I do miss the friends I really value.' She urged Fry to visit her, and bring his grandchildren. 'It seems my life is only full of acquaintances these days. I'm thinking seriously of trying to stop work, or most of it, but I suppose I've been talking about this for a year and don't know if I'll ever do it.'

Kaye was only fifty-nine, but perceptive friends had suggested that she should consider retiring. She hated the very idea, but while in New York the previous year she had already discussed this possibility with the wise and sympathetic Grace Hogarth. Now she admitted to Joan Aiken that during her three weeks in a clinic that November, the office seemed to tick along, so she no longer felt she was indispensable. But she could not face leaving Puffin. It was her life. Even when 'I'm sitting at home with great fat puffy legs and aching shoulders . . . having had a tooth out, and having got ulcers on my eye! lame, blind, halt, a real old cripple', she knew she would 'bob back'. 'Dear old Prince Charles has agreed to choose a favourite picture for the *Puffin Annual*, where The Faithless Lollybird (by J. Aiken) will go.'

Penguin Books moved to Grosvenor Gardens, Victoria, in February 1974. This meant being separated from the Puffin Club office, which stayed in Harmondsworth. It was a bleak time ('the winter of discontent'), with petrol shortages and strikes, though Kaye found 'the Victorian melodrama of Lord Lucan's homicide and flight were a bit of cheer'. The takeover by Pearson had brought in a hardback children's imprint, Longman Young Books, renamed Kestrel. It was run by Patrick Hardy, aided by Tony Lacey (from Penguin Education) and Ruth Petrie, a forceful Canadian feminist. Lacey was one of those who found the Puffin office über-feminine ('the dominant Kaye, with Dorothy, Felicity and Doreen'), 'entirely bound up in their club, their magazine, their jolly parties and weekends away with the children. Kaye was a force of nature, surrounded by giggling and adoring women. In my chippy male way I found it all too cosy – but it was commercial. It was their patch and they were very, very successful – especially with *Watership Down*.'

Kaye's enthusiasm for Richard Adams's *Watership Down* mystified some colleagues, including Judy Taylor, who had summarily rejected it for the Bodley Head, but Kaye knew it would be a winner: 'I was so impressed by the way the rabbits talked. Richard Adams had made them all sound like civil servants and it was frightfully funny.' When Rex Collings published it,

Kaye got the paperback rights (after just a month) for Puffin, despite Penguin board resistance. Jacquie Graham (now Pan's publicity supremo) ran the publicity campaign for the unknown Adams, and it was a freak success, selling a million in the first year and even more on the back of the animated film, with its song 'Bright Eyes'.

At the end of 1974 Kaye moved into a mansion flat. Lampard House, found by Kate, was near Kate's own flat in Randolph Crescent. Dorothea Duncan stayed behind in Montrose Villas, and, together with Dorothy Wood and *Puffin Post*'s designer Gerry Downes, became part of an 'uproariously happy' household.

Kaye's fifth-floor flat overlooked the picturesque canal at Little Venice, and she lived there for the rest of her life. Elvira, the cook-housekeeper who had worked for her since Newton Road, went with her on a living-in basis, becoming a 'ferocious' presence, occupying the largest room in the flat, running the old-fashioned kitchen at the back. (Kaye was terrified of her, some thought.) Her flat was filled with books and pictures, a singing clockwork bird in a cage, a ship's figurehead by the door. On the walls were many relics of Ronald: his prison-camp pictures, a Webb toy theatre which he had painted, and a damaged Rowlandson drawing into which he had inserted a Ronald Searle figure.

On 10 November Kaye had a date: to go to Buckingham Palace, in hat and gloves, to get 'my little medal', her MBE, which placed her on the same low rung of the honours ladder as the Beatles. Kate would accompany her, but John couldn't get an extra day off from the local paper where he was now a reporter. So she asked her brother Bill, and he dutifully agreed, although 'his vast bulk won't sit happily on those small golden chairs'. (Bill now weighed seventeen stone.) 'I hated it to seem as if I had absolutely no males in my life,' she told Richard Kennedy, 'although God help me, it's the truth.'

There was soon, however, a useful man in her life: Patrick Crosse, former head of Reuters in Rome, who had been married to Jenny Nicholson, daughter of Robert Graves. He became an available walker and travelling companion, and he lived in the heart of Covent Garden – convenient for theatres, as he told Kaye. 'Your mention of theatres in the plural fills me with delighted expectation – when can we start? I'm free next Tuesday and Wednesday, and the Tuesday after, and the Tuesday and Wednesday after . . .' Kaye had to dictate this letter; 'my hands are rotten today'. 'Up and down like a yo-yo' is an accurate description of her spirits, almost wholly health-induced.

Joan Aiken had had a dream that she was reading Kaye's autobiography, 'published by Gollancz; it was called *Adventure in the Dark* and it was very good . . . So you had better get going!' Kaye had, in fact, already been discussing her autobiography with Richard Kennedy, who wrote a draft outline for her. She wanted to call it 'An Ordinary Girl' and it would not be strictly an autobiography ('She does not like autobiographies') but would tell the story of how 'an ordinary girl who takes a secretarial course without the advantages of higher education could become a successful editor'.

The book would tell how she had been a reporter during the Battle of Britain, lost a cherished brother in the war, and had interviewed many writers and artists, for whom, it seemed to her, 'their talent was a burden, like the stone of Sisyphus'. The most telling paragraph is the one in which Kennedy expresses, in Kaye's voice, her lack of intellectual confidence. 'I had to skip out of an editorial meeting at *Lilliput* to consult the local library and discover who the Post-Impressionists were. When someone quoted Proust I had to disguise the fact that I had never heard of the fellow let alone read him in the original French. I was constantly having to hide my guilty secret.' Male colleagues had helped: 'There is nothing a man likes better than enlightening the unenlightened female.' Since then she had proved that an English literature degree was not necessary: 'It may be that what one snatches at greedily on the wing while involved in earning a living has more impact.' She had shared whatever she learned with Puffin readers, revolutionizing their reading while not being spared 'the emotional claims which are a feature of every woman's life, looking after ageing mother and children'.

Kaye's greatest unhappiness, she told Kennedy, was that 'I have always been trying to find solutions for other people's problems and finding that I couldn't'. The question she felt 'acutely' was, 'What can we offer children in the way of a faith in the ultimate goodness of life?' This, Kennedy decided, was Kaye's expertise: she should produce an anthology of the inspiration people had derived from their childhood reading. Kaye was 'not especially saintly', said Kennedy, and had read no philosophy. She was 'by some standards a poor ignorant woman with a lively sense of self-preservation'. In one sense she was 'an archetypal Jewish momma', he wrote, since children all over the world, from the Malay States to Surbiton, looked to her for spiritual sustenance. Puffin Books had become a sort of substitute for the Bible and Shakespeare, 'since they contain a dynamic force, a human inspiration' (i.e. Kaye). 'They constitute one of the great cultural moments of recent years.'

Kaye's female authors were a constant reminder of the indomitable qualities women need, as they soldiered on alone in the face of adversity. Philippa Pearce's husband, who had been a PoW in Japan, had died within a year of her marriage; Rumer Godden had overcome financial disaster and once found her house ablaze from end to end. Ursula Moray Williams was recently widowed when she reported to Kaye about going to a Puffin 'Witches and Wizards' event at Bolton (involving four changes of train, standing for the last hour). She'd met thousands of 'splendid' children who had queued in the rain, and had never signed so many autographs in her life. 'The one I liked was a small & grubby boy who demanded a signature and then waved it in my face saying, "Wot's it for?" "Your guess is as good as mine," I replied.' Children who had never been into a bookshop before had bought books: 'They just went mad on the bookshelves as if they were in a sweetshop, and there were lots of Puffineers there, some of whom had been to Featherstone, & they bought *Castle Merlin*' (Ursula's book inspired by the Winter Whoopee). One 'dear little Puffineer' who had won a Puffin holiday this summer, 'sent you her love 3 times'.

Ursula, whose first success had been *The Little Wooden Horse* in the 1930s, had never (until the Puffin Club) been out to meet readers. As well as running her farmhouse, and being a magistrate, she always had another book on the go, busy from 6.30 a.m. to 10 p.m. It was inbred in women of Ursula's spirit to concentrate on the pleasures and consolations of life, such as gardening – a conspicuous lack in Kaye's life in her eyrie, where her friends felt she was somewhat 'marooned'. Ursula sent Kaye a photo of her crocuses: 'I get such a kick out of it, and the birds are singing.' Ursula had eleven godchildren and several grandchildren, who were 'so nice & funny, I wish I could give some of them to you, it wracks me that you have no grandchildren'. But she added, mollifyingly, 'On the other hand you have thousands and they adore you. Life is the strangest thing, how it is parcelled out in various ways & we all want somebody else's . . . You are so famous and wonderful.' Kaye increasingly needed this bolstering from her authors. She sent a bronze puffin to Helen Cresswell, who wrote her thanks in a verse. Helen had given up 'puffin' at fags' in 1975, and the puffin now stood on her desk where her ashtray had been. 'If I weaken, / She'll lift her beak'n / Cough / To tell me off.' Dorothy Edwards, another author who loved visiting schools and Puffin parties ('it's so pleasant to meet people') echoed the thoughts of many when she assured Kaye how admired she was for carrying on even when in pain. 'I just cannot see why anyone who does so much good & works so honestly should have to suffer as you do.'

But 1975 was a bad year. She missed Kate, who had gone to work in Canada, and she was repeatedly 'back in the bloody hospital'. She was just home from hospital in June when Keith Hunter called unannounced one day while she was taking an afternoon nap. When she found Keith's card on the doormat, 'I sat down and cried from sheer frustration. It would have been so nice . . . but there you go.' Joan Aiken wrote, wondering if Kaye had watched the recent television programme about Ronald, 'and if so what you were thinking – must have been strange for you. He's very like both John and Katie, isn't he – but especially John.' Joan had been amazed by Ronald's drawings from Changi. 'What a thing to have been through. No one could ever be normal after that.'

It was 'foul' doing things from her hospital bed that summer, but Kaye rallied when Penguin called on her to give their fortieth birthday party 'a bit of panache'. She wrote to Cyril Ray, the *Punch* wine writer, 'Do you think your brilliant invention could discover a Penguin drink?' His pink Puffin drink, Puffin's Pleasure, had 'a kick like nobody's business'. Could he now devise an orange-coloured cocktail with forty ingredients? 'And come and help us drink it!'

Penguin paid her hospital costs and sent 'gratitude and appreciation for all you have contributed to excellent results in a difficult year'. She was happy to be with Nina Bawden and Nicholas Fisk at the Edinburgh Festival, addressing a throng 'with great éclat', says Fisk. 'She was good at audiences.' Afterwards the threesome couldn't find a taxi ('Kaye's taxis never came'), and stumbled in a rainstorm down Princes Street, Kaye hailing a group of American naval men with 'Hello, sailor! Want a good time?' Fisk, a tall, handsome figure, real name David Higginbottom, was Kaye's 'devoted admirer and occasional companion'. They enjoyed a chaste but flirtatious relationship. 'She was a life force, and must have been ravishing as a girl. I once found her on hands and knees on bare boards, pinning up pictures of puffins. I totally admired her personality and drive.'

At a time of social unease (bombs in Mayfair, rising street crime) Kaye felt, like many, that central London had changed since her youth, and was a difficult, threatening place. Most of her authors inhabited rural havens. After a visit to Jan Pieńkowski's idiosyncratically beautiful old house on the river in Barnes, with its rustic setting and roaring fires, 'the only nice place to be is in the country, quite far away from most people', she wrote to Joan Aiken. 'Just for a little while [life] felt good and simple again.'

13: The Succession

1976–9

'The magic never fails. Each birthday when we meet you draw me back through the years & neither your eyes nor time nor memory dim. You have been charmed by some power not of mortal weakness . . .' Laurie Lee was always florid when writing to ladies, and he and Kaye, who were both now sixty-two, went back a long way. 'Do you know, dear friend, that it was 1944 when we met? I look forward – Penguin & G Orwell willing – to 1984 with you. I'll be thinking of you as you go off to South Africa.' Kaye was leaving in February for 'this damn stupid South Africa trip', another Penguin mission, and she was ailing again: back pain this time, and an eye problem. '1976 has been pretty grim for me,' Kaye wrote at the end of the year. 'I think I've been four or five times in hospital. I can't do stairs and I hobble around like an old lady in the flat. But . . . I'm always rather dramatic about things I do know.'

That summer Kaye was promoted to 'Editorial Director, Children's Division', responsible for Kestrel hardbacks, as well as managing director of Puffin. Her salary was £10,000 a year, and she would get two-thirds of that on retiring at sixty-five. 'A decent pension arrangement', Kaye thought – which may have been the chairman Jim Rose's motive, as there had been murmurings about her retirement. It may also have been his consolation for their letting her down over her Children's Bookshop project. She had found an excellent freehold property next to the Unicorn Theatre, where many schoolchildren, parents and teachers would be passing through. 'Charing Cross Road is a book area and far more attractive to staff than Victoria,' she wrote reproachfully. Their only rival would be the Children's Book Centre in Notting Hill. She planned to put in two of her girls, Sylvia Mogg and Annabel Bartlett, as managers. Penguin could sub-let the offices above. She thought Pearsons had guaranteed the money, but now she was told they could not afford it.

These were bad times at Penguin and she worried about the way the company was going. A young marketing executive called Tony Mott was appointed to the board: 'a splendid chap', said Kaye, but coming from the hard end of marketing, he was interested in big sales. Penguin was losing its identity, Kaye told Rose: 'I firmly believe that a company's ultimate reputation is built up on the shape of the list, and the odd bestsellers simply don't give it its identity.'

The *Puffin Annual* was a lively and rather highbrow production, strong on photographs and well-researched original articles. The new one was called *Puffin's Pleasure*, a title she regretted, but the cover was done before she could change it. The Puffin Exhibition had been unusually chaotic: the girls were mounting exhibits on the eve of opening. Kaye's top authors showed up – her visitors' book was signed by all the usual suspects, plus two of her bestselling authors, Barbara Willard and Russell Hoban, and a few show-business friends like the actor Bernard Cribbins – but Kaye was on the point of collapse afterwards. Dorothy Edwards thought she should stop the Exhibitions 'if they affect you so badly'. Kaye's perfectionism meant she 'just couldn't sit around letting other people create your "thing" . . . That, of course, is why the Exhibitions have been so unique & so successful – & why no-one else could do them as well! It's often better to stop when a thing is good rather than let it run down.'

'I do seem to find it awfully difficult to cope with just ordinary work,' Kaye confessed to Polly Hope, the painter and sculptor who had created one of her famous tapestries and written its story for the *Puffin Annual*, 'and shed my friends like flowers.' Reviving old friendships had begun to nag at her. She told the Fergussons, Bernard and Laura, that she wished they hadn't disappeared from her life. 'Perhaps it's something to do with you both being so super to me when Ronnie went off . . . you are part of my eternal circle of friends as opposed to the ones who come and go because of work. And yet I never seem to do anything about it.'

Kaye no longer went on Colony Holidays with her Puffineers. She would send Philippa and Jane, and simply arrange the visiting authors. The organizer, Chris Green, had come to find Kaye's presence awkward: she was 'a little too keen on taking charge'. 'She was lovely, and so charismatic,' he says. 'But she would tell the matron what to do, and the cook how to cook the meals, and me how to run Colony Holidays.'

But she did need holidays. She needed sunshine to ease her arthritis. Polly Hope's house at picturesque Lindos on the island of Rhodes was one she was hoping to get to, with her brother Bill and his wife 'who's a bit of a painter'. She might also bring John Phillips, her TV director friend, and his future wife and her 'very manageable little boy called Charles' – 'we could all fit in, couldn't we?' In return she offered to send 'my little Marianne', the seamstress from the Unicorn Theatre, to help with Polly's tapestry-sewing. She even advised Polly on problems with her maid, who had abandoned spring-cleaning to go off and milk her cow. Polly should get tough and 'make the bloody woman do it', wrote Kaye. 'Just say: "I'm a creative artist . . . and you've got to do the lot."' Polly said this was pointless: Greek village women were 'too aristocratic' for work. 'Yes, aristocratic is a real Greek word; it means more or less the same as our usage, snotty.'

She also asked Keith if she might rent his place in Spain. He demurred: 'Quite honestly we wouldn't recommend this place to our worst enemy, outside the winter months. Things have changed enormously since we first arrived. Now it is not just the heat but "the noise, the people".'

So Kaye went to stay with her *Lilliput* friend Alison (Blair) Hooper in her charming, colourful and artistic house in the Algarve. On her return, much invigorated, she had thoughts of finding a seaside place of her own. She went to see (with John Phillips) a pair of coastguard cottages in a beautiful village, Abbotsbury in Dorset. The writers Katherine Mansfield and John Middleton Murry had lived there, and D. H. Lawrence, so the cottages had 'a bit of an aura', with a garden that swept down to the sea in front and up to the hills behind.

Nothing came of this plan, but she desperately needed friends and diversions. The twins, now in their thirtieth year, had long since flown her nest. John was married and working on a paper in Abergavenny, but 'spends all his time hang-gliding – he would choose something as alarming as that'. John says hang-gliding induced 'feelings of magnificence'. 'It forced upon me a level of awareness and focus that I had never experienced before. I felt integrated with nature and the world, and released from troubling thoughts.' From there he went to live off the west coast of Ireland, on Valencia Island, where he rebuilt a cottage – he could build anything – and became a fisherman, bravely going out in the teeth of Atlantic gales. Once, every phone line in Ireland was cut off for several days. 'Journalists couldn't get their copy through, or anything,' John says. 'But one day Mrs Ring the postmistress came along and said, "I don't know how she's done it! That mother of yours is on the line down there in the post office" – Kaye had got through, by sheer force of personality.'

Kate was planning to get married to a Canadian, and to live in Ottawa. Kaye seemed excited about this, and even thought briefly of emigrating with her. She wanted to help with the wedding, and when Richard Usborne reminded her that he still had some of Ronald's drawings on loan, and offered to buy them, she suggested £80, which 'might buy Katie a jolly good going-away outfit'. Kate, however, abandoned the marriage plans; but she did go back to live in Canada for another five years. Kaye rented out Kate's garden flat to Jill Murphy, and also arranged for Jill's highly obedient dog, Lottie, to star in a film of one of Helen Cresswell's Bagthorpe stories, earning Jill a much-needed £3,000.

Puffineers, growing up and in need of guidance, became a substitute for Kaye's absent family. When Puffin member 359, Charlotte Cory, had sent Kaye a chapter of her work in progress, *The Wandering Wind*, Kaye was 'riveted', and longed to know what befell 'the wretched Derrick (what a good name!)'. But she gently pointed out that other books, like *Moonfleet*, told the adventures of a boy on a ship; it might appear 'derivative'. 'I think you write vividly and well, and you've got a great sense of developing the excitement of the story, but it may be that it is going to be a bit predictable.' This would not matter to child readers, but it would 'when you're measuring yourself against professional writers like Rosemary Sutcliff'. Kaye's response galvanized Charlotte's ambition to write.

The future playwright Paul Godfrey, a bright, sensitive only child whose parents never travelled outside Devon, really did become Kaye's substitute son. He had joined the Puffin Club at eleven, winning so many competitions he had to be restricted (as were others) from competing again. When he first went to London in 1976, on a school trip to the America Bicentennial exhibition at Greenwich, he broke away from the group and took the District Line to Kaye's office at Victoria. She was welcoming, and not at all surprised to see him. He told her he admired *Watership Down* and that his favourite Puffin was *Hobberdy Dick*, the story by the great folklorist K. M. Briggs about a hobgoblin in a seventeenth-century manor house. When he noticed on the wall a Quentin Blake drawing of Kaye, prancing through fields surrounded by puffins, and said he wanted to be an illustrator, she gave him a story to illustrate for *Puffin Post*. Every Easter for the next five years he helped to design the Puffin Exhibition, staying at Kaye's flat, hanging pictures, organizing bookstalls, painting walls, amusing the heaving throng of Puffineers, shepherding the artists and writers. 'There was a gang of us who took care of Quentin Blake and Roald Dahl. Kaye had this radical quality. You could see the other Penguin executives thinking, what on earth is Kaye Webb doing with all these wild cards, these teenagers?' They appeared to be irked by her 'inspired idiosyncracy'.

Kaye was at 'the bloody Exhibition' (in the Mall Galleries), 'pinning up puffins and working robots and setting competitions', when she wrote to her companionable friend Patrick Crosse proposing a motoring trip around Devon. Patrick was feeling low and listless, so it was nice to know that someone felt even lower and less energetic than herself: she had been having dental work ('ordeals by mouth') so there would be many silences, and occasional sibilances. And would Patrick come to her opening party? 'We've got lots of lovely Cranks food and some good wine – Berry Bros – because we're really doing it in style as we are doing it for each other and not for the rotten old Press.'

Patrick was not a lover, and after Jenny he was not the marrying kind, but she found him a perfect companion. When her accountant said her shares looked 'dicey' she seriously considered Patrick's suggestion that she put her capital into a half-share in his big house in Putney; Kate could live upstairs. But Kate vetoed the idea, suspecting that she would become 'a dogsbody' to the ageing pair. To make up for her dithering, Kaye offered Patrick a quarter's rent: she said she was 'frightened to death' that she might lose his friendship over this. 'When we started talking about it, I thought how heavenly it would be to live near you . . . just to know that I'd see you occasionally for dinner or something without all the journeying . . .'

Increasingly lame, and living sixty stairs up, she was grounded when the lift at Lampard House was out of action for six months and she had to camp at Kate's flat. For much of the summer of 1977 she was in hospital. Nina Bawden – another of the wise and splendid authors who helped Kaye to see her own miseries in perspective – wrote her a long, bolstering letter. She admired the way Kaye carried on working when laid up: if ever she wanted to put her feet up, she thought of Kaye, and stopped moaning. She reported that her son Niki, who was schizophrenic (and later tragically drowned himself in the Thames), had bought himself a motorbike, was happy for several weeks, acquired a lovely girl, then was knocked off his bike by a car, which 'started up all the old delusions'. She asked, might Kaye come to a screening of the film of Nina's *The Peppermint Pig*? She enclosed a picture of the two pigs in the film, Big Johnnie and Smaller Johnnie. Smaller Johnnie had unfortunately died of a heart attack just as the filming finished. And she said writing novels got harder, not easier, with time: a young editor had changed all her grammar in her new one, *The Rebel on a Rock*, and 'I completely lost faith in my ability to put two words together let alone 75,000 or so.'

Paul Godfrey became Kaye's protégé, urged by her to do whatever delighted him, and always to aim for the first-rate. They went often to the National Theatre, where she could get free tickets. When she promised to take the chief buyer from James Thin bookshop in Edinburgh to the theatre, and couldn't go, she sent Paul in her place. 'The prim lady from Edinburgh was incredibly disappointed to be with this kid of seventeen, instead of Kaye Webb,' he recalls, 'and the show was *Bubblin' Brown Sugar*, full of scantily clad negro women doing lively dances. We both sat there in excruciating embarrassment.'

With Kaye's encouragement Paul applied to Oxford. His grammar school laughed at such presumption, but he got in to read English at St Edmund Hall. When Kaye visited him in his handsome room in the lovely old quad, he held a party for her. His fellow undergraduates, all brought up on Puffins, were thrilled to meet the great Kaye Webb: 'But she was in awe of students. She said, "Everyone's so clever," which just wasn't true. She had an inferiority complex about being under-educated and non-intellectual.'

Paul would get messages in his pigeon-hole summoning him to come and put on a puffin costume at events like the opening of the Penguin bookshop in Covent Garden. She paid him £150, but he earned it: 'It was quite rough – you're vulnerable because the kids come up and punch you in the stomach, and you can't even speak.' Kaye was 'the perfect grandmother, helped by the fact that we weren't related'. While her son John found Kaye's disabilities increasingly hard to cope with, Paul found her 'terrifically brave', and spent weekends in her flat, doing illustrations and setting competitions, even painting a mural of birds dancing across her bathroom wall.

There was a telling moment for Kaye when Paul was asked by Jane Nissen to look carefully at a Rosa Guy novel for the Peacock list. 'The story included a girl taking a drug overdose in a toilet. Kaye was very worried about this. Jane asked me to read it to see if I found it shocking. I found it not shocking at all, and Jane asked me to tell Kaye, which I did.' Rosa Guy, a Trinidadian who grew up rootless in Harlem and knew the gritty reality of which she wrote, was a big success with teenage readers in her rite-of-passage novels of the 1970s.

The loss of readers in their teens was a preoccupation of that decade. How to get fifteen-year-olds, especially boys, to read? Kaye had created Peacocks in 1962 to be a bridge between Puffins and Penguins. Her first Peacock was Enid Bagnold's *National Velvet* in 1962; others were *Walkabout* by James Vance Marshall, *The Greengage Summer* by Rumer Godden, and *Fifteen* by Beverly Cleary (which starts, 'Today I am going to meet a boy.'). Early in Kaye's time at Puffin, the intellectually snobbish Marghanita Laski infuriated her by saying young people she knew were intelligent enough to decide for themselves what to read. Even allies like Ian Norrie had doubts about Peacocks: 'Children make their own natural transition, and I think some sensed patronage when they were offered *The Catcher in the Rye*, a hugely successful Penguin already, as a Peacock.' In 1971 Kaye had invited fifty Puffin Club members for a 'Peacock Think-In' weekend at a college in Reading. The publisher Andrew Franklin, then aged twelve, was one. It was a Puffin-style weekend that featured a visit to an animal sanctuary, but they also wrote critical reports on Peacock books. Andrew's was the new William Mayne, *A Game of Dark*.

Margaret Clark at the Bodley Head had introduced 'New Adult' fiction, with teenage novels by Paul Zindel, Emma Smith and Aidan Chambers, among others, a conspicuous success. But Kaye published many novels with a perennial appeal to older children, by Alan Garner, Jane Gardam and Jill Paton Walsh. (Ten years later, Kaye appeared on a radio programme about books written 'for the awkward age', and said the most sensible thing ever said on the subject: 'It may be that the teenagers who don't read, have never really read.') But in her heart she knew that her personal taste had become ossified. 'I don't think you can get rid of your own datedness, after nineteen years,' she said in a *Woman's Hour* broadcast the following year. 'You can try very hard to be modern, but I know the kind of books I'm very fond of might not be the kind of books children want now.' She sounded self-conscious and defensive. Puffin had the unique advantage, she would emphasize, of its contact with readers through the Club: 'We see them and talk to them . . . so we're aware of what they like. And of course the sales figures tell us that too.' She felt beleaguered by pressures, sociological and economic. Her original criteria – that books should have 'quality', should enrich the reader's life, and should make the child want to read them again

– were muddled by the need to think of different types of child. 'It meant taking on books you wouldn't have particularly liked yourself.'

Children's book publishing had changed with the social climate of the 1970s. It was all very well for bright, well-behaved children from book-lined homes to be given fun things to do with authors. But Elaine Moss identified the 'nowhere child' (like the Beatles' 'Nowhere Man'), disadvantaged and deprived, simply because their parents were totally ignorant of books. Kaye had never found any shortage of literate, articulate readers, and she would sigh when asked for dogma about 'reaching out' to reluctant readers: her sole mantra was that parents should read aloud to their children, even after they can read perfectly well for themselves. She told me, in 1988, 'If only families would read together as they watch TV together. It would give them shared references and stories and bywords – and laughter.' She was right: nothing ensnares a child reader like family laughter. P. G. Wodehouse, Thurber, *Diary of a Nobody* are all excellent family fodder. But that still excludes the nowhere child. She told a putative successor that she felt guilty about it. 'I feel I've failed in one particular direction . . . We've still not tackled head-on the problem of getting to the generally under-privileged children.'*

There was also the question of how far children's books should reflect the troubles of the modern world. 'Children can face the realities of life without suffering fearful damage,' John Rowe Townsend had written in *Puffin Post*. Puffin, Peacock and Kestrel books often confronted challenging themes: poverty, violent crime, broken marriages. Nina Bawden, as a magistrate in north London, saw vulnerable children every day exposed to social evils and the inadequacies of their parents, and never flinched from writing about them. But Kaye began to feel that her treasured

*Letter from Kaye Webb to Julia MacRae, 1978.

concept of a lasting children's library of high-quality writing, much of it written in a completely different era, was threatened by these distracting contemporary obsessions.

How should Puffin deal with the competition they now faced from rival imprints? Kaye set out her Puffin Strategy for chairman Jim Rose in March 1977. It was more defensive than proactive. The 1,000th Puffin would be published in March 1978. Seven hundred Puffin titles were still in print – a testimony to their staying power. She listed those with a strong selling life of five more years. She was adamant that they should 'nurse our list, to reinforce its excellence and maintain the standards which have made us the leading children's paperback imprint, sticking to our policy of acquiring enduring books'. Eleanor Graham's dictum, that books kept in print for five years will endure another twenty, 'is constantly being endorsed'.

'We cannot hope to get into the mass-media market with quick, cheap sellers,' Kaye wrote – though they had 'succumbed to this once or twice' – 'without sacrificing the reputation we have built up in the last 38 years.' That reputation among parents and teachers would survive if they stuck it out. Kaye could do nothing about the loss of titles whose licence had reverted (for example C. S. Lewis), 'and unless we can find another great seller like *Watership Down*, or spend an enormous amount of money making best-sellers out of what we currently hold, we cannot avoid facing the fact that for the next 2 or 3 years sales will drop'. She thought they might get back *The Borrowers*, and should look to media tie-ins and spend money promoting authors into big sellers. 'We have got, and I think will safely keep, the Roald Dahls,' she wrote. (She had written to her ex-husband to warn him that he might be asked to illustrate the new Roald Dahl, *The Enormous Crocodile*. 'Before you turn it down out of hand I just would like to say that . . . he really does make a fortune,' she told Ronald. 'We must have sold a million of the kids' books he has done so far . . .' In the event, thanks to Tom Maschler at Cape, this was Quentin Blake's first collaboration with Dahl, an inspired alliance.)

She undertook to prune the backlist, to re-jacket titles that looked old-fashioned, to commission books with Oxford (with which Penguin now had an arrangement) and Kestrel, instead of luring authors from other publishers, and to find family books and series: 'There is no doubt that children like to "settle down" with a series of books, such as Laura Ingalls Wilder or the Nesbits.' She wanted to revive the American idea of Easy Readers – she preferred 'Beginning Readers' – by fine writers. Above all, she would continue to promote Puffins on the grounds of the excellence of the list. To remind the chairman of her track record, she added that the Puffin Club was so successful that its age range had extended upwards, which left out the under-eights. Might she start a separate club for them? The Junior Puffin Club, for the four-to-sevens, was launched the following year, with a magazine called *The Egg*, edited by Helen Nicoll and designed and illustrated by Jan Pieńkowski (the *Meg and Mog* team). It was launched on the same day that the Time Capsule was buried.

The Time Capsule was a grandly defiant gesture, the moment when Kaye tried to ensure that her taste and choice would be recognized in perpetuity. In January that year, Elaine Moss had published an article on 'Television's Effects on Publishing', criticizing the superficiality of children's TV programmes, in which presenters seemed terrified of boring the children by length. Books, by contrast, demanded concentration. Everybody was aware of television's threat to the reading habit. 'We were worried,' Kaye wrote a decade later, 'that many of the marvellous books we published might be forgotten by children 100 years in the future.'

She cancelled her mission to Australia that spring. Publishing the 1,000th Puffin (*The Crack-a-Joke Book*) was more important, and so was the Puffin Exhibition, where the children of 1978 could write messages 'for the children of the future' to be put inside the Time Capsule. Hundreds of Puffineers, from all over the Britain, wrote vignettes of their lives, wrapped in silver foil, encased inside horse-pills and placed in the casket, which was ceremoniously buried beneath a cherry tree, as described in Chapter 1. 'Funny to think of all those books sleeping under the soil on the hill at Harmondsworth,' wrote Ursula Moray Williams. 'What kind of a world will read them in 2078? Books are a tremendous responsibility aren't they? ... it's quite frightening. One thing – you will have had an enormous influence on this half century's reading.' That was the legacy Kaye wanted to cement, literally, inside the capsule.

Her sixty-fifth birthday loomed in 1979. But she could not retire unless she knew that her successor would carry on her work. Her choice was Julia MacRae, who edited children's books with great flair at Hamish Hamilton. Born in Australia, Julia had trained as a children's librarian and had worked with Grace Hogarth. She was duly wined and dined by Penguin's men in suits. Kaye wrote her a five-page letter hoping to persuade her, describing the sterling qualities of her staff (Felicity Trotman was 'a past master at the art of a good intelligent reply to difficult letters'; Doreen Scott was 'the key person in our outfit', etc.) and outlining her week, with its time-consuming sales meetings and board meetings. She even recommended Penguin's 'absolutely first-rate canteen'. She told Julia she got 'an immense number of letters addressed to me personally' because of having her name on the books, which hadn't been her idea. She had 'never had much talent for delegation' and said that even if her staff felt she was wrong, 'they sometimes find it hard to say so!'

Her hopes that Julia would take over were heartfelt. 'I've put such a lot of myself into Puffins, I'm really desperately apprehensive about falling into the wrong hands, and that's why I'm trying to do such a hard selling job on you,' she ended. 'I know, even if you change the direction of the list quite a bit, you would still not buy rubbish, you would still care what we made available to children, and that to me is the most important thing.' But Julia, though honoured, turned down the job. 'Kaye would have been a hard act to follow,' she says, 'and I realized I wasn't really a paperback publisher.' The ingenious Eric Carle's *The Very Hungry Caterpillar* was the kind of book she had published at Hamish Hamilton (and remains, she says, her claim to fame when meeting new people). She really wanted to found her own hardback imprint, Julia MacRae Books – and did so, the following year, with great success.

That summer, Dorothy Wood moved after nine 'treasured' years at Puffin to a job with Scholastic. Penguin called in a head-hunting service (at £1,000 a head) to find a substitute, and Kaye was appalled: this was not her way at all. Instead, her colleague Liz Attenborough recommended Julia Eccleshare of the *Times Literary Supplement*. 'Get her in, darling!' cried Kaye. Julia was a Cambridge graduate, daughter of Colin who had published Ronald Searle's first book. Kaye took Julia to lunch at the Arts Club and, impressed by her vitality, enthusiasm and excellent judgement, despite lack of publishing experience, hired her to do fiction and picture-books. 'By the time I arrived,' says Julia, 'someone had taken half my job, which was a classic Kaye thing to happen. I was left with non-fiction, such as the *Puffin Book of Flags*, in which I had very little interest.' It was the tail-end of Kaye's regime. She had to be collected and delivered home, 'and you often had to stop and pick up something like a Hoover on the way'. 'But when she said, "Darling, I think we should do a book on . . . " or "Go and find . . . " or "I've heard of a person who . . . " she was inspirational,' Julia says. 'It was ad hoc, but it worked because she gave people their head, but she was also hands-on.'

Kaye's succession was a botched business. A young man from BBC Education was appointed to replace her. Even Julia, the newest Puffin staffer, could see at once that 'he did not have the personality for Puffin. Perfectly nice, but with no publishing experience, no charisma, no communications skills. The poor guy was given a windowless cupboard-sized space of three walls, with no privacy, no daylight, while Kaye still sat in her huge office at her big curved desk. One day he looked in Kaye's diary and saw that she had appointments fixed up for the next three months. He had nothing to do, and he resigned.' Jane Nissen says it was rather funny, 'but Kaye behaved terribly. She just couldn't bear to think of Puffin being in his hands.'

Then, in November 1978, Peter Mayer blew in from the USA, to be Penguin's new supremo. Mayer, born in London but brought up in America, was a big, broad, brash figure. Chain-smoking, gravel-voiced, in his smooth black polo-neck sweaters, armed with a salary said to be the largest in publishing, he set out to reinvigorate an ailing company with his commercial know-how, energy and aplomb. Kaye was filled with trepidation. She and Mayer had crossed swords before, when she had published *Watership Down* and he had bought it for the US as an adult title for Avon Books, just when Penguin were getting copies distributed there via Penguin Canada. 'I wrote many letters to Kaye at that time,' Mayer recalls. 'I was mad at mighty Penguin. But now, suddenly, I was looking forward to working with Kaye Webb.'

When he was told that Kaye had announced her retirement he called her in and said: 'You can't do this! Penguin is going to have a renaissance. I don't know the children's scene, and I need you.' So she un-retired herself – for another year.

Days before, Kaye had accepted Hilary Rubinstein's suggestion that she should edit *The Oxford Book of Twentieth Century Children's Literature* – a rash promise instantly regretted, and rescinded as soon as Mayer rescued her. 'It looks as if Mr Mayer has heard such good things about me that he wants me to stick around!'

she told Rubinstein. And anyway, she added, a big Oxford volume was not her thing. 'You know my talents are not particularly scholarly, and my reactions are very individual ones, and my taste is pretty individual too . . .'

Rubinstein was unruffled: 'I rejoice that Peter Mayer appreciates you, and long may you flourish together.' He would shelve the project *sine die*. So off Kaye went to New York for the Viking sales conference in December, and stayed to spend Christmas in California with the actress Gloria (Stuart) Sheekman, one of the old friendships she had lately revived.

The new lease of work improved her health. Mayer found her more engaging, and a better listener, than he had expected. But her sixty-fifth birthday in January 1979, 'a bit of a milestone', made her realize the sad truth: 'how much I depend on the people I work with to have really any kind of life at all', she told Gloria, 'because in a sense they were the only people who remembered it. I'm not saying that plaintively, it's just a fact.'

At Easter Kaye was happy and busy. They were launching Puffin number 1295, *I Like This Poem*, in aid of the International Year of the Child. She had asked readers which poems meant a lot to them and got 1,000 entries. Kipling's 'If' was there, and 'The Charge of the Light Brigade', and de la Mare, and 'I Like Mice', and 'lots and lots of Spike Milligan'. She was pinning up puffins for her exhibition in the Commonwealth Institute, telling Yehudi Menuhin what to say in his opening speech, when Kate arrived with the news that her uncle Bill had had a stroke. Kaye was devastated. Bill had been enjoying his retirement, firing off letters on racing matters to *Sporting Life* ('Sir, I was appalled to read that . . .'), signing himself Bill Louis of Kew. 'As always Kaye blamed herself that Bill died,' Kate says. 'He'd suggested that they should get a flat in Brighton together. Perhaps if they'd done that, Kaye thought, Bill might have relaxed and rested more.'

The exhibition went ahead as usual: Peter Mayer took his

four-year-old daughter Liese along – she was frightened at first by someone dressed as Raymond Briggs's Fungus the Bogeyman – and saw for himself Kaye in her element among the children, in complete command. But he still needed to plan for her successor. The jovial Tony Lacey, who had been running a successful children's list at Granada, was Kaye's choice. ('He's absolutely super and I'm delighted,' said Kaye on radio.) Lacey agreed to come as long as he could take Puffin in a new direction. 'The Puffin list had become very middle-class,' Mayer says. 'Things were going on in the minds and lives of children that were hipper, edgier, and Kaye wasn't moving forward. If you're successful and loved, as she was, that's not a fertile ground to try out new things. Judy Blume was an issue between us. Every young girl read Judy Blume, Judy was a friend of mine, and I mentioned the success Pan was having with her, and Kaye told me proudly that she had turned them down. "American kids are different," she said. I told her there were fresh winds blowing.'

Mayer moved the Penguin operation to a modern, faceless office block on the King's Road at World's End, Chelsea, but the Puffin Club, which would in future be Kaye's only fiefdom, would remain at Harmondsworth.

'This is a funny old week for me,' she wrote to Joan Aiken in November 1979. 'I'm clearing up and clearing out . . . Friday's my last day in my lovely new office in really quite interesting Chelsea, after which I'm an old has-been hacking away down in Harmondsworth at the Puffin Club, and named "A Consultant", but God knows what they'll consult me on! And I'm staying on the main Board, so I'll have some slight involvement with Penguins.

'Everybody's being extraordinarily nice and making a fuss of me, but that somehow makes it worse . . .' There would be a farewell lunch where she would probably shed tears, and a party was promised on her sixty-sixth birthday in January. She had been doing broadcasts, but 'it isn't so much fun when you know it's valedictory'. Julia MacRae had asked her to write her life story 'if Denise can stand hearing somebody being egotistic day after day on tape'. (Her secretary Denise, who typed this dictated letter, inserted here, 'Yes she can.')

Kaye truly did not relish the prospect of a solitary life in her flat. 'What will you DO anyway?' asked Ursula Moray Williams. 'Will you write The Story of the Puffin Club?' She wished, she told Ursula, who had four sons and many grandchildren, that she had a 'your-sized' family. 'They do rally round, don't they? I'm jealous of that. I mean, nobody could be nicer than Katie, but I just wish there were more grandchildren around.'

Letters of thanks came in from parents, full of gratitude 'for helping over the years to introduce my children to the immeasurable delights of reading'. There was a party at the Children's Book Circle, after which Grace Hogarth wrote recalling the conversation they had had in Maine six years ago about Kaye's horror of retiring. 'Now that it has come I hope you feel differently,' she wrote. 'Good children's editors are capable of being the children they once were. You have this ability to a remarkable degree . . . And it is closeness to children that makes you the remarkable and successful woman you are.'

She would 'sail out in full glory, having handed over, it seems, to a team you trust,' wrote Ursula, sure that 'the intangible state of Puffinhood, founded by yourself, will carry things on I know'. Anyway, she reassured Kaye, all their 'darling Puffineers' were 'growing up and leaving us . . .' She graphically recalled their Puffin Club activities. 'The Exhibitions – all those eager little faces & dear Noel sitting in a corner signing autographs . . . And you coming for the party here in the rain & you rushing off to Tewkesbury to pinch that tarpaulin from the Fire station for the children to sit on . . . And all the occasions of swarming happy Puffins with you dashing about in the middle of them like what Peter called a blue arsed fly dispensing such love and interest and inspiration . . . But managing to retain a personal relationship with everyone from the smallest Puffineer to the oldest author, like being all of our mother! Those things don't stop with retirement, they build future foundations.'

One of Kaye's valedictory interviews was on *Woman's Hour*, when the interviewer, Teresa Birch, called her 'a powerful person'. 'I never wielded a big stick as far as I know,' replied Kaye. 'I used to think I was rather a mild woman, and tentative, but lately people have been saying to me that I cast a long shadow and that I'm rather strong . . . I used to call my staff "the girls" and I don't think they minded. They used to send me Christmas cards, "from Kaye's girls".'

Would she have terrible withdrawal symptoms?

'Ooh! I'm not going to stop,' said Kaye. 'I'm giving up the editing, but I'm going to keep the club going, and . . . well, there's a great many things I could help with at Penguins, and I have ideas . . .'

One of the last Puffins with her name on it was *I Like This Poem*. Teresa suggested that poetry was for middle-class children.

'Poetry middle-class? Oh, no! Every child in the world likes rhymes, starting with Hickory Dickory Dock. We asked them why they like each poem – it's usually "because it makes me happy", or "because I like the rhythm", or "because it's easy to remember".'

Do you think you will ever completely retire?

'No. I know I won't.'

When Peter Mayer left Penguin eighteen years later, in 1996, he looked around the office to see what souvenir he might take with him. And he chose Kaye's big curved desk, which reposes today in his country house at Woodstock in upstate New York.

14: Post Puffin

1980–85

I first met Kaye Webb in 1981, to write an article celebrating Puffin's fortieth birthday. With three daughters under five, I was well aware of Puffins, and of Kaye's heroine status. I found her in her book-and-picture-lined flat, seated by the window overlooking the canal, white-haired, still pretty and excellent company: quick-witted, amusing, and as enthiusiastic as ever about *Puffin Post*. I remarked on the 'fearsomely curious and polite' Puffineers. 'They have such zest,' Kaye said. 'That's what keeps us fresh.' And the Ronald Searle connection fascinated me. The walls of her flat still displayed Ronald's work. In the 1950s my cartoonist father had brought home all Searle's books, and I loved Molesworth. Being married to Ronald, Kaye said, had been 'a remarkable experience'. 'He's a genius, really.' Ronald's life had kept her busy for ten years, she said: but then she confessed that she really ought to have stayed married to Keith. 'All my life,' she said, 'my business life has worked out beautifully, with perfect timing. My private life has been the reverse.'

Iona Opie, who had recently lost her husband and collaborator Peter, pondered on these words when she read my *Evening Standard* interview, and wrote to Kaye: 'Looking back over my life & your life, it was just not possible for you & Ronald Searle to have our sort of marriage. I am the sacrificial sort; I was not so much subjugated as gave myself – eventually. And you are not that kind at all – much too splendidly outgoing (not the best word but I can't think of a better).'

My eldest daughter, Lucy, became (of course) a Puffin Club member. The next year, her name was picked from a hat to win a 'Golden Ticket' to visit Roald Dahl's home. I waved her off from outside Penguin's office at World's End, an apprehensive face in a coach packed with bright chattering Puffineers. But they had a marvellous day at Gipsy House. Dahl's daughter Lucy showed them the gypsy caravan in the garden, and the nicotine-stained hut where Dahl worked 'which had never been cleaned', and the BFG's sandals, which were actually Dahl's own. As they left, Roald himself came out and presented each child with a Jiffy bag full of Mars Bars, Maltesers, etc.

But after meeting Kaye I remember an impression of her wistfulness. She was so bitterly conscious of no longer being in charge at Puffin. It had been her emotional life as well as her job. 'I find really I'm only going on working to fill spaces between the morning and the night,' she would write to friends. She was 'in a sort of no man's land', feeling 'bereft and odd, not knowing quite what to do', she told busy Patrick Moore. 'Unlike you, I don't seem to have any great demands being made on me now, and I'm not used to that.'

Moore had been having a 'grim time' caring for his frail old mother, and Kaye, as always, offered help. Being semi-retired, she said, 'I can do a bit more travelling and seeing my friends'. He must not get into a frenzy about 'the wretched book' he had failed to deliver to Puffin. She longed to spend time by the sea: could she perhaps come down and help look after his mother? 'It really would feel quite nice to be useful, and Selsey sounds a wonderful place.' There was a note of desperation as she clung on to her author friends. To Mary Norton, whose new *Borrowers* book was 'enormous fun', she wrote: 'This is just to remind you that although I know I'm no longer your editor, sadly, I still hope that I'm your friend, and next time you come I would love to see you if you have a moment – I could buy you lunch or something.' When a postcard came from Laurie Lee after a long delay she wrote: 'I had thought perhaps you had decided that we weren't really to be part of your life in future.' Could she give him 'lunch, dinner, a movie, a theatre . . .'?

The Puffin exhibition was more exhausting than ever. Apart from Sylvia Mogg and Jill McDonald, her staff had gone: Felicity Trotman had an allergy to the new Penguin building, and left, eventually to start up Signpost Books with Dorothy Wood. Helen Nicoll resigned from *The Egg* after a falling-out with Kaye over a photograph of a mare giving birth to a foal. Ruth Petrie had left, and Philippa Dickinson was now Tony Lacey's deputy, leaving Kaye with 'young, inexperienced and somehow less imaginative people'. The magazines took up swathes of time, under new economic restraints. She had to turn down an invitation to New Zealand from Dorothy Butler (author of *Babies Need Books*) because 'overseas trips are no longer allowed'.

She had plenty of invitations – to Ursula Moray Williams's farmhouse or Joan Aiken's Hermitage, a rambling book-lined Regency house with log fires. But plans would be scuppered by the weather ('I seem to mind the cold so much') or her wretched arthritis, which sapped her energy and robbed her of mobility. She had a summer holiday in Canada with Kate, and spent Christmas in Tunisia with 'misanthropic' Patrick Crosse, to escape the festive season. With her twins both away, her alternative would have been 'whipping up friends to come, or being a poor sad lady joining in someone else's Christmas, neither an attractive prospect'. She went to Lyme Regis with Dorothea Duncan, but was too lame to walk along the front, didn't enjoy reading *Persuasion* and refrained from calling on John Fowles because Dorothea teased her so much about him ('Wasn't that silly?'). She had a new neighbour: Michael Bond, author of *Paddington*, a fan of Kaye's since 1947, when he had won a case of wine in a *Lilliput* caption contest. He had now bought a pretty house on the grander side of her street. The new Mrs Bond cooked lunch for Kaye, who carried off the leftovers, saying, 'Roald Dahl's coming, and he likes turkey legs.'

But unlike Noel Streatfeild, 'heroically un-sorry for herself' after a stroke – Noel had said she did not expect to be 'on this earth' much longer – Kaye could not stave off self-pity. 'I'm feeling just a little bit low at the moment because of not being at the centre of things,' she told Joan Aiken.

Most gallingly, the new Puffin team of Tony Lacey, Patrick Hardy and their sales director Barry Cunningham (who later discovered the Harry Potter books for Bloomsbury, which Penguin had turned down) quickly gave the Puffin imprint a revamp, making it more male, reaching a new type of reader. Lacey had gone to the 1980 Puffin Exhibition, manning the tills, and had to admit that 'for a publisher, seeing queues of children buying books was rather enjoyable'. But he deliberately made the Puffin covers 'less girly' and introduced the Fighting Fantasy interactive game books by Ian Livingstone and Steve Jackson. Twelve-year-old Patrick Bossert was selling 'how to solve the Rubik cube' sheets in his school playground in Richmond, Surrey, so Lacey paid him £100 to see if he could work his notes into a book, in which Puffin then acquired world rights. *You Can Do the Cube*, subtitled 'Simple step-by-step instructions on how to complete Rubik's Cube by schoolboy cubemaster Patrick Bossert', sold a million copies in six months. The Fighting Fantasy series was followed by Dungeons and Dragons. It was a highly successful period for Puffin, reaping immediate sales, but they were aware of Kaye's disapproval. Established authors, previously secure in the longevity of their esteem, found themselves labelled 'old-fashioned' and 'too literary'. 'The feeling of responsibility has gone,' Kaye told Nick Tucker, 'and it's been replaced by making money and selling any kind of book.' But Lacey's strategy was effective, after the limbo of Kaye's last years.

Kaye was not the first retiree to bridle thus. Eunice Frost, was edged out in her forties after devoting twenty years to Penguin, and 'spent the rest of her life in exile in Lewes, grumbling about the sad falling-off of the firm, bombarding former colleagues with letters and phone-calls, nursing that sense of grievance that is all too liable to afflict those who have entrusted their all to a firm or institution'.*

However, Kaye filled in time with reviews, broadcasting, hosting a party for Rosemary Sutcliff, and keeping in touch with 'her' authors. She and Joan Aiken exchanged views on 'poor old Richard Adams's' *Girl in a Swing*, which was withdrawn from circulation because Adams had used the real name of a woman friend. He had been devastated by this, said Kaye, but he 'bloody well deserved it'. She had acupuncture and other new treatments, and went to retreats in Sussex and Kent set in pleasant parkland, providing 'angelic people waiting to discuss your problems with you'. Tom Hopkinson, writing his memoirs, tapped into her memory bank about *Lilliput*. Kaye told Tom she was feeling 'forlorn'. With Kate in Canada, 'I don't seem to have any relatives left' and 'I can't bear to spend the rest of my days just lying around reading the odd book'. (Patrick Hardy would get regular memos from Peter Mayer instructing him to keep Kaye happy by sending a book.) 'You know me, I'm so gregarious I just don't like living alone, and working does at least mean you keep in contact with people.'

She wrote to Thora Hird, praising her performance on the *Parkinson* show, for 'telling it the way it was', unlike entertainers who embellished their stories. She sent her a copy of her 1949 interview with Thora 'for the autobiography which you will undoubtedly write one day', and invited Thora's grandchildren to join the Puffin Club. Thora replied that her grandchildren, the children of her actress daughter Janette Scott, lived in Beverly

* Jeremy Lewis, *Penguin Special*, Viking, 2005.

Hills; and she had already written her autobiography, *Scene and Hird*, years before. But she remembered Kaye: 'You were always so very smart,' she wrote.

Kaye did not lack projects and ideas. She said on radio that she would like to run a children's radio programme, and wrote to the *Telegraph* offering children's TV reviews because she had to watch the programmes for the magazine *Books for Your Children*. Sean Day-Lewis responded ('I think you knew my father') with apologies: he was 'unable to arouse any enthusiasm' for children's TV reviews. In the ensuing years, she was consulted by anyone starting a children's magazine (such as Thames TV's short-lived *Tele-reporter*) or a children's newspaper (Julia Watson was just getting her newspaper idea financed when she had to decamp to Moscow with her *Guardian* reporter husband.) She briefly became an agent for children's books, with Curtis Brown. But what excited her most was becoming a consultant to Jake Eberts's company, Goldcrest Films, suggesting children's stories that could be filmed for TV. In 1981 she became a limited company, Kaye Webb Productions, splitting profits with Goldcrest fifty-fifty. James Mason, at his 4 July fireworks party, wished her luck as 'the emerging David Puttnam'.

Her first film project was Ursula K. Le Guin's *The Wizard of Earthsea*. The great veteran British film director Michael Powell, aged seventy-six, had written to Le Guin asking why her book was a mere Puffin; Ursula replied, 'Because Kaye Webb's a smart cookie.' Armed with Powell's script and Le Guin's blessing, Kaye went to Sag Harbor in June 1981 to stay with a Goldcrest colleague: 'You see, I'm really getting into this wheeler-dealing aren't I?' she wrote to James Lee of Pearson Longman. But then came the rejection letter from Goldcrest: Powell's script was exotic, clever, original, and his name added to the project's potential, they said, but it would be expensive, and anyway they were 'committed to a very similar project entitled *Mandrake the* '

Magician'. Typical of the film world, but Kaye ground her teeth in frustration, she told Powell. Ursula wrote from Portland, Oregon, refraining from saying what she thought of Goldcrest: 'I'm sure the Post Office would confiscate the letter.'

Kaye next turned her attention to Rumer Godden's *The Dolls' House*. Rumer, in the highlands of Scotland, had just suffered a Christmas flood in her library that had ruined all her Puffins, but voiced a biblical stoicism: 'Oh well. He did not say "you will not be afflicted" but He said "you shall not be overcome".' Tony Lacey had offered to replace her Puffins for one-third the cover price, 'which is unexpectedly kind of him'. (Kaye intervened and had them sent without charge.) *The Dolls' House* was eventually made by Goldcrest into an animated TV series, with Oliver Postgate narrating, and the voice of Anna Calder-Marshall for Tottie Plantagenet.

It was now a struggle even to persuade her authors to contribute to *Puffin Post*. Everybody was so busy, partly thanks to her ('I'm committed up to my neck,' said the poet Charles Causley), and she had to pay them in books, not cash. 'Puffins and the Puffin Club have turned out to be rather like Ronald and St Trinian's,' she told Tom Hopkinson, 'a monster (except that it's a pleasant one) that I can't shake off.' She wanted to hand it on – but who else would spend the amount of time she did 'for so little financial reward, the Club being what it is – always hard up and trying to think of new ways of doing things on the cheap?'

But *Puffin Post* retained the Kaye Webb stamp, inspiring creativity in its readers. They still made fantastic collages of sandcastles with shells, lolly sticks, feathers, gorse and sand. Did you know, *Puffin Post* asked, you could roll a hibernating dormouse in a ball across the dining-room table without waking it up? Why not adopt a goose (£6) or a swan (£7.50) or a duck (£4) from Sir Peter Scott's Wildfowl Trust? Readers were invited to write a story about a stone. 'No stone books, please. Five stony prizes.' The 'Puffinvite' page contained a dozen children's book fairs, with Roald Dahl, Jan Pieńkowski and Errol Le Cain, the illustrator and animator with whom Kaye had recently established a fond rapport. TOMCAT the computer answered queries such as 'Do computers ever fall in love?' Uniquely among magazines, *Puffin Post* featured Fattening Food recipes, such as Sweet Fried Eggs, using Swiss roll, tinned peach halves and cream. (Kaye now styled herself not just Fat Puffin but the Fattest Puffin.) Nina Bawden wrote about her new book, *The Robbers*, and Jane Allan visited the set of *Stig of the Dump*, which Thames TV were making into a series. There were Puffin events at Madame Tussaud's, and on the *Tattershall Castle* on the Thames, got up as a pirate ship.

Imaginative readers submitted diaries of a Rolls-Royce owner, a workman with measles, a Cockney layabout, a uniformed nanny ('heart beating under that apron'), a burglar, an executive having a nervous breakdown, a tramp sharing his Christmas with a lonely puffin, an escaped convict going home to see his new baby 'for a few brief days of sweetness'. One young reader, Claire Rumball, produced the diary of a thoroughly unpleasant woman which began 'Why I married Norman I'll never know.' 'Louise Rowe's Henry Horrabil Hamwiche was a most attractive chap,' reported Kaye. Another prize-winner, Emmeline E. Vault, aged twelve, wrote a macabre diary of an obsessive cat collector. 'We'd like to see a short story by her one day,' wrote Kaye. Puffineers were preparing a 'Loving Tree' for Noel Streatfeild's eighty-fifth birthday: they painted little symbols from her books (a ballet shoe, an ice-skate, a tiny violin) to be hung on the tree, which Kaye would deliver to Noel at the Home for Distressed Gentlefolk at Vicarage Gate, Kensington, on her birthday, Christmas Eve. (She found the uncomplaining Noel sitting in the corridor in her nightie because she said it was 'less lonely' there.)

The Puffin Club was now fifteen, with a quarter of a million members past and present. Kaye went on the Noel Edmonds radio show for Puffin's fortieth birthday on 2 December 1981, celebrated with a new edition of *Worzel Gummidge*. She was robustly on the defensive with Edmonds. Don't the kids in the 1980s get their entertainment from other sources? he asked her. Oh no, Kaye said, under-twelves still got a kick from seeing their names in print. One Puffineer had published *The Pirate's Tale* at age five and three-quarters, and got into *The Guinness Book of Records*. Wasn't it all frightfully middle-class? 'No, because we have a schools' membership.' Edmonds turned to her private life: 'You were in the gossip columns in the 1950s, with Ronald Searle. What was that like?' 'Oh, it was marvellous,' said Kaye. 'You can't imagine anything more exciting than being married to someone who's so clever . . . It was like having a performance going on, I would go up to the studio and he'd be doing yet another wonderful drawing. It was fun, being married to a rising star, who became a star.'

The 1981 Puffin exhibition, at the Bishopsgate Institute in the City of London, was almost the last. Arthritis was 'giving me the devil' and poor Jill McDonald, so vital to the whole enterprise, was seriously ill. Kaye wrote the *Times* obituary when Jill died a few months later. It was a terrible blow. She had been 'a very special friend and a great source of inspiration', Kaye wrote to Jill's aunt, Lady Fleming, in New Zealand. 'There isn't any way that she can be replaced. In fact for various reasons – some of them of my making – I've decided not to go on editing *Puffin Post* in future but to hand it over to younger people. I think if it's going to have a new image, it should be altogether fresh and different – we can't just go on imitating darling Jill.'

So said Kaye, but she was not quite so robust when the axe actually fell. In 1982, there was another upheaval at Puffin. Peter Mayer set up the new adult hardback imprint Viking and appointed Tony Lacey as editorial director. Liz Attenborough, who knew Kaye well, took over at Puffin. Liz had joined Penguin in 1977 from

Heinemann, and had found it 'overwhelmingly wonderful to be in a company that loved children's books'; her office had been just outside Kaye's, so she had witnessed the 'Kaye-os', the authors coming and going, the excitement of birthdays when everyone wore Puffin pink, and glasses of Puffin's Pleasure were served.

But Liz, who had published the Ahlbergs' *Each Peach Pear Plum* (which Kaye had turned down for Puffin), had to deal with a far tougher children's book scene. Fighting Fantasy books were still top sellers, along with Dahl; every year she would send Dahl his personal bestseller list as *Fantastic Mr Fox*, or *The BFG*, or *Matilda*, or *The Witches*, or *Charlie*, or *Danny*, vied with one another. Dahl naturally loved this. 'We needed these big sales,' Liz says, 'because so many licences, Arthur Ransome for instance, had reverted to their hardback publisher. People still assumed that anything good would be in Puffins, so it was quite a reputation to maintain.'

The Penguin children's division now embraced Longmans, Blackie, Hamish Hamilton and Frederick Warne, which gave them Beatrix Potter – which Kaye later tried to get filmed for television. But Kaye was about to go into hospital again, and Liz appointed a bright young teacher, Eunice McMullen, to run the Puffin Club.

'I nearly rang you up to weep on your shoulder,' Kaye told Joan Aiken. She was trying to be rational, knowing she could not have gone on for ever. She knew she would never find another Jill McDonald. 'Besides which, I do realize that younger people have to move in. They're not kicking me out, they're just making me a consultant, whatever that means . . . They want me to be around to discuss general Puffin publishing, which is a bit ironic since I've not had anything to do with it for two years, and . . . I don't really know what's going on in the children's book world any more.'

But she had not realized how deeply attached she was to her Club. 'I suppose it was really a home from home, a makeup for all the grandchildren they've never seen fit to present me with,' she told Joan. 'I'm beginning to think that neither of my kids will produce.' Liz Attenborough learned a lesson from observing Kaye that year. 'One day Kaye came into the office and seemed shocked to find Tony Lacey sitting at her old curved desk. She came through to my office and wept. "I know I'm an old has-been and nobody wants me around," she said. What was worse, her authors had stopped ringing her, stopped writing to her and coming for Sunday lunch: "And I thought they were my friends!" This was a fundamental lesson to us all. I always tell new staff, you must not put everything into your job. You must have a life outside.'

Kaye tried to be robust after that day in June 1982: 'I've just come back from Penguins,' she told Gloria Sheekman, 'and am feeling very doleful because they're quite happily running the Puffin Club without me – I'd always felt that they simply wouldn't be able to cope and would have to call me back. They're doing very well, unfortunately, so it's a pretty salutory [*sic*] lesson!'

William Mayne dedicated his new book, *Winter Quarters*, to Kaye. Joan Aiken dedicated *How to Write for Children* to her, telling her, 'You should have written it really.' Patrick Crosse took her off to the Dead Sea 'for a bit of treatment and sun'. She resolved to become a New Woman after she'd got her new hip that summer. Her surgeon instructed her to lose a stone, and she managed to shed 10lb. She had the operation at St Thomas' Hospital, in a room with a view of the House of Commons terrace. Paul Godfrey, who was doing a summer vac job at Harrods, knew she longed for ice-cream; he took the tube to Westminster, bought a cone from a street vendor and sprinted over Westminster Bridge like an Olympic athlete with a torch, the ice dripping, to her fifth-floor room.

Paul's success in Oxford theatre was a source of maternal pride for Kaye. She went to see his production of *Peer Gynt*, and warned him not to get too distracted by theatre: 'You really would feel annoyed with yourself if you left Oxford without at least a 2nd

– and I'm afraid it is going to make a difference in the work stakes later on. Gosh I sound like your Mum!' she wrote. But as Paul says, he left Oxford with a third, 'and it never made any difference'. After Oxford he became a trainee director at Perth Rep, where he was soon adapting *A Christmas Carol*.

Kaye was pessimistic about her son John's imminent return from Ireland too. 'At the age of 35 with no training except in journalism, goodness knows what my poor son will do,' she told Gloria Sheekman. 'I wish I could think of a business we could start.' However, she reported to Ronald, now living in Provence, that the twins were both well and happy. 'I hope you are also – certainly the article in the *Sunday Times* gave that impression,' she wrote.★

Patrick Crosse restored Kaye's joie-de-vivre in the spring of 1983 by taking her to Sri Lanka, a land 'full of charm and smiles and niceness'. Patrick organized it beautifully, she told Gloria. 'I had a perfectly lovely carefree time with him paying the bills and the waiters and checking on the hotel rooms, the lot. In fact, although there was no personal relationship in it, it was just like being married again and taken care of – my goodness, doesn't that make a difference to one.'

As she approached her seventieth birthday, she became less confident about her Goldcrest job; but without that, 'what would I do when I woke up in the mornings?' she asked Gloria. 'One

★ Philip Norman, who wrote the 1982 *Sunday Times* article about the Searles in Provence, had found that Ronald was still working 'like a man possessed' at sixty. 'He gets up at six, fetches the bread and reads the paper,' Monica told Philip. 'Then he works for eleven hours. It's all he ever wants to do.' This was a rare intrusion from the British press. But anyone who breached the Searle stronghold received a gratifying welcome. Martin Amis, who wrote about the Searles in 1977 for the *Sunday Telegraph*, said he was 'greeted as if my presence were a key part of some rare and complicated treat they had long promised themselves'.

has to have A Purpose . . . and I'm not a wonderful painter like you, and my writing is definitely on the commonplace side.' She felt out of touch, no longer interested in children's current passions. 'Space fiction bores me, as does all that wretched rock and roll. I need to have grandchildren to keep me up to the mark, and they haven't turned up.'

Julia Watson's bold but abortive children's newspaper project (in the face of W. H. Smith's warning that the only successful kids' magazines were called *Soccer* or *Pop Hits*) excited her for a while, as did her brief time as an agent at Curtis Brown, until disillusion set in. 'I think I get too involved with the authors and worry in case they haven't been sent to the right publishers. Nice people in the office, but can't spend all my time worrying.'

Her seventieth birthday was duly celebrated by Puffin with tributes from her authors and illustrators. At home, in the flat where she now felt restless – it was 'too big and not too tidily planned' and the main rooms faced north and saw no sun – she began to sort out her things so that the children wouldn't have too much to deal with 'in 5 or 10 years time, or whatever it is', she told her old boss John Grigg. She had just sold Grigg's gift of a George Orwell holograph, which she had always kept in her box of treasures. University College, home of the Orwell archive, had bought it 'for a really most impressive sum', and she proposed giving Grigg half the money. (Grigg spurned her cheque. 'A present is a present – absolute and unqualified. You wouldn't expect me to compensate you if it went down in value, so why should I be rewarded if it goes up?') Liz Attenborough too was summoned by Kaye, and offered Quentin Blake's drawing of Kaye surrounded by puffins. 'She thought Puffin should have it, she said, and added, "I could do with the money."' The price was £80, so Liz, bemused, bought it. (Kaye later discovered that the drawings she possessed were worth considerably more. In 1988, Richard Usborne had Sotheby's estimate the value of the half-dozen she had lent him, including a Ronald Searle, a Pont, a Brockbank and an Emett, and they came to £4,000.)

In the past decade Kaye had been sporadically collecting material for a *Lilliput* anthology, tracing writers and photographers to get their permissions – 'What idiots we were not to keep everything!' – and this now bore fruit: *Lilliput Goes to War* was published in July 1984. She hated Hutchinson's 'horrible' cover, 'which has taken all the fun out of it for me'. 'It really is vulgar and yet the Hutchinson sales people like it,' she told Alison (Blair) Hooper. But Tom Hopkinson hosted a launch party at the Photographers' Gallery, and the book got excellent notices. Kaye was interviewed on Radio 4's *Bookshelf* by Hunter Davies, who played a hilarious example of one of *Lilliput*'s features – the excuses heard by a billeting officer for not taking in evacuee children, including 'My husband snores'; 'My husband keeps his fishing tackle in the spare room'; 'My house is nicely furnished'; 'Not a London child! We have heard such things about London children'; and 'I'm sorry but I can't be doing with this war at all.' They talked of the 'kindlier sense of humour' of the 1940s, represented by the ironies in the juxtaposed photographs. 'What about the nudes then?' asked Davies. 'Well, Stefan liked nudes. And it was the pictures of the girls that got the fan-mail,' said Kaye. Alas, her book flopped. Four years later she told one friend it had sold just 300 copies, and no friend had ever been able to find it in any shop, ever.

Everyone continued to be concerned for Kaye's bones and joints. Roald Dahl, in a poor state himself ('nearly snuffed it'), recommended his own homoeopathic doctor. Dahl would drop him a note telling him to treat Kaye with respect. 'After the session, you shyly hand him a ten pound note which he folds into a little square and slips into his waistcoat pocket . . . Do go, then pop in here afterwards.' Kaye became a great enthusiast for homoeopathy.

But she felt like an 'old crock' and had a shoulder operation.
Keith and Barbara sent her a bedcape, as she recuperated at
Osborne House, alongside old generals and colonels with new
hips, telling Keith that 'claiming to be the ex-wife of a Group-
Captain got me in!' Mary Norton offered Kaye her houses in
Devon or Ireland. Maurice Edelman's sister Sophia in Santa
Monica offered a holiday in the California sun. (Sophia proposed
a biography of Edelman, but Kaye had to remind her that with
Edelman's books out of print, it would not be commercially
viable 'in this rotten publishing climate'.) But travelling was now
impossible. She could not even visit Richard Kennedy ('I do miss
you – I do wish you lived nearer'). Life was beginning to be 'quite
boring when you can't get out'. But in May 1985 she was, at last,
a grandmother, as John's wife Gisele had a 'glorious' son, Daniel.
Everyone was sent snaps of 'John's wonderful, wonderful baby'
. . . 'a super child'.

15: 'I like things to end happily'

1986–96

'It may be that my publishing experience is now becoming a little old-fashioned,' Kaye wrote to Quentin Blake. 'I certainly find myself baring my teeth at some of the illustrations I see, and some of the covers even good old Puffins are using, so I think I'm perhaps moving into the Eleanor Graham area now – "what was good was in the past".' Q had invited her to address his Royal College of Art students about illustration in June 1986, when he declined (too busy) her request to illustrate her revived 'Birthday Books'.

Q sent her a drawing of an old lady sitting at her virginals, while two dancing mice chant 'We're doing our "get-well-soon-please-Kaye" dance.' Yes, Kaye was in hospital again: the leitmotif of her last decade. She had a second hip replacement, an ankle fused, a shoulder operation, treatment for a slipped vertebra. Much correspondence was conducted from hospital beds, by dictation to her secretary Denise Pearce. 'I really must be one of the most boring friends anybody has ever had,' she would write. Increasingly stoical, she carried on trying to get *The Borrowers* televised, and always bolstered her correspondents. When Ted Hughes wrote to Charles Causley about Causley's anthology *Early in the Morning*, saying it was 'full of little masterpieces', and suggested making it into a musical ('a Chagall sort of *Under Milk Wood* Cornish dream'), Causley sought Kaye's advice: wasn't she connected with a children's theatre? Kaye, instantly enthusiastic, said the Unicorn would do it charmingly – but lightness and fantasy might be hard to achieve because 'the little darlings could be so very solid, and perhaps heavy-footed'. She saw it more ambitiously as a television film, set on a fairground merry-go-round, 'boats swinging backwards and forwards, slides, anything which made the effect of light movement – of poetry'. Perhaps the imaginative new head of Thames TV children's programmes would do it. 'I do hope something comes out of all this. It's nice to think this rotten stay in hospital has given me time to push it on a bit.'

Causley got it right when he imagined Kaye finding hospital exasperating, 'with so many notions, ideas, commitments sculling round inside your head'. She so wanted to be occupied and needed. She was often asked to speak, or to read the stories people had written, or to help raise funds; the Opies' fine collection of rare children's books could go to the Bodleian Library if they could raise half a million pounds. In her fund-raising experience, wrote Kaye, 'you scream with delight if you get £100 from a donor'. And she was constantly urged to write her life story. 'How is the autobiography going?' friends would ask. She must have time on her hands, said Richard Kennedy: her memoirs 'would be very therapeutic for both of us & I could illustrate it'. (When Kaye sent her recollections about Mervyn Peake to Brian Sibley, she asked him to put 'copyright Kaye Webb' beneath, 'as I need it for my reminiscences'.)

What she wanted more than anything was to have people around her. 'I'm pretty housebound at the moment, but delighted to have visitors . . . I live in a most convenient place overlooking the Canal,' became a refrain. Luckily Kate returned from Canada in the summer of 1986 and started work in props at the Royal Opera House, Covent Garden. Kaye was thrilled, proud of her daughter's artistic skill and inventiveness. Kate bought a house in Hove, because Kaye so loved being by the sea.

Noel Streatfeild died on 11 September 1986, at ninety-one. Seven years later Kaye wrote the *Dictionary of National Biography* entry on Noel, for their usual fee of £50. She extolled her generosity in encouraging young writers, and in replying to every child who wrote to her. 'Noel was a tall woman with a fine carriage, perhaps the result of her stage training,' Kaye wrote, 'and famous for elegance. She often wore a mink coat and her very lovely hands were regularly manicured with red nail polish. Even in her last months in a nursing home, she had red reading glasses.'

Kaye knew exactly how her authors felt as they got older: she was their confidante. They were a preternaturally upbeat set of women, but even Rumer Godden bridled at younger, unfamiliar publishers ('Philippa Harrison being very Queen Bee . . . I should so like to end my days in peace with a publisher') as decreasing royalties diminished her freedom, 'which is what I mind most'. Joan Aiken had written, 'I know you say I write too much, but I really have to, to keep afloat. Oh to sell just ONE film right, or have just ONE TV serial, so I could lay off for a year.' One highly successful young author confessed to being in a gloom about her unlucky choice of men. Kaye told her that the next time she met a man, she must bring him for her to vet. 'I suppose in the end we really do have to become satisfied with our own lives and take any outside affection and love as a trimming,' Kaye wrote. 'I'm a fine one to talk – but the seven weeks in hospital with absolutely nobody I could talk to except my occasional visitors has led me to a lot of self-examination.'

The Whittington Hospital, then a bleak and depressing place, sorely tried Kaye in the winter of 1986–7, leaving her in plaster, with metal bits in her ankle, unable to walk for a month. 'I've learned a lot being in hospital. I mean I've learned a lot about the desperate awful sadness of being old and alone.' She had met five old ladies with broken hips who could not return to their flats, and would 'have to end up in any old home that will have them, plus one who's going to a hospice, never to come out again. If I really let myself, I would weep from morning until night, though most of the time I get so bloody angry about how insensitive people are.'

Helpless old patients were treated casually and heartlessly, she told Gloria Sheekman. 'There's so much tragedy in this 22-bed ward that it's almost unbearable. Really the most important thing in life is for everybody to have a lot of family, half these old ladies haven't got a soul in the world (and will have to go into Homes where they will sit around until they die).'

Paul Godfrey left Perth Rep, having already achieved an impressive body of work. His adaptation of *James and the Giant Peach* was staged at the Westminster Theatre, and Roald Dahl came to see it, thanks to Kaye. In March 1987, after a silence, Paul got back in touch with Kaye. He recalled 'opening *The Times* and seeing Philip's face on the front'. (This was Philip Geddes, another devotee of Kaye's, a Time Capsule guardian, who was one of six people killed by the IRA bomb outside Harrods in December 1983. Geddes, a journalist, had been at the same Oxford college as Paul, and once took Kaye to a Commem Ball, and gave a black-tie dinner beforehand with the menu written in Puffin-ese.)

Kaye expressed relief at hearing from Paul again. She sent him the Causley poems which she 'and Ted Hughes too' thought would make 'a frightfully good children's show'. Paul's lovely mural in her bathroom, she had to tell him, was no more. Having failed to sell her flat, she had had her bathroom adapted, and when a wall came down, the mural came with it. (Paul said he was sad about it, 'but I've never claimed to be Michelangelo'.)

She was glad to have Paul's good memories of Puffin Club times. 'Mine are a bit low at the moment because they're closing it down,' she told him. 'At the end of this year there'll be no more Puffin Club members. The magazine will just be sent to schoolteachers and sold directly to children, but the Club side of it is going to evaporate because they say it was costing them too much money. They also said it wasn't reaching a wide enough audience – I thought we had been building up a pretty good membership in schools, but it did take a lot of devoted work, and once I'd gone, and practically everybody who had been on the Club had gone off to be editors and things, the new girls saw it much more as a job.'

Closing the Puffin Club was Liz Attenborough's decision. 'We were down to under 20,000 members and spending a fortune on getting new members. Children would be given membership by their grandparents, but wouldn't renew when it expired. We had more staff running the club, writing personal letters to the children, than on Puffin publicity and marketing. So we decided to keep the brilliant magazine and send it out through our schools' book club. Oddly enough it was parents who most objected – "We are appalled to learn that you are closing the Puffin Club," they would write. "We loved it even though our children have long left home."'

Paul Godfrey wrote consolingly. His work was ephemeral – 'Theatre is gone like air,' he said – but Kaye's inspiration to children would always remain. 'Wasn't it H. G. Wells who described immortality as achievable when your name was printed more than eight thousand times? If that's true you've done it several times over.' Paul was writing his first original verse play, *Inventing a New Colour*. 'There's suddenly been a flow of words within me, unstoppable and like never before.' Kaye told him to send it to the Royal Court. A week before Paul's twenty-seventh birthday, Kate Harwood at the Royal Court told Paul she found the verse 'direct and expressive', 'and the characters really lived with all their imperfections and dilemmas'. The Royal Court would stage a reading – and so would the National.

In a state of euphoria, Paul waxed lyrical about his new riverside home at Strand-on-the-Green, with a view of boats and willows. He described the sparkling water reflected on the ceiling of his room, a cobweb strung with dewdrops by the railway, and the fun of going out rowing at night. Three doors away lived another Time Capsule guardian, Zoë Teale. He discovered this when he rang Sylvia Mogg to suggest a tenth anniversary reunion of the guardians 'to emphasize our existence to Penguin Books'. Zoë was going up to Oxford to read English and Paul gave her his old wind-up gramophone, to use when punting on the Cherwell.

When his play opened at the Royal Court, Kaye had to be hoisted into her seat by stage-hands. She hadn't cared for the script, but was 'knocked out' by the performance, Paul says, and she told him: 'What I've learned is that I don't know anything about theatre.'

Laid out flat for several months, in hospitals in London and Hove, Kaye was an object of much sympathy. Joan Aiken encouraged her to draw, enclosing some chalks and a little sketch book, 'and two postcards to fill you with emulation – do please try them – it really is a wonderfully peaceful occupation'. Keith Hunter wrote, sorry not to be there to dole out sympathy, a 'reversal of roles from 1938 eh? Heavens that's almost half a century ago.'

By 1988 most Time Capsule guardians were into their twenties, and their newsletter resembled a college yearbook. Its editor, Sarah Davnall, had produced a 'guardianship heir', now eight months old. Other guardians were equally busy: one was a local councillor, working for the rehabilitation of prisoners; one was the mother of three children and was running a Lake District farm. One Puffineer, doing a PhD at Cambridge, sang in a university choir, was learning book-binding, and was secretary of the Cambridge Antiquarian Society. One was doing a degree in speech therapy. Alison Cartledge was in her final year in theatre design, writing a thesis on the Russian Revolution and the arts.

Niall Mackenzie was in the Cabinet Office and rowed for the Civil Service team. Catherine Badger, an Oxford graduate, had been interviewed in the *Observer* as a 'City High Flier!' And Paul Godfrey was about to have his second play, *A Bucket of Eels*, performed at the Royal Court.

With regret Sarah reported that the Puffin Club was to close, deemed 'not cost-effective'. 'Where does this leave us?' she wondered. Did anybody, apart from the Guardians, care about the Time Capsule any more? Should they just forget about it? Should they pass their guardianship over to the Puffin Schools Club? Professor Akers, who had masterminded the Time Capsule, hoped it would endure, since 'paper conservators of the 21st century would be able to gain much useful information from it, and it would be of immense educational value . . . to librarians and archivists'.

Brian Alderson had been re-reading early *Puffin Post*s 'with unalloyed delight', and wrote to remind Kaye 'what wonders you performed with that magazine – and that Club – and to bemoan how much we have now lost. The "industrialization" of children's books – the manipulation of responses – the neglect of the free enjoyment so evident in those old *Post*s, is a sad decline. How could it have happened when you showed everyone what was possible?' Kaye agreed, wistfully: *Puffin Post* had become 'commonplace' and she was wondering 'if that 20 years hard slog was a bit of a waste'.

The inexorable rise of the computer was a fact of life. Whenever possible Kaye spoke on radio about encouraging children's book-reading habits. She took part in a lengthy LBC phone-in, during which she admitted that her Peacocks series had failed: 'Teenagers didn't really want to be seen among the children's books. Now they call them Puffin Plus, which is much more sensible.' Parents, she said again, had to communicate their own enthusiasm, and demonstrate to their children that books were useful when travelling, in trains or at airports. 'Books are about the only thing children can take with them, anywhere at any time.'

Listeners rang in asking about Sue Townsend, Anthony Horowitz and other recent top-selling children's authors. Kaye felt on safer ground talking of Rosemary Sutcliff and Roald Dahl, whose autobiography, *Boy*, she commended; otherwise she advised parents to consult children's bookshops like the Puffin Bookshop in Covent Garden, which 'gives you a jolly good day out too', and magazines like *Books for Children*, *Books for Keeps*, *The Good Book Guide* and *The Best Books of the Year*. Lynne Reid Banks, Joan Lingard and Susan Cooper wrote intelligent books about current problems, she said, and she recommended *On Your Bike*, about jobs children can do to make money. When Judy Blume was mentioned, she quickly rejoined, 'Oh, Betsy Byars is far better than her.' Most of all she wanted to stress that 'a book is going to go on. A book doesn't need any other mechanical device.'

Many Puffins had become television drama serials – Nina Bawden's *Carrie's War*, Joan Aiken's *Arabel and Mortimer*, the Narnia books. ('Do you watch *Narnia*?' asked Joan Aiken. 'I think it disgusting, but then I always hated the books. Can't stand that mix of father Xmas, fauns, nymphs, dreadfully plain 1930s-style children & Christian religion – ugh!') Anna Home, who ran the BBC children's drama department, hosted a seventy-fifth birthday lunch for Kaye, who was hoping she would ask her to be a consultant, 'but no', Kaye told Rumer Godden, 'I just have to accept that my days are past and I'm just thought of affectionately as a good old girl who did the job once.'

Jenni Murray asked her, on *Woman's Hour*, how to recommend books to 'the child of today'. Kaye replied that she would say, 'if you don't read, you won't get to learn a lot of words, and if you don't have a good vocabulary, you're never going to be able to say what you really think or feel about anything. So as well as all the fun of having adventures by yourself – and it's the only thing you can do by yourself – you will learn to say exactly what you feel and what you want, and that will be very useful when you grow up.'

Age did not wither her keenness to take on new projects. She asked Christopher Fry to write a novel for Ladybird, who paid 'quite decently' – £1,000 and a 3 per cent royalty – and sold in enormous quantities. 'I know it sounds rather odd to have me, the Puffin perfectionist, having to do with Ladybird but nobody else has offered me a job,' she told Fry. 'At least it keeps me living in this flat which otherwise I probably couldn't afford.' She was still working on her 'Birthday Books' idea – now for Paul Hamlyn's Octopus Books. She hoped to produce (with John Phillips directing) a TV film about Michael and Clare Morpurgo's Farms for City Children, which every year provided 1,000 children from the inner cities with the experience of country life at their farm in Devon. Kingfisher Books asked her to find 'books that aren't quite classics but which people treasure' to reprint: the omnivorous reader Joan Aiken sent a list of possibles from the 1920s and 30s, including *Lost Legends of the Nursery Songs* by Mary Senior Clark, 'with fine pictures in *Yellow Book* style by Alice B. Woodward'. But the series foundered.

In idle moments Kaye looked into her Webb family history, and discovered Laurence Webb, son of her father's brother Harold, with whom Arthur had fallen out. She told Laurence of another cousin, her uncle Fred's daughter, Joyce Cassettari, a successful businesswoman who ran the Chinacraft shop in Bath, and proposed opening a shop called Penny Plain Tuppence Coloured. Any new person coming into Kaye's life caused great delight and would be invited to tea: Keith's daughter, the publisher Angela Elkins, went regularly, and the children's illustrator and writer Joanna Carey held a tea-party for Kaye at her home, complete with a musical cabaret. Hannah Cole, the ex-Puffineer who now wrote children's books, offered to drive Kaye to see friends in her VW Polo, 'not too encrusted with crisp-packets'. When Kaye needed someone to help rearrange her furniture and books, Ruth McCarthy (a friendly publisher who often rang just to chat) sent along 'a nice, polite, strong sixth-former' who, to Kaye's delight, proved to be Stephen Kinnock, son of Neil. And best of all, the new star comedienne Victoria Wood had come to live in the flat next door, having just moved from the north, with two-year-old daughter Grace, and pregnant with son Harry. Victoria knew Kaye's name from Puffins in her childhood – Eve Garnett was a favourite, and Molesworth was one of her heroes. So she was thrilled when Kaye knocked on her door, with her flat full of books and fascinating stuff: she was 'the perfect neighbour'. 'For Grace's third birthday party we sat in our flat with paper hats on, just the three of us, having cherry cake.' Later Grace and Harry were allowed to ride on Kaye's electric wheelchair, pressing the buttons, whizzing about and cannoning into Kaye's hatstand, laughing hysterically. 'She used to say about the children, "Don't you just want to sit and look at them all the time?" and when I moved out and bought a house I felt bad about leaving Kaye.'

Friends dwindled, as they were bound to: Tom Hopkinson died, Rosemary Sutcliff died, Alison Blair died. James Mason had died in 1985: Kaye was incensed to find, in Sheridan Morley's biography of Mason, *Odd Man Out*, that she had been quoted verbatim. 'I would certainly never have said I thought James married Clarissa because he was lonely (I know how deeply in love he was).' She claimed not to have realized, when she chatted to Morley on tape, that her words would be used. 'I . . . thought we were having an informal talk.' Morley, Kate wrote, had 'damaged a very important friendship', and she begged to be removed altogether from any reprint.

Having managed to rush down to console Pauline Baynes when her husband Fritz suddenly died, Kaye remained a steadfast friend, sending cheering letters and flowers at Christmas. Pauline was still in great demand, working feverishly on Narnia illustrations for Brian Sibley's C. S. Lewis biography, and a new Tolkien; she felt 'like a bit of elastic, fully stretched'. 'It's wonderful to be <u>asked</u> – but, with 6 acres – a huge garden – & dogs' walks – hoovering, dusting etc & shopping – all the things that Fritz used to look after so efficiently – to cope with – it's almost too much!' Her Rottweilers anchored her to her cottage, and often got into chases or fights with foxes and badgers. But they were 'worth the anchoring. It's an enormous comfort to have Bertha stretched out on Fritz's bed – especially if I've just listened to something frightening on the radio & TV.'

Kaye was even more anchored, being housebound, but it did not cramp her sociable instincts. She was always willing to be wheeled into a party, and was winched aboard the *Barracuda* on the Thames for a celebration of forty years at Penguin for Betty Hartel, once Allen Lane's secretary and now Peter Mayer's. And the anthologies Kaye edited in her last years were an ideal sedentary occupation. *I Like This Story* in 1986 contained 'a taste of' her fifty favourite children's books. As editor of 1,000 Puffins, choosing just fifty was hard, and she dismissed it as 'a rather awful book', guilty at leaving out so many of her authors. *Meet My Friends* in 1991 was another set of Puffin extracts, featuring characters like Mole, Ratty, Badger and Toad, Milly-Molly-Mandy, Ramona, Captain Pugwash and Olga da Polga. An anthology of poems for six-year-olds, *Round About Six*, was launched at the Canonbury Academy in 1992, but she felt it didn't merit a launch. It was no longer her book, since artwork and verses she hadn't wanted had been added. (But Charles Causley told her: '*Round About Six* is a peach of a book!')

By far the best and most enduring anthology was *Family Tree*, published in 1994. She compiled it 'because a little girl wrote and asked me, are there any books with quarrels in them, because my family always seems to be quarrelling but no one else's does'. Inspired to look into a cornucopia of literature proving that there are many different kinds of family, and supplied with a sheaf of lists from the London Library, she soon regretted having begun. 'I realized I was into anthropology in a big way . . . It shows that when you're not educated you shouldn't take on educated ideas,' she confessed, appealing for help from friends. Felicity Trotman proposed some excellent material; others Kaye rejected, including Joan Aiken's suggestion of mawkish Victorian pieces like Coventry Patmore's 'The Toys' ('My little son, who looked from thoughtful eyes . . .'). She divided her volume into parents, siblings and grandparents, ending with 'Aunts, Uncles and Some Disagreeable Cousins'. The result was lively, comprehensive and witty, mixing classics by Edmund Gosse and Mark Twain with contemporary verses from Spike Milligan, Roger McGough and Kit Wright. It remains the kind of anthology that yields plums on every page: Eleanor Farjeon's 'I quarrelled with my brother'; Eve Garnett's Mr Ruggles, contented father of seven; Michael Rosen's 'I'm Waiting for My Mum'; Charles Causley's forgetful Reverend Sabine Baring-Gould, who asked his own daughter, 'Whose pretty child are you?' Every entry was meant to be read aloud. Kaye was rightly proud of this, her last book, eventually published on her eightieth birthday.

As she began her research in 1990, Roald Dahl, 'feeling rotten what with gout and complicated blood disorders', was asked to edit an anthology of stories, and proposed that Kaye do it instead; he and Kaye could each contribute a short preface. 'I'm buggered if I am going to do 5,000 words,' he wrote. 'And obviously there's no money in it for either of us as it's for charity.' (But Kaye was going 'back to hospital again, dammit' for a synovectomy or a pair of new knees.) Five months later Roald died, aged seventy-four, on 23 November 1990. At his funeral Peter Mayer paid tribute to a Big Friendly Giant 'whose kindness and help to others seemed boundless', who 'had far, far more than his fair share of life's tragedies and illnesses'. Dahl's widow, Liccy, wrote to Kaye: 'During his life he failed at very few things but I know that one thing he always felt he had failed with was getting you made a Dame of the British Empire. His respect for the work you did for children's literature was gigantic and splendiferous.'

Kaye, too, unabashedly felt that she deserved a greater honour than her MBE of fifteen years before. In July 1990, she sent *Stig of the Dump* and the *Puffin Annual* to Prince Charles, for his sons. Alistair Watson, RN, wrote from St James's Palace: 'I have laid these before His Royal Highness who, I know, would wish me to thank you very much indeed for sending them.' Charlotte Cory took up her case and told her, 'I am writing to Buck House regarding you-know-what, and shall pursue the matter remorselessly because if anyone ought to be a Dame and wear one of those cloaks and great glittering badges (after all the treasured badges you used to bestow) it's you! I shall get up a bit of a lobby – so, let's hope!'

Charlotte, not knowing that Kaye already had an MBE, did write to 10 Downing Street, and got a letter from Lindsay Wilkinson about 'further recognition for Miss Webb' which would be considered 'fully and carefully'. No further recognition came. Kaye's unfulfilled and 'absurd' desire to be a Dame mystified friends. At her funeral, Naomi Lewis said: 'A Dame? Pshaw. Ridiculous. She was a Queen, and her wand wasn't made of tinsel.'

Roald Dahl had been expected to be the cornerstone of Puffin's fiftieth anniversary celebrations in 1991; his daughter Tessa, a former Puffineer, took his place. Liz Attenborough appointed Sally Gritten, newly arrived from America, to organize the celebration and to write a short history of Puffin. Charlotte

Cory, who had just had her first novel accepted by Faber, organized a Puffin Club reunion where everyone read out their winning entries from *Puffin Post* to put on the wall. 'We were all pretending to be Puffin members again. Then Kaye mentioned Philip Geddes. I opened a *Puffin Post* and there was his name – Volume 5 number 4, page 24 – with a picture of the elements, and ohmigod, his story was about a bomb. It ended: "Bang! Dust." The room had been full of laughter; and suddenly we all stopped and looked at each other and were moved to tears.'

The latest Puffin Guardians' newsletter, in 1991, gave further updates on the lives of Puffineers. One was a nurse, married to an inner-city minister in London. One was not only a personnel officer in the probation service, but also a Tawny Owl for a Brownie pack, and was trying her hand at pottery. One was painting cork boxes, and another was a hydro-geologist in America. One was working for the Northumbrian Wildlife Trust. Zoë Teale was teaching English in Japan, before starting a Master's degree in anthropology at the LSE; Paul Godfrey had written the libretto for an opera at Covent Garden. Not everyone had achievements to report: one Puffineer confessed to having had 'a quiet year' but had made a number of new friends. 'That's always good news!' wrote the newsletter editor, in true Puffineer style.

They were all invited to the V&A on 20 June, where there was a Giant Puffin Birthday Cake created by Jan Pieńkowski, which you could walk inside to find a display of Puffin books and which would go on show at the Edinburgh Festival in August. Kaye arrived in her wheelchair ('trapped in your chariot' as Haro Hodson put it). Yehudi Menuhin could not be there, but sent 'particular love and admiration to our wonderful Kaye Webb'. Kaye, everyone agreed, still looked beautiful, and made a memorable and witty speech about the Puffin Club, taking in all the triumphs and the disasters like Lundy Island. 'I must say I have enjoyed myself these past few weeks,' she wrote, 'and only wish I still had something to do with the books.'

She asked Rumer Godden, 'Do you wake up in the morning being glad for the day?' and Rumer replied that she did. But Rumer also sent her some consoling lines from Frances Cornford's poem 'A Wasted Day':

> Let me forget,
> Let me embark,
> Sleep for my boat,
> And sail through the dark.
>
> Till a new day
> Heaven shall send,
> Whole as an apple,
> Kind as a friend.

Kaye wrote to Rumer, who persisted in urging her to start on her memoirs: 'The idea of writing my life story fills me with greater trepidation every single day. I'm more and more convinced that I've nothing particularly interesting to say and as I find typing tiresome and writing worse, and I don't seem to have much flair for dictating, I don't see how it will ever get done. And if it doesn't, why then I've got nothing else to do. I keep looking at these little books they keep pushing out as easy readers, Kites and so on, and they seem so thin and unsatisfactory . . .' (Michael Morpurgo was judging the Smarties Prize that year, and agreed with her: 'A mass of badly written stories, mediocre and imitative, poorly illustrated and unimaginatively designed.')

'Oh Kaye,' Rumer responded, 'you have so much to tell that no one else can tell that I wish, in spite of all the difficulties, that you would write this book.' If only she would start, a book would come. 'Even if you only do a little every day. It's an amazing thing with writers, all of us. When we know in our inmost hearts that there is something we should do. Even when we want above all else to do it, mysteriously we put it off and find every excuse not to. I do this all the time – one has to be stern with oneself.'

The only evidence that she did make a start are the notes on her early life, and some brief tape-recordings, in her archives. Kate, busy at the Opera House, would often stay overnight at Kaye's flat. On most weekends they would go down to Kate's house by the sea at Hove, where John, by now a single parent, would bring Danny, her adored grandson. These were the times Kaye enjoyed most in her last years, otherwise bedevilled by pain and sleeplessness. One day Kate found a kitten in the rain in King's Cross and brought her home to Kaye: Polly was quite feral, not a cuddlesome cat, but 'I hadn't realized what a difference it makes,' Kaye wrote to Rumer, 'to be greeted when you come back into the flat by something affectionate – or perhaps not affectionate so much as cheerful.'

Late in 1993, *Stig of the Dump* was relaunched as the first Puffin Modern Classic, along with others from Kaye's era: Russell Hoban's *The Mouse and His Child*, *Watership Down*, *Carrie's War*, *The Borrowers*, *The Silver Sword*, *Charlotte's Web* and *Tom's Midnight Garden*. Kaye wrote the introduction to *Stig*, and rang Clive King, now aged seventy-one, at his cottage in Norfolk. 'Your voice on the telephone really cheered up a drizzling February day. And it seems that, thirty years on, I am once again indebted to you for lifting STIG out of his dump and into Classic (as against classic) status. Indeed the debt is incalculable,' Clive wrote. 'STIG already contributes one of three pensions on which I subsist very comfortably in semi-retirement, enforced by recession and the refusal of publishers to publish anything new.' He enclosed an extract from his memoirs, which he would never complete because he had 'a superstitious reluctance to draw a bottom line under my own life'.

She continued to help other biographers. Miranda Seymour spent a morning discussing Robert Graves for her definitive life. She loved Kaye's treetop-level flat with its green shade, but felt sad for Kaye, and 'a life that had not got quite so much going for it after the glory of the Puffin years'. Kaye lent her some Graves manuscripts which showed how he revised his poems. If she wanted to sell these, Miranda said, she should offer them to the Berg Collection in New York or the University of Buffalo. She enclosed two of her own stories for Kaye's opinion: Kaye liked them, 'beautiful words, beautifully phrased, and imagination on top of that'.

On 30 May 1993 Kaye's turn came to star on *Desert Island Discs*, which fulfilled its usual purpose of giving the subject the chance to edit down their life to its pleasantest essentials. 'Approaching your ninth decade,' said Sue Lawley, 'do you still read children's books?' 'I'm astonished to find I prefer them,' said Kaye. 'I think because I'm a fairly soppy person and I like things to end happily.'

She chose Dame Janet Baker singing 'Where Corals Lie' ('I go to sleep by this music') and Jack Buchanan's 'Goodnight Vienna', remembering meeting Buchanan at a dinner party in Worthing in the 1930s. He had driven her, in her car, 'at breakneck speed' to Brighton. 'His wife was on the doorstep, and said I was the bravest woman — "Jack hasn't driven for years, he was stopped for dangerous driving."' She played her tape of Walter de la Mare talking to her ('What a lovely day it is . . .') that day in 1958, telling her about the night when his great tree was struck by lightning, and lost all its bark, and he watched the flames and sparks reflected in a looking-glass. 'I was in bed,' he said. 'Best place you can be, isn't it?' There followed the unmistakable voice, reading Browning's 'My Last Duchess', of James Mason, whom Kaye described as one of the 'perks' of having worked at *Lilliput*:

they had dined at the Savoy, 'and he's always been part of our lives'. From the 1950s, she recalled walking along the Champs-Elysées with Ronald, seeing a crowd of people, joining the queue, and so discovering the tiny figure of Edith Piaf singing 'De l'autre Côté de la Rue'. 'Your marriage broke up,' said Sue Lawley. 'That must have been quite a blow.' 'Yes it was, I suppose,' said Kaye, 'but I can understand many of the reasons for it. He wanted a completely other kind of life, not a domesticated life with kids bawling. I was always shouting up and down, organizing parties which he probably didn't want. Anyway, it was obvious it wasn't a good thing to go on.'

'And the call from Puffin helped you through.' 'Yes, my whole life has been like that, I've had very good luck in the working sense, and not such good luck in the private life.'

This was the cue for the Puffin Song, in the delightful recording by Nonnie Locke, daughter of Ronald's American agent, and a guitarist friend of Kate's. 'When I ring people,' said Kaye, 'they still sing it.' She recalled how the Puffin Club had become a cult among young readers. 'Yes I do miss it all,' she said. 'I thought I was going to enjoy not having the responsibility. But now I miss it really quite a lot.' She also chose 'It's Easy to Sing (a simple song if you sing it after me)' from *Salad Days*, because Yehudi Menuhin, her president on *Young Elizabethan*, said everybody should sing every day; and a chorus from *Die Fledermaus*, 'to think of all the happy times we had'. Asked which one record she would take, she picked 'Where Corals Lie', 'to make the dolphins come'. Her chosen book was the anthology of poems to learn by heart, *Messages* by Naomi Lewis, 'one of the best children's reviewers in the business'. Her luxury was a photo album on a wheeling table, so that she could spend the rest of her life arranging the photos and sticking them in. 'I'd hate being cast away and I'd behave very badly,' she said. 'I really don't like being alone. All the records I've chosen are happy ones, because I want to hear human voices.'

A month later, her eightieth birthday was celebrated with a tea-party at Claridge's. Raymond Briggs, Nina Bawden, Shirley Hughes, Philippa Pearce, Nicholas Fisk and Leon Garfield were all there; and Victoria Wood with Grace and Harry. Before the party, I went to Kaye's flat for another interview, for *The Times*. 'The world is now full of ageing Puffineers. Poets, playwrights, senior executives on *The Times*, and the new editor of the *Observer* were all first published in *Puffin Post*,' I wrote. But Puffins had changed: the 1994 catalogue favoured themes of violent crime and murder, in an effort to lure readers of the Gameboy generation. I quoted a recent letter Kaye had received: 'Dear Ms Webb. Me and my friend Larrisa are interested in writing books. We are ten years old and Larrisa has already wrote a book and sent it to the publisher but they have not wrote back yet. The book Larrisa wrote was named Pure Madness. I started a book called Tabatha Tallulah. Please if you do have some advice please tell us, please please write back.' Kaye told me she already felt that the Time Capsule would have to be opened much sooner than 100 years hence: fifty years perhaps, possibly even thirty – 'things are changing so fast'.

Kaye's lively mind was unimpaired, but in October 1994 she had to apologize to Polly Hope that she had just found Polly's book of Greek folk songs, a present from the previous Christmas. She asked Polly to come and read it to her in the Middlesex Hospital – 'that would be very spoiling!' – as she was having a knee fixed. 'And thank you for continuing to be a friend in spite of all my casualness – I'm 80 now and a bit forgetful!' She wrote to Yehudi Menuhin to say bravo for defending Prince Charles in the *Evening Standard*. Yehudi had written that 'we are privileged to have in Prince Charles the ideal candidate for the Crown . . . in every way fit to be king'. 'You put it so lucidly,' Kaye wrote, 'I can't help feeling it must arouse a few other people to think of the difficulty Charles has endured.'

Kaye's last year was spent in and out of hospitals, having broken her arm in a fall. Unable to write, she dictated a letter to Ursula Moray Williams about missing Penguin's sixtieth anniversary celebrations, so she could not see 'my dearest Puffin authors get some appropriate praise for their loyalty and enthusiasm'. She had also missed the AGM of the Penguin Collectors Society, a canal cruise that passed her flat. She put a large cardboard Puffin in her window, so that everyone would see it as they sailed by.

In January 1996, the day before Kaye died in her sleep, Dorothea Duncan had paid her a chance visit. Kaye was sitting looking out at the canal, and told Dorothea she had become aware of her mother sitting at the other side of the room. Dorothea glanced at Kaye's Australian girl carer: she had heard that this was a sign of imminent death, as it proved to be. Kaye died that night, on 16 January, just ten days before her eighty-second birthday.

There were warm obituaries and tributes from Michael Bond, Alan Garner, Raymond Briggs. Naomi Lewis wrote to Kate: 'I still find myself looking about for little surprises to amuse Kaye . . . have to stop myself picking up the telephone for a chat. How can she not be here? She was such a vital part of my life. . . Her real charisma stayed with her always. To hear her speak on the air, in her young, beguiling voice, dipping into a deep well of observation, reminiscence, personal anecdote, always so lightly and casually thrown off, was a treat indeed.'

Jane Nissen wrote: 'Your mother was one of the most fascinating and talented people I have ever met and everyone will remember her for her enormous creative abilities. "The end of an era" so many people have said to me today – and it's true. There won't be another Kaye, ever . . . I do think Kaye was the right person at the right time, and with this she was able to build a truly glorious Puffin Books and Puffin Club . . . without her we'd be nowhere.' After her family, Jane said, Kaye was probably the most important person in her life. 'She gave me much more than just a job. Children's publishing has been an absorbing passion . . . and I owe it all to Kaye . . . Katie, I truly loved Kaye. And I know it was easy for me because I wasn't her daughter. But in the last couple of years she has spoken of you with such deep affection. You have been magnificent.'

The *Daily Telegraph* ran an editorial, with a gloomy warning. 'Puffins, and Miss Webb herself, did not share the current view that literature is a pill which children can be persuaded to take only if sugared. She knew that children would love it all the more the earlier they entered its secret garden. She knew exactly the distinction between what is childish and what is childlike. Kaye Webb's Puffins catered for the child who has an education so sound that he or she can read large chunks of sophisticated, and in that sense adult, prose and yet remain utterly a child, preferably pre-adolescent. The problem today is that such a child barely exists.'

At Kaye's memorial in St Martin-in-the-Fields, John Grigg recalled in his eulogy: 'She really cared about children, listing "children and their interests" as her principal recreation in *Who's Who*. Last year we asked for her advice on books to read out to our three-year-old granddaughter, and she sent us detailed suggestions, ending the letter: "I'm sorry this is a bit messy, but to be asked to find the right books is very flattering – I wouldn't want to let her down."

'Kaye,' said Grigg, 'had the mind of a shrewd and street-wise adult, while retaining the spirit of a child – excited, restless, enthusiastic and inquisitive. She was also extraordinarily brave, as her long endurance of pain and disability showed. Her spirit will live on through innumerable children, now middle-aged men and women with children of their own, whose lives were touched by her creative and imaginative spark.'

Afterword

Having an eye on posterity, Kaye left behind a mass of letters, manuscripts, scrapbooks, diaries, drafts of her radio scripts, and Puffin Club memorabilia. The immense task of sorting out these papers was undertaken by Dorothea Duncan, who speedily classified everything in time for Sotheby's sale the following year. But before the sale, with funding from the Heritage Lottery Fund and the Friends of the National Libraries, Kaye's archive, including her priceless library, was bought by the newly created Seven Stories, the Centre for Children's Books, in Newcastle. Here it was catalogued and stored – an invaluable springboard for the first national collection of children's literature. Seven Stories remains a living, growing collection of work by more than seventy writers and artists, with about 25,000 books. Kaye would have been gratified to know she was a vital part of it.

Shortly after her death, Radio 4's *Treasure Islands* broadcast a tribute to Kaye. Elaine Moss called her 'the golden girl' who could recognize good children's books 'even if she didn't care for them herself', and whose gift was being able to entertain children through their reading, 'so children who might otherwise have been quite quiet and isolated came together to have fun with books'. Victoria Wood fondly remembered her good neighbour. Philippa Pearce said Kaye 'pitchforked her authors into a sort of man-trap friendship'. Raymond Briggs recalled her fantastic enthusiasm and declared that she was 'too nice, too kind and too good' for the publishing scene she left behind. 'She and Allen Lane belonged to a different era, not so concerned with accounts.' One of the Puffineers recalled the excitement of *Puffin Post*, with its passwords, coded language, meet-the-author events and holiday camps 'where you could meet new friends, with Kaye at the centre, this infectious person opening up the world of learning'.

Nicholas Tucker was at that time editing, with Kimberley Reynolds, a book about children's book publishing since 1945. In his closing paragraphs, he acknowledged that contemporary society was turning increasingly towards the electronic media, and despite large book sales, 'the habit of reading for pleasure can no longer be taken for granted, even among those who seem naturally good readers'. In 1945 there had been plenty of child readers, he wrote, but suitable reading material was scant. Now the situation was reversed: 'an abundance of well-written, entertaining books, but far fewer children for whom reading is still the main leisure-time pursuit'.

In the decade and a half since Kaye's death, children have not completely lost their appetite for books, despite competition from the electronic media. The explosion on to the scene of the Harry Potter books by J. K. Rowling – who had been influenced as a child by books such as Dodie Smith's *I Capture the Castle* – and the continuing popularity of writers such as Philip Pullman, Anthony Horowitz, Anne Fine and Michael Morpurgo testify to the health of children's literature. Kaye's Puffineers are now parents and grandparents, who communicate the pleasure of reading to the next generations. When *The Times* launched its Books for Schools campaign in November 2008, to provide free copies of 'the best children's fiction', they asked some of their columnists to recall their favourite childhood reading. Puffins predominated. Libby Purves chose *Moonfleet* by J. Meade Falkner. Erica Wagner, *The Times*'s American-born literary editor, chose *A Wizard of Earthsea* by Ursula K. Le Guin. Caitlin Moran, who was educated at home and grew up to be a voracious reader, chose *The Horse and His Boy*, the sixth in C. S. Lewis's Narnia sequence. Simon Barnes chose *The Jungle Book* by Rudyard Kipling. Similarly, in

April 2009, when the Radio 4 *Today* programme asked Anne Fine and Michael Morpurgo what books are 'must-reads' for children, several of the titles they mentioned, apart from the William books, were in the Puffin list: *The Wolves of Willoughby Chase*, *Treasure Island*, Oscar Wilde's *A Happy Prince*, *Ballet Shoes*, *Mary Poppins*, and T. H. White's *The Sword in the Stone*.

In October 2008 *Puffin Post* was revived by a company called The Book People. It was launched (just as the prime minister, Gordon Brown, announced that every child in the land would be assured of Internet access) with a Puffinesque party at the Roof Gardens in Kensington, complete with Penguin-orange and Puffin-pink balloons, jellies and cakes. The magazine, which retained a look of the original, would be sent out through schools – but no club was attached. Judy Taylor thought Kaye would have approved, as the magazine had 'all the right personal touches' with lots of competitions. Rosemary Sandberg was less enthusiastic: 'It's a manufactured project. The original *Puffin Post* was organic.' In the *Sunday Times*, the founder-Puffineer Nicolette Jones wrote her reminiscences of the original *Puffin Post*, which was 'more about creativity than commerce. There were no ads, except to show the jackets of upcoming Puffin books. There were no concessions to popular culture beyond a few stills from new films of books: *The Railway Children*, *Swallows and Amazons*, *Doctor Dolittle* . . . Prizes were imaginative but minimal: "stringy things" in a competition to make pictures out of string . . . Grand prizes were book tokens, or the juvenilia of established authors. And the competitions themselves were like exercises in a creative writing course, about favourite words and concrete poems, reportage, or stories based on a theme or an opening sentence.' The achievements of old Puffineers were the legacy of Kaye's influence, Nicolette wrote. She wondered whether the new magazine would be so nurturing of writers and illustrators. 'No doubt it will at least be less middle-class. In the originals, nonwhite faces in the photographs of Puffin events were few. One contest invited members to draw their cleaning lady.'

The most dispiriting development in the world of children's reading in the last two decades – which would certainly have horrified Kaye – is the acceptance of the low boredom threshold and the 'work-sheet culture' which delivers only snippets of books to schoolchildren, out of fear that they would never be able to get through a complete book. In 2009 the publishers Heinemann commissioned independent research which revealed that many children never read a complete book at school, and launched a literacy project to encourage teachers to make their schools into 'whole-book-reading schools'.

A Postscript

Ronald Searle turned ninety this year. Having been given, at the age of twenty, the gift of survival when so many friends died, his determination to 'make the best of every second' has been fulfilled. He and Monica, together for half a century now, live in a spiralling warren of a tower in Tourtour, 'the village in the clouds' in Haute-Provence. They decamped there from Paris in 1975, after Monica had undergone a revolutionary treatment for breast cancer; when diagnosed in 1969, she had been given only six months to live. Miraculously granted a new lease of life, she created a home where Ronald's passion for order is everywhere apparent: 'roomfuls of books, carefully sorted by subject; a huge video library of films and TV programmes; a magazine rack with all the latest English-language publications,' as one interviewer noted. 'All correspondence is filed carefully into boxes, and he has a collection of nibs – annotated in minute writing – attached to a sheet of card on the wall.' He communicates with the world chiefly by fax and post. His industry remains impressive: he draws with a Mont Blanc fountain pen and shows no sign of diminishing in strength or accuracy. In 2005, aged eighty-five, he was given an honorary degree – collected on his behalf by Quentin Blake – by his old art school, now called Anglia Ruskin University, in Cambridge.

When Ronald took part in *Desert Island Discs* in the same year (Sue Lawley had to go to France to record his first broadcast interview in more than thirty years), the programme was received with universal warmth and admiration. His engaging voice, his modest charm, and the terrible wartime story he had to tell, captivated a new generation of listeners who had never seen him.

He related how his mad productivity in the 1950s had induced a state of panic. 'If you come back and find yourself with two children, freelancing, belting away and taking any jobs available, you have to earn money, it was really a marathon, to keep going and keep your head above water, there comes a breaking point. When you come out of the world I came out of, a world of total unreality, into post-war Britain, the whole thing was not only transitory, it was ephemeral.' Sue Lawley: 'You decided to turn your back on it.' 'Absolutely.' 'You wrote a note saying I've gone.' 'Yes – and I think it was the best decision I ever made. I think it took a long time for the relationship between myself and the children to sort itself out. The decision itself was correct I think. But a decision like that has to be brutal.' 'You are a very well-known personality, at that time in England, you'd suddenly decided to disappear and to start from zero.' 'It didn't worry me, because I'd been to zero before. When you've been the lowest of the low, you can never go down lower.' 'You didn't care what anybody you left behind said about you?' 'No, totally egocentric. It was really a question of survival, and I decided, I'm sorry, but I had to abandon my wife, abandon my children, abandon my house, my career, abandon my reputation, and start from zero.'

After forty-four years with Monica, 'I think it's going to work out,' he laughed. One of the records he chose was the second movement of Mozart's Piano Concerto no. 21 in C major, which had been played in the background of the French television programme Monica made about her cancer treatment in 1969, a time when cancer was rarely mentioned openly.

Later Sue Lawley asked whether he felt 'passed over' by his fellow countrymen. 'Well, not really, one doesn't demand anything. I am very aware of my English roots, and certainly as far as humour is concerned, one can't escape from the fact that the origins of the area one is working in are Hogarth, Gillray, Rowlandson and Cruikshank, a great century and a half of genius creation . . . I want to express myself to the maximum, I'm not parochial, I don't think about the recognition side.' 'If you hear that one of your drawings sold for £10,000?' 'I say who got the money? I sold it for five guineas,' he laughed.

His last record was the 'Champagne Song' from *Die Fledermaus*. His chosen book was the *Dictionary of National Biography*, all sixty volumes. His luxury was a bottle of champagne 'and when I finish that I can send a note in it saying please send another one'.

I finally went to visit Ronald, for *The Times*, for his ninetieth birthday in March 2010, in his labyrinthine Provençal fastness. Lean, trim, mentally alert, he exuded bonhomie and genial charm, offering pink Billecart-Salmon champagne, which he called his 'engine fuel'. He was still working daily at his drawing-board, still guarding his cherished solitude, not minding the widespread British assumption that he must be dead. Three London exhibitions (at the Cartoon Museum, Chris Beetles gallery and Maggs, the antiquarian booksellers) opened on his birthday, celebrating the full range of his work. He could no longer travel, but he was touchingly gratified that fellow artists, from Gerald Scarfe and Ralph Steadman to Martin Rowson, Steve Bell, Posy Simmonds, Quentin Blake and the film director Mike Leigh, paid their homage to Ronald Searle as the most significant comic and literary influence, paving the way for 1960s satire, and who remained – in absentia – their inspiration and their hero. 'To have the respect of one's peers,' he told me, 'makes it all worthwhile.'

He had resigned himself to his St Trinian's cartoons being regarded as his best-known legacy. He'd killed off the girls in 1953, but they refused to lie down. In 2009 the film company re-making the films starring Rupert Everett paid him £100,000 for the rights.

In Hanover, a much bigger exhibition opened at the Wilhelm-Busch Museum, which houses Ronald's vast collection of caricatures and books. He had chosen to bequeath everything to them because (unlike the British Library and the Bibliothèque Nationale) they were prepared to take his entire archive. He did not want his collections scattered piecemeal. The Wilhelm-Busch had even photographed his bookshelves to display them in the same order, and rebuilt his library in the museum ('very Germanic'). 'We are Europeans,' he said of himself and Monica. 'Not parochial.' The devotion of the Searles to one another was always remarked upon by every visitor.

I will resist drawing any conclusions about Kaye and Ronald Searle, other than the certainty that their marriage was congenial and mutually productive for much of the decade it lasted. Ronald has never made any adverse comments to me about Kaye: I believe he departed because he had simply fallen in love with another. The drastic effect of his departure on the three lives he left behind cannot be ignored. Today, Kate, an accomplished and much-admired designer of sets at the Royal Opera House, is still in constant touch with her father; but with John, who farms in southern Spain, there is no contact. Ronald has never met his only grandson, now in his twenties and a scholar of Japanese.

The loss of Ronald was an abiding tragedy for Kaye Webb, who had invested so much in her family. Her ability to triumph over this blow remains a measure of her spirit and personality, the ingenuity of her ideas, and her energy and drive. By dedicating herself to another cause, she brought pleasure and inspiration to generations of young people lucky enough to be born in a book-friendly era, and opened worlds of adventure and creativity for them. They will not forget Fat Puffin and the fun she gave them.

Bibliography

Books consulted

Humphrey Carpenter, *Secret Gardens*, George Allen & Unwin, 1985.

Russell Davies, *Ronald Searle, The Biography*, Sinclair-Stevenson, 1990.

Julia Eccleshare, *From Beatrix Potter to Harry Potter*, National Portrait Gallery, 2002.

Annabel Farjeon, *Morning Has Broken*, Julia MacRae Books, 1986.

Paul Hogarth, *The Artist as Reporter*, Gordon Fraser, 1986.

Tom Hopkinson, *Of This Our Time*, Hutchinson, 1982.

Valerie Lawson, *Out of the Sky She Came*, Hodder/Belladonna Books, Sydney, 1999.

Elaine Moss, *Part of the Pattern*, The Bodley Head, 1986.

Ian Norrie, *Mentors and Friends*, Elliott & Thompson, 2006.

Mairi Pritchard and Humphrey Carpenter, *The Oxford Companion to Children's Literature*, OUP, 1984.

Nicholas Tucker, *The Child and the Book*, Cambridge, 1981.

Nicholas Tucker and Kimberley Reynolds (eds.), *Children's Book Publishing in Britain since 1945*, Scolar Press, 1997.

Ronald and Monica Searle, *Searle & Searle*, Hirmer Verlag, 2001.

Books by Kaye Webb and Ronald Searle

Paris Sketchbook, Michael Joseph, 1950; Perpetua Books, 1957.

Looking at London, News Chronicle Publications, 1953.

The St Trinian's Story, Perpetua Books, 1959.
Refugees, Penguin, 1960.

Books edited and compiled by Kaye Webb

The Crack-a-Joke Book, Puffin, 1978.
I Like This Poem, Puffin, 1979.
Lilliput Goes to War, Hutchinson, 1984.
I Like This Story, Puffin, 1986.
Meet My Friends, Puffin, 1991.
Family Tree, Hamish Hamilton, 1994.

Acknowledgements

I could not have written this book without the help and co-operation of Kate and John Searle, and their father, Ronald Searle. Corresponding with all three has been a great pleasure. Special thanks to Kate Searle for permission to use family photographs from her private collection.

I am especially indebted to Brian Alderson, Russell Davies and Laurence Webb, who very kindly read parts of the manuscript dealing with subjects about which they know a great deal more than I.

I must also thank: Lizza Aiken (Brown), Jane Allen (Macnabb), Liz Attenborough, the late Jill Balcon (Day-Lewis), Annabel Bartlett, Jessica Bawden, Nina Bawden, Chris Beetles, Miranda Birch, Quentin Blake, Michael Bond, Raymond Briggs, Mark Bryant, John Burningham, Rachel Calder, Laura Cecil, Susan Chitty, Christianna Clements, Hannah Cole, Charlotte Cory, Hunter Davies, Sarah Davnall, Philippa Dickinson, Dorothea Duncan, Julia Eccleshare, Angela Elkins, Jonathan Fenby, Sally Fenby, Nicholas Fisk, Margaret Forster, Andrew Franklin, Jill Freud, Paul Godfrey, Joanna Goldsworthy, Griselda Greaves, Chris Green, Anne Harvey, Professor Eric Hobsbawm, Betty Hartel, Polly Hope, Judy Taylor Hough, Shirley Hughes, Barbara Hunter, Roland Huntford, Nicolette Jones, Kate Kellaway, Clive King, Tony Lacey, Jeremy Lewis, the late Naomi Lewis, Francis Long, Clare Lyons, Julia MacRae, Kate McFarlan, Peter Mayer, Marion Milne, Clare and Michael Morpurgo, Elaine Moss, Jill Murphy, Helen Nicoll, Jane Nissen, the late Ian Norrie, John Phillips, Jan Pieńkowski, Rosalind and John Randle, Rosemary

Sandberg, Doreen Scott, Brian Sibley, Christine Teale, Ion Trewin, the late Wendy Toye, Felicity Trotman, Nicholas Tucker, John Patrick Webb, Laurence Webb, Nick Webb, Clodagh Wilkinson and Linda (Villiers) Yeatman.

At Seven Stories I thank Kate Wright, Lucy Pearson and all the others who work in the old chocolate factory near Gateshead which houses the treasures of the Children's Book Centre; and I thank the editor of the *Penguin Collectors*, Jo Lunt, whose magazine is a treat for everyone who admires the artistic and editorial wizardry of Allen Lane's Penguin Books.

Permissions

I am grateful for permission to quote from the letters and published works of Kaye Webb and Ronald Searle, courtesy of Kate and John Searle and Ronald Searle. Elaine Moss kindly allowed me to quote from her article on *Puffin Post* in the *Children's Book Review* of spring 1970. I thank all the erstwhile Puffin Club members – now long grown up – whose competition entries, published in *Puffin Post*, I have singled out for mention. I also thank Sarah Davnall, for allowing me to glean information from the Puffin Time Capsule Guardians' newsletters.

Extracts from the letters of Andrew Keith Hunter are reproduced by kind permission of his widow, Mrs Barbara Hunter. Extracts from Richard Kennedy's letters by kind permission of his daughter, Mrs Rachel Ansari.

Letters from Joan Aiken are quoted copyright © 2010 by kind permission of the Estate of Joan Aiken. Letters from Pauline Baynes are quoted by permission of the Chapin Library, Williams College, Williamstown, Massachusetts, on behalf of the Williams College Oxford Programme. Letters from Eleanor Farjeon are copyright © Anne Harvey (repository of all knowledge on children's books) for the Eleanor Farjeon Estate. Letters from Rumer Godden are quoted by kind permission of the Rumer Godden Literary Trust. Extract from Noel Streatfeild's letter by kind permission of the Noel Streatfeild Estate. Letters from Ursula Moray Williams are copyright © the Estate of Ursula John, reproduced with permission of Curtis Brown Group Ltd, London.

The poem 'A Wasted Day' by Frances Cornford is reprinted

Index

Abbotsbury, Dorset, 212
Adams, Douglas, 108
Adams, John Bodkin, 111
Adams, Richard: *Watership Down*,
    4–5, 202–3, 219; *Girl in a
    Swing*, 232
Adler, Jankel, 54, 67
Adler, Larry, 115
Aiken, Joan: advises KW on
    children's books, 178, 251,
    254; home at Petworth, 182,
    230; and KW's outings and
    events, 190, 201; considers
    changing publishers, 192;
    and KW's anxieties over son
    John, 193; and KW's ill-
    health, 202; dreams of KW
    writing autobiography, 204;
    sees TV programme on
    Ronald Searle, 207; and
    KW's visit to Jan
    Pieńkowski, 208; and KW's
    retirement, 225, 232, 237; on
    Richard Adams's *Girl in a
    Swing*, 232; concerns over
    decreasing royalties, 245;
    encourages KW to draw,
    248; *Arabel and Mortimer*: TV
    version, 250; *How to Write for
    Children*, 238; *Winterthing*
    (play), 180

Aiken, John Sebastian, 178
Akers, Professor (of Camberwell
    School of Arts), 5, 249
Alderson, Brian, 148, 249
Algarve: KW visits, 212
Allan, Jane, 190, 235
Alvarez, Elvira Martín
    (housekeeper), 108, 132–3,
    141, 143, 145, 203
Amis, Martin, 239n
Andrews, Julie, 125
Ardizzone, Catherine, 93
Ardizzone, Edward, 46n, 93, 112,
    137, 148, 153
Ashburton Book of Verse, The, 18
Ashburton School, Devon, 16–20
At the Drop of a Hat (revue), 113
Atkinson, Alex, 111
Atlantic Charter, 45
Attenborough, Liz, 222, 236–7, 238,
    240, 247, 255
Australia: KW visits, 156–7, 186
Austria: KW's skiing holiday in,
    103
Ayckbourn, Alan, 113

Badger, Catherine, 249
Bagnold, Enid: *National Velvet*, 216
Baker, Dame Janet, 259
Balcon, Jill (Mrs Cecil Day-Lewis),
    90, 124, 144

Balfour, Honor, 32

Banks, Lynne Reid, 250

Barnes, Simon, 266

Baron (photographer), 110

Bartlett, Annabel, 174, 210

Baruch, Emmanuel de Marney, 109

Basie, Count, 117

Bateman, Michael: *Funny Way to Earn a Living*, 67n

Bawden, Niki, 215

Bawden, Nina, 7, 201, 207, 215, 218, 261; *Carrie's War*, 4; TV version, 250; *The Peppermint Pig*: filmed, 215; *The Rebel on a Rock*, 215; *The Robbers*, 235

Baxter, Biddy, 187–8

Baylis, Lilian, 20

Baynes, Pauline (*later* Gasch), 146, 148, 156, 253

Beardsley, Aubrey, 12

Bedford Gardens, off Kensington Church Street, 67, 83, 90

Beerbohm, Sir Max, 39, 68, 82, 98

Beirut, 160

Bell, Cressida, 169

Belles of St Trinian's, The (film), 99

Belsky, Franta, 39, 93, 124

Belsky, Margaret, 39

Ben-Hur (film), 120

Bennett, Richard, 71, 74–5

Bentine, Michael, 124

Bentley, Nicolas, 84, 93, 124

Bergman, Ingrid, 89

Best, Herbert: *Garram the Hunter*, 3

Betjeman, (Sir) John, 39

Birch, Lionel ('Bobby'), 31–2, 42

Birch, Miranda, 174

Birch, Teresa, 227

Bird, Kenneth ('Fougasse'), 82

Birthday Book of Ten, The, 156

Blair, Alison (*née* Hooper), 30, 32, 128, 212, 241; death, 252

Blake, Quentin: on KW's frankness with child reader, 4; first meets Ronald Searle, 94; illustrates Roald Dahl, 148, 220; paints caravan for KW, 173; popularity, 174; at *Jackanory* party, 201; drawing of KW surrounded by puffins, 213, 240; and Paul Godfrey, 213–14; KW confesses to being old-fashioned, 243; collects honorary degree on behalf of Ronald Searle, 269; Searle's influence on, 271

Bloom, Claire, 93–4

Blue Murder at St Trinian's (film), 118

Blue Peter (TV programme), 187

Blume, Judy, 225, 250

Blyton, Enid, 164; *The Famous Five*, 150

Bologna Children's Book Fair, 148

Bond, Michael, 200, 230; *Paddington*, 134

Book People, The (company), 267

Bookman (magazine), 126

Books for Your Children (magazine), 233

Bookshelf (radio programme), 241

Bossert, Patrick: *You Can Do the Cube*, 231

Boyle, Edward, 177, 197

Braddon, Russell, 58, 67, 87; *The Naked Island*, 93
Brandt, Bill, 40
Bredin, Lucinda, 167
Brierley, Christopher Eustace Desmond (Kit): marriage to KW, 28–9; in India, 29, 32–3; KW divorces, 34–5; naval service in war, 34; offers insurance money to KW, 79
Brierley, Ursula, 35, 67
Briggs, Katharine M.: *Hobberdy Dick*, 5, 213
Briggs, Raymond, 196, 261–2, 265
Brighton, 137
Brisley, Joyce Lankester, 7
Brittany, 117
Britten, Benjamin (*later* Baron), 101
Brook, Peter, 125
Brown, Elizabeth ('Lizza'), 174–5, 178, 180
Brown, Gordon, 267
Bruges, Belgium: KW in, 21, 24
Brunhoff, Laurent de, 137
Buchan, John (1st Baron Tweedsmuir), 18
Buchanan, Jack, 259
Bucknell, Barry, 171
Bumpus Books (London), 2
Burnett, Frances Hodgson: *The Secret Garden*, 5
Burnham Court, Moscow Road, Bayswater, 83, 93
Burnier, Raymond, 21
Burningham, John: *Borka*, 8
Burns, Tania, 256
Butler, Dorothy, 230

Butler, Richard Austen: Education Act (1944), 148
Byars, Betsy, 250

Calder-Marshall, Anna, 234
Calder-Marshall, Arthur, 93–4, 164
Calkin, Jessamy, 168
Call My Bluff (TV word game), 156
Calvocoressi, Peter, 193
Camden School for Girls, 153
Campbell, Cherry, 69, 70n
Campbell, Pat (Mrs John Grigg), 120
Campbell, Patrick, 67, 69–71, 82
Canard Enchaîné, Le (magazine), 85, 103
Cape, Jonathan, 3
Carey, Joanna, 252
Carle, Eric: *The Very Hungry Caterpillar*, 222
Carpenter, Richard, 190
Carr, Mary, 256
Carrington, Dora, 1
Carrington, Noel, 1–2, 177
Cartledge, Alison, 7, 248
Cassettari, Joyce (KW's cousin), 251
Casson, (Sir) Hugh, 124
Castle, Barbara (*later* Baroness), 84
Causley, Charles, 234, 244, 253; *Early in the Morning* (anthology), 243, 246; *The Puffin Book of Magic Verse* (ed.), 9
Cecil, Lord David, 101, 163
Cecil, Eustace, 163
Cecil, Jim, 163, 191–2

Centre for Children's Books (Seven
    Stories), Felling, near
    Newcastle upon Tyne, 10, 265
Chamberlain, Neville, 31, 54
Chambers, Aidan, 217
Chambers, Harry, 198–9
Chapmansford, Hampshire, 183
Charles, Prince of Wales, 202, 255,
    261
Chelsea Arts Ball, 103
Childrens Book Centre, Notting
    Hill, 210
Children's Book Circle, 136, 182,
    226
children's books: flowering, 147–8;
    and social and class changes,
    158–9, 218, 267–8; favourites,
    266–7
Children's Bookshop project, 209–
    10
Chiswick *see* Montrose Villas
Chivers, Violet, 17
Christiansen, Rupert, 166
Christmas Carol, A (proposed
    animated show), 125–6
Churchill, (Sir) Winston, 13, 45
Clark, Margaret, 129–30, 137, 217
Clark, Mary Senior: *Lost Legends of
    the Nursery Songs*, 251
Cleary, Beverly: *Fifteen*, 216
Clunes, Alec, 20
Cochran, (Sir) Charles B., 12
Cochrane, Willie, 180
Cockburn, Claud, 30
Cole, Hannah, 166, 252
Coleridge, Nicholas, 166
Collings, Rex, 202
Collins Magazine, 99

Collins, William, 99, 135, 191
Colony Holidays, 179, 211
Colquhoun, Robert, 67
Connolly, Cyril, 30
Connolly, Sybil, 105
Constable Young Books, 134
Conway, Robert, 92
Cooksey, Arthur, 151
Coolidge, Calvin, 16
Coolidge, Susan: *What Katy Did*, 11
Cooper, Susan, 250
Cooper, Tommy, 115
Cornford, Frances: 'A Wasted Day',
    257
Cory, Charlotte (*earlier* Everest-
    Phillips), 160, 167, 174, 255–6;
    The Wandering Wind, 213
Cowdrey, Colin, 101
Cowper, William: *John Gilpin*, 84
Cresswell, Helen, 201, 206, 213
Cribbins, Bernard, 210
Crompton, Richmal: William
    books, 134, 148
Crosse, Patrick, 204, 214, 230, 238–9
Crossman, Richard, 58
Crowley, Aleister, 46n
Cudlipp, Percy, 48, 97
Cunningham, Barry, 231
Curtis Brown (literary agents), 233,
    240
Cyprus, 193

Dahl, Liccy (Roald's wife), 255
Dahl, Lucy (Roald's daughter), 229
Dahl, Roald: collaboration with
    Quentin Blake, 148, 220;
    Lucy Grove visits, 229;
    participates in Puffin events,

235; as bestseller, 237; recommends homoeopathic doctor to KW, 241; KW speaks on, 250; death, 254–5; declines to compile anthology, 254; *Boy*, 250; *Charlie and the Chocolate Factory*, 5, 176; *The Enormous Crocodile*, 219; *James and the Giant Peach*, 176; dramatized, 246; *The Twits*, 176

Dahl, Tessa (Roald's daughter), 166, 255

Dahl, Theo (Roald's son), 176

Daily Herald: KW's father at, 20, 22

Daily News, 23

Daily Telegraph, 263

d'Ancona, Matthew, 166

Dankworth, John, 173, 182

Davies, Hunter, 241

Davies, Russell, 125, 139, 142–3

Davnall, Sarah, 248, 256

Day-Lewis, Cecil, 90–91, 124

Day-Lewis, Sean, 233

Dead Sea: KW visits, 238

de la Mare, Walter, 18–20, 111–13, 164, 259; *Peacock Pie*, 146

Dent, Martin, 191

Desert Island Discs (radio programme), 124, 259–60, 269–71

de Wolfe, Terence, 78

Dickinson, Peter, 196, 201

Dickinson, Philippa, 196–7, 211, 230

Dietrich, Marlene, 30

Disney, Walt, 117

Donlan, Yolande, 93

Dover, 122

Downes, Gerry, 203

Drabble, (Dame) Margaret, 186

Driberg, Tom (*later* Baron Bradwell), 50, 59, 67, 93

Drysdale, Russell, 186

Dublin, 104

Duke, Neville, 101

Dulles, John Foster, 107

du Maurier, Sir Gerald, 25

Duncan, Dorothea, 154, 173, 197, 199, 202–3, 230, 262, 265

Dungeons and Dragons, 231

Durrell, Gerald, 135

Ebert, Jake, 233

Eccleshare, Colin, 67, 222

Eccleshare, Julia, 166, 222

Edelman, Maurice, 42–3, 50, 58, 242; *Who Goes Home?*, 94

Edelman, Sophia, 43, 242

Edelman, Tilly, 43

Edinburgh Festival (1975), 207

Edmonds, Noel, 235–6

Edwards, Dorothy, 206, 210; *My Naughty Little Sister*, 149

Egg, The (magazine), 220, 230

Eichmann, Adolf, 134–5

Eisenhower, Dwight D., 96

Eleanor Farjeon Award, 153, 182, 184

Elizabeth the Queen Mother, 124

Elkins, Angela (*née* Hunter), 200, 252

Elliott, Denholm, 93

Ellsmoor, Jean, 140, 145

Elsie (Webb family housemaid), 46, 132

Eluard, Paul, 81
Energetically Yours (film), 117
Enid Blyton Magazine, 164
Epstein, Sir Jacob, 87
Ethel (Arthur Webb's girlfriend),
    131–2, 138, 179, 193
Evans, (Dame) Edith, 125
Evans, Isla, 196
Everest-Phillips, Lalage *see* Cory,
    Charlotte
Everywoman (magazine), 84
Exeter University: annual
    conference of children's
    authors and teachers, 201
Exile, The (prisoner-of-war
    magazine), 57–8, 60

Fahy, Kate (KW's maternal
    grandmother), 14
Falkner, J. Meade: *Moonfleet*, 121, 266
Family Tree (anthology; ed. KW),
    254
Farjeon, Eleanor, 116, 120, 138–9,
    151–3; *The Little Bookroom*, 153
Farms for City Children, 251
Fassi, Allal el, 87
Fay, Steffan, 256
Featherstone Castle,
    Northumberland, 179–80
Fedden, Mary, 84, 172
Feiffer, Jules, 126
Fenby, Charles, 32, 75–6, 90, 200
Fenby, Jonathan, 114, 117–18, 124,
    197
Fenby, June, 200
Fenby, Sally, 174, 180
Fenice, El (house), Cavajal, near
    Malaga, 177

Fergusson, Sir Bernard (*later* Baron
    Ballantrae), 110, 122, 157, 211
Fergusson, Laura, Lady, 99, 122,
    157, 211
Fernandel, 86
ffolkes, Michael, 67
Finch, Peter, 84, 124, 931
Findlay, Deborah, 174
Fine, Anne, 266–7
Finney, Albert, 126
Fisher, Margery, 147
Fisk, Nicholas (David
    Higginbottom), 173, 207–8,
    261
Fitzpatrick, 'Pasty', 14, 28n
Flanders, Michael, 113, 156
Fleming, Lady (Jill McDonald's
    aunt), 236
Forester, C. S., 39
Fortnum, Peggy, 148
Fougasse *see* Bird, Kenneth
Fowles, John, 230
Foyle, Christina, 84
François, André, 85, 95, 101
Franklin, Andrew, 166, 217
Freud, (Sir) Clement, 90–91, 93, 145
Freud, Jill, 144–5
Frost, Eunice, 157, 177, 232
Fry, Christopher, 84–5, 89, 93, 115–
    16, 120, 151, 168, 201, 251;
    Curtmantel, 115; *An Experience
    of Critics*, 95; *The Lark*
    (adapted from Jean Anouilh),
    105
Fuchs, Klaus, 84

Gage, Henry Rainald Gage, 6th
    Viscount, 163

Gaitskell, Julia, 101
Gallico, Paul: *The Snow Goose*, 136
Gandhi, Mohandas Karamchand, 48
Gardam, Jane, 217
Garfield, Leon, 7, 201, 261
Garland, Sarah, 136
Garman, Kathleen, 87
Garner, Alan, 169, 175, 182, 201, 217, 262
Garnett, Eve, 252; *The Family from One End Street*, 3
Garrick Club, 110
Gasch, Fritz Otto, 146, 253
Gaulle, Charles de, 50, 123
Geddes, Philip, 7, 246, 256
Gen (forces newsletter), 44, 59
George VI, King: funeral, 89
George, Mabel, 134
Germany: Ronald Searle visits, 125
Gibbs, Ben R., 17–20
Gielgud, (Sir) John, 125
Gili, Phillida, 114
Gill, Eric, 94
Gilliatt, Penelope, 124
Gingold, Hermione, 91, 93, 125
Go (magazine), 88
Goddard, Rayner, Baron, 84
Goddard, Theodore, 34
Godden, Rumer, 133, 205, 245, 250, 257–8; *The Dolls' House*, 234; *The Greengage Summer*, 216
Godfrey, Paul, 7, 213, 215–16, 238–9, 246–8, 256; *A Bucket of Eels* (play), 249; *Inventing a New Colour* (play), 247
Godwin, Tony: commissions Paris book from KW and Ronald Searle, 85; at KW–Searle New Year party, 124; offers post of 'Outside Editor' at Penguin to KW, 129–30; puts KW on Penguin staff, 132; negotiates with Collins, 135; offers own desk to KW, 145; overspends budget, 154; ends 'Birthday Books', 156; and Puffin Club, 166
Goebbels, Joseph, 30
Goldcrest Films, 233–4, 239
Golding, William, 126
Gollancz, Livia, 158
Goodman, Arnold (*later* Baron), 125, 137
Graham, Eleanor, 2–3, 129–30, 137, 159, 177, 219
Graham, Jacquie, 191, 203
Graves, Diana, 87
Graves, Lucia, 197
Graves, Robert, 106, 121, 134, 259
Greaves, Griselda (*later* Garner), 199
Greco, Juliette, 86
Green, Chris, 179–80, 211
Green, Roger Lancelyn, 137; *The Adventures of Robin Hood*, 8
Grenfell, Joyce, 111, 115, 168
Grigg, John (*sometime* 2nd Baron Altrincham): publishes *Young Elizabethan*, 99; on KW's Christmas party, 102; attends Chelsea Arts Ball with KW and Ronald Searle, 103; takes KW to tea with de la Mare, 111, 113; offers shares to Searles, 113; sees Flanders and Swann review, 113; on space

Grigg, John – *cont.*
in *Young Elizabethan*, 114–15; and KW's road accident, 116; criticizes Royal Family, 118; and KW's giving up editorship of *Young Elizabethan*, 119; attends Searles' New Year party, 128; KW sells Orwell holograph gift, 240; gives address at KW's memorial service, 263
Grigson, Sophie, 167
Gritten, Sally, 255
Grossmith, George and Weedon: *Diary of a Nobody*, 218
Grove, Lucy, 229
Growing Point (magazine), 147
Guinness, (Sir) Alec, 87, 89, 93–4, 124–6
Guinness, Merula (Lady), 87, 93
Guy, Rosa, 216

Hadrian's Wall, 179–80
Hale, Kathleen: *Orlando's Evening Out*, 3
Hambrook, Katie, 256
Hamlyn, Paul, 251
Hanover: Wilhelm-Busch museum of graphic art, 271
Harburg, Yip, 125
Hardy, Patrick, 202, 231–2
Harmondsworth, Middlesex, 2, 6; *see also* Penguin Books
'Haro' *see* Hodson, 'Haro'
Harris, Clare Laurel, 115
Harris, Rolf, 115
Harrison, Philippa, 245

Hartel, Betty, 253
Harwood, Kate, 247
Hastings, Macdonald, 32
Heaslip, Susan, 256
Hebden, Peter, 136
Heinemann (publishers), 268
Hellman, Jerome, 125
Hemingway, Ernest, 38
Henry, Thomas, 148
Herbert, (Sir) A. P., 172–3
Herbison, Cyril, 31
High Hill Bookshop, Hampstead, 135, 160
Hilberman, David, 125–6
Hird, Thora, 76–7, 232
Hoban, Russell, 210
Hobsbawm, Eric, 53–4
Hodgkin, Marni, 134, 158
Hodson, 'Haro', 150, 154, 256
Hoffnung, Gerard, 39
Hogarth, Grace, 134, 136, 202, 221, 226
Hogarth, Paul, 74, 79–81, 135
Holiday magazine, 135
Holloway, Stanley, 117, 125
Home, Anna, 250
Hope, Polly, 210–11, 261
Hope-Wallace, Philip, 124
Hopkinson, Sir Tom: edits *Picture Post* and *Lilliput*, 32, 46; supports Hoffnung drawings, 39; and Dylan Thomases, 42; on appeal of *Lilliput*, 44; and Ronald Searle's silence during war, 55; and KW's visit to New York, 71; as protégé of Arthur Webb, 195; and effect of Puffin on

KW, 234; and launch of
  Lilliput Goes to War, 241;
  death, 252
Horowitz, Anthony, 250, 266
Hough, Charlotte, 136
Hough, Richard, 136, 192–3
Howard, Leslie, 27
Howes, Sally Ann, 82
Hughes, Richard, 81
Hughes, Shirley, 130, 136, 148, 261;
  Dogger, 191
Hughes, Ted, 243, 246
Hulton Press, 31–2
Hundred and One Dalmatians, The
  (film), 117
Hunt, Brigadier Sir John, 101, 114
Hunter, Andrew Keith: marriage
  to KW, 35–8, 228; wartime
  absence, 46; and KW's
  falling for Ronald Searle, 66;
  divorce from KW, 68–9, 72,
  78; marriage to Barbara
  Woosnam, 68–9, 74, 79;
  visits KW after birth of
  twins, 74; KW's twins meet,
  150; lives in Spain, 200, 211;
  misses KW on visit, 207;
  sends bedcape to KW in
  hospital, 242; writes to KW
  in hospital, 248
Hunter, Angela *see* Elkins, Angela
Hunter, Norman, 7, 177, 201; *The
  Incredible Adventures of Professor
  Branestawm*, 3
Huntford, Roland, 127–8, 144
Hutchinson's (publishers), 241
Huxley, Aldous, 81
Huxley, Sir Julian, 101

I Like This Poem (ed. KW), 224, 227
I Like This Story (ed. KW), 253
Illingworth, Leslie, 93
Illustrated Weekly, 676
India: independence movement, 48
International Congress of
  Intellectuals for Peace,
  Wrocław (1948), 81
International Year of the Child
  (1979), 224
Irons, Evelyn, 45
Israel: KW visits, 160
Italy: Ronald Searle in, 98

Jacobson, Sydney (*later* Baron),
  30–32, 50
Jacques, Hattie, 115
James, Will: *Smoky*, 3
Jansson, Tove, 189
Jaques, Faith, 148
Jaques, Robin, 82
Jay, Douglas, 195
Jerusalem: Ronald Searle in, 134
Johnston, Cecile and Pat, 54
Jones, Nicolette, 166, 168, 267
Jones, Rachel, 168
Jordan, Martha, 44
Julia MacRae Books, 222
Junior Puffin Club, 220

Kath (Webb family housemaid), 46
Kaye, Danny, 117
Kaye Webb Productions, 233
Kaye Webb's Scrapbook (TV
  programme), 106
Keevil, Mrs (Ann Webb's nurse-
  companion), 118, 132
Kellaway, Kate, 166, 168

Kelly, Gene, 105

Kendal Milnes (Manchester store), 115

Kendon, Frank, 67

Kennedy, Richard, 155, 198, 201, 203–5, 242, 244; *A Boy at the Hogarth Press*, 155, 189

Keown, Eric, 83, 91, 93, 104, 111

Kerr, Judith: *The Tiger Who Came to Tea*, 19

Kestrel (*formerly* Longman Young Books), 202, 209, 220

Kettlebrook Meadows (house), 124

Keynes, John Maynard, Baron, 49

Kiki de Montparnasse, 86

King, Clive, 155, 160, 258–9; *Stig of the Dump*, 149, 159, 255, 258; TV version, 235; *The Twenty-Two Letters*, 160

Kingfisher Books, 251

Kinnock, Stephen, 252

Kipling, Rudyard, 136; *The Jungle Book*, 266

Knight, Myfanwy (*née* Gibbs), 20

Koenig, Charles, 123

Konig, George, 144

Kunzle, Christian, 84

Lacey, Tony, 202, 225, 230–31, 234, 236, 238

Ladybird Books, 251

Laine, Cleo, 118

Lampard House, Randolph Crescent, 203, 214

Lane, Sir Allen: launches Penguin Books, 1–2; KW meets, 129; offers post to KW at Penguin, 129; success at Penguin, 147; attends KW's dinner at L'Écu de France, 155; interest in 'making readers', 159; doubts on profitability of Puffin Club, 163–4; and KW's marriage problems, 163; and Puffin Club trip to Lundy Island, 170; Alan Garner on, 175; bowel cancer, 177; offers picnic at Chapmansford, 183; death, 183

Lane, Burton, 125

Langdon, David, 46

Langley, Noel, 82

Lansbury, George, 44

Lasdun, (Sir) Denys, 92, 93

Laski, Marghanita, 216–17

Laughton, Charles, 125

Lawley, Sue, 259–60, 269

Lawrence, D. H., 31, 212; *Lady Chatterley's Lover*, 1

Leader (magazine), 75–6, 83, 127

Lebanon, 160

Le Cain, Errol, 235

Le Corbusier (Charles-Edouard Jeanneret), 107

Lee, James, 233

Lee, Laurie, 40, 132, 160, 165, 190, 209, 230; *Cider with Rosie*, 132

Le Guin, Ursula K., *The Wizard of Earthsea*, 149, 266; film project, 233

Leicester Galleries, London, 89

Lennon, John: *In His Own Write*, 155

Lewis, C. S., 148, 219, 253; *The Lion, The Witch and the Wardrobe*, 5; Narnia books, 250, 266

Lewis, D. B. Wyndham *see* Wyndham Lewis, D. B.

Lewis, Jeremy, 164; *Penguin Special*, 232n

Lewis, Naomi, 147–8, 155, 173–4, 255, 262; *Messages* (anthology), 260

Life magazine, 134

Lilliput (magazine): KW works on, 29, 31, 35, 38–40, 44, 46–7, 58, 68; character and popularity, 30–31, 38–9, 43; Hultons buy, 31; Roosevelt reads copy, 46; on Ronald Searle's return from prison camp, 60; publishes Searle drawings, 65–6; dismisses KW, 75; ceases publication, 127

Lilliput Goes to War (anthology; ed. KW), 32, 46n, 241

Lindgren, Astrid, 187

Lindos, Rhodes, 211

Lingard, Joan, 250

Little Pines, Sussex, 119, 132

Livingstone, Ian and Steve Jackson: Fighting Fantasy game books, 231, 237

Locke, Nonnie, 260

Lofting, Hugh, 159; *Dr Dolittle*, 3, 134

Longleat, Wiltshire, 201

Lorant, Stefan, 30–32

Lowerson, Mary, 115

Lundy Island, 170–71, 256

MacBryde, Robert, 67

McCarthy, Ruth, 252

McCulloch, Derek: *Cornish Adventure*, 3

McDonald, Jill, 165–6, 181, 230; death, 236

McFarlan, Kate, 167

Mackenzie, Niall, 249

MacLiammoir, Micheál, 105

MacRae, Julia, 218n, 221–2, 225

Madame Bovary (film), 74

Magnani, Anna, 102

Majorca, 121

Málaga *see* Fenice, El

Malcolm, Mary, 175

Mandrake the Magician (film), 233

Mansfield, Katherine, 212

Margaret, Princess, 22

Marshall, James Vance: *Walkabout*, 216

Martin, Kingsley, 81

Maschler, Tom, 148, 220

Masefield, John: *The Midnight Folk*, 136

Mason, James: friendship wth KW, 43; writes article for *Lilliput*, 43; emigrates to USA, 74, 83; and KW's first TV appearance, 106; KW meets in Hollywood, 117; as godfather to John Searle, 121; as Marley's ghost in *A Christmas Carol* (proposed), 126; KW entertains, 132; Dorothea Duncan meets, 154; returns to London after divorce, 157; names favourite children's book, 168; on KW as film producer, 233; death, 252; KW's choice on *Desert Island Discs*, 259

Mason, Pamela, 74, 157

Mason, Portland, 74, 115, 117

Mates, Sally, 180

Maude, Joan, 87

Mayer, Liese, 224

Mayer, Peter, 223–4, 227, 232, 236

Mayne, William, 165, 180, 181, 189, 199 & n, 201; *A Game of Dark*, 217; *A Parcel of Trees*, 159; *Winter Quarters*, 238

Meet My Friends (anthology; ed. KW), 253

Menuhin, Yehudi (*later* Baron), 101, 224, 256, 260–61

Mickey Mouse (magazine), 26

Miles, Sir Bernard (*later* Baron), 129

Mili, Gjon, 71

Milligan, Spike, 168, 174; *Silly Verse for Kids*, 9

Mills, Annette, 98

Mills, (Sir) John, 94, 125

Milne, A. A., 148

Milne, Marion, 187–8

Milner, A. J., 187

Minton, John, 67

Mogg, Sylvia, 182, 191, 210, 230, 248

Moggach, Deborah, 136

Moir, Vivien, 7, 256

Molesworth, Mary Louise: *The Cuckoo Clock*, 3

Montrose Villas, Hammersmith Terrace, Chiswick, 172–3, 203

Moore, Henry, 40

Moore, (Sir) Patrick, 6–7, 229

Moran, Caitlin, 266

More, Kenneth, 105

Morley, Robert, 125

Morley, Sheridan, 157; *Odd Man Out*, 252

Morocco, 87

Morpurgo, Clare, 251

Morpurgo, Michael, 251, 257, 266–7

Morrison, Herbert (*later* Baron), 89

Moscow Road *see* Burnham Court

Mosley, Sir Oswald, 50

Moss, Elaine, 148, 158, 176, 181, 199, 218, 220, 265

Mott, Tony, 210

Mountbatten, Lord Louis (*later* 1st Earl), 58

Muggeridge, Malcolm, 16, 97, 105, 168

Murphy, Jill, 245

Murray, Jenni, 251

Murry, John Middleton, 212

Musset, Alfred de: *On ne badine pas avec l'amour*, 43

Myers, Amy, 190

Nabokov, Vladimir: *Lolita*, 94

National Review, 118, 120

Naylor (Ashburton headmaster), 17

Neal, Patricia, 176

New York, 117–18

New Zealand: KW visits, 157, 186

News Chronicle, 23, 87, 89, 92, 103; ceases publication, 127

Newton Road, Bayswater: KW's house in, 91, 95, 119, 133, 153, 172; sold, 192

Nicholson, Jenny (*née* Graves), 82, 204, 214

Nicholson, Virginia (*née* Bell), 166, 169

Nicoll, Helen, 7, 220, 230
Nissen, Jane, 4, 173, 197, 211, 216, 223, 262
Norman, Philip, 239
Norrie, Amanda, 166
Norrie, Ian, 135–6, 160, 186, 217
Norrie, Jessica, 166
Norton, Mary, 136, 229, 242; *The Borrowers*, 219, 243
Novello, Ivor, 27
Nuremberg, 80

Oakwood School, Lavant, 189
Octopus Books, 251
Odhams Press, 27
O'Hara, John, 126
Olivier, Laurence (*later* Baron), 77
On the Twelfth Day (Wendy Toye film), 98
Opie, Iona, 155–6, 228, 244
Opie, Peter, 155–6, 244
Orwell, George: KW sells holograph, 240
Our Time (magazine), 127
Oxford Book of Twentieth Century Children's Literature, The, 223

Paint Manufacturing Journal, 26
Palk, Harold, 18
Paris: KW visits, 68, 146; KW and Ronald Searle write joint book on, 85–6; Searle meets Monica Stirling in, 122–3; KW takes twins to, 128; Searle in, 132, 142, 146; events of 1968, 177
Parrish, Max, 91
Patmore, Coventry: 'The Toys', 254

Paton Walsh, Jill, 201, 217; *The Dolphin Crossing*, 9
Peacock Books, 154, 216–17, 250
Peake, Mervyn, 41–2, 244
Pearce, Denise, 226, 243
Pearce, Philippa, 134, 136, 205, 261, 265; *Tom's Midnight Garden*, 5, 7, 136
Pearson Longman (publishers), 182, 202
Penguin Books: launched, 1, 3; Lane offers post to KW, 129; and KW's salary, 145; goes public, 154; KW promoted to board, 157; passes to Pearson Longman on death of Allen Lane, 183; under Peter Calvocoressi, 192; women's bonding at, 197; moves to Grosvenor Gardens, Victoria, 202; fortieth birthday party, 207; under Peter Mayer, 223; moves to King's Road, 225; children's division takes over other publishers, 237; sixtieth anniversary celebrations, 262
Penguin Collectors Society, 262
Penguin Ronald Searle, The, 126
Perpetua Books (publishing house), 94–5
Perski, Ludwik, 80
Petrie, Ruth, 202, 230
Peynet, Raymond: *The Lover's Keepsake*, 124
Phillips, John, 178, 180, 211, 212, 251
Phillips, Siân, 118
Phillpotts, Eden, 18
Piaf, Edith, 260

Picasso, Pablo, 81, 118

Picture Post (magazine), 29, 31, 40, 75, 180; ceases publication, 127

Picturegoer (magazine), 26–7, 44

Picturegoer's Who's Who and Encyclopaedia, The, 27

Piddington, Syd, 67, 87

Pieńkowski, Jan, 208, 220, 256

Pimlott, Ben, 113

Pocock, Tom, 120

Pollinger, Murray, 149

Pollock's Toy Museum, 11–12

Pope, W. Macqueen, 25, 77

Portofino, 82

Postgate, Oliver, 234

Potter, Beatrix, 237

Powell, Michael, 233

Prague, 79–80

Priestley, J. B., 19

Priestley, Mary (*née* Wyndham Lewis), 77

Pritchard, Gwynn, 115

Pritchett, (Sir) V. S., 40

Pudney, John, 40

Puffin Annual, 210–11

Puffin Books: launched, 2; Kaye Webb takes over, 3; Time Capsule, 4–10, 221, 249; KW appointed to, 129–37, 145, 147; Doreen Scott joins as editorial manager, 132; publishes books from hardback publishers, 134–5; KW's credo at, 147; and social class of books, 159; sales, 181; bookplates, 188; staff recruitment, 190–91; Exhibitions, 193, 210, 214, 230, 236; competitors, 219; keeps books in print, 219; thousandth title, 219–20; under Tony Lacey, 231; Liz Attenborough heads, 236–7; fiftieth anniversary celebrations, 255–6

Puffin Bookshop, Covent Garden, 250

Puffin Club: membership, 4, 166–8, 188–9, 235; formed, 101, 163; graphics and presentation, 165–6; prizes, 169, 175, 181; outings, events and holidays, 170–72, 179–81, 189–90, 201, 205, 235; exhibition of children's work, 174; correspondence, 181–2; badge, 188; makes demands on KW in retirement, 234; Eunice McMullen runs, 237; closed, 246–7

Puffin Modern Classics, 258

Puffin Plus Books, 250

Puffin Post: founded, 101, 166; readers, 166–9; introduces authors, 167–8; contents, 168, 234–5; payments to contributors, 175; KW gives up editorship, 236; decline, 249; remembered, 265–6; revived by The Book People (2008), 267

Puffin Song, 160–61, 163, 260

Puffin's Pleasure, 210

Pullman, Philip, 266

Punch (magazine), 66, 82, 91, 97, 110, 125, 135

Purves, Libby, 266

Queen's College, Harley Street, 110, 153

Querschnitt, Der (German magazine), 30

Quigley, Janet, 98

Radio Times (magazine), 67

Raison, Maxwell, 32, 75

'Rake's Progress, The' (Ronald Searle drawings), 97–8

Randle, John, 189

Randle, Rose, 189

Ransome, Arthur, 136, 237; *Swallows and Amazons*, 3, 140

Rawlings, Marjorie Kinnan: *The Yearling*, 36

Ray, Cyril, 207

Raymond, Jill (Mrs Clement Freud), 90–91, 93

Redgrave, (Sir) Michael, 132

Rees, Nigel, 114

Reeves, James, 148

Reinhardt, Max, 130

Reynolds, Kimberley: *Children's Book Publishing since 1945* (with Nicholas Tucker), 158n, 266

Reynolds' News, 66

Rice, Peter, 172

Richardson, Maurice, 74

Richardson, (Sir) Ralph, 77

Robson, (Dame) Flora, 77

Rome, 102

Romersa, Anna, 94

Roosevelt, Franklin D., 45–6

Rose, Jim, 209, 219

Rosenberg, Alison, 7, 196

Ross, Billy, 18

Round About Six (anthology; ed. KW), 253

Rowallan, Thomas Godfrey Polson Corbett, 2nd Baron, 101

Rowe, Louise, 235

Rowling, J.K.: Harry Potter books, 266

Royal Court Theatre, London, 247–9

Rubinstein, Hilary, 223–4

Rumball, Claire, 235

Russell, Leonard, 88

Russell, Victor, 35

St Trinnean's girls' school, Edinburgh, 54

Saki (H. H. Munro), 47

Salinger, J. D.: *The Catcher in the Rye*, 217

Salzburg, 127

Sandberg, Robin, 174

Sandberg, Rosemary, 164–6, 169, 171, 191, 267

Saville-Sneath, R. A.: *Aircraft Recognition*, 1

Saxton, Miss (Walter de la Mare's carer), 111

Scarfe, Gerald, 271

Scott, Doreen, 132, 145, 173, 177, 191, 200, 202

Scott, Janette, 232

Scott, J. D., 93

Scott-James, Anne, 32

Scott-Moncrieff, Joanna, 112

Scrooge – The Musical, 126

Searle, Daniel (John/Gisele's son), 242, 258, 272

Searle, Gisele (John's wife), 242

Searle, John (KW–Ronald Searle's son): birth, 73–4; and parents' absences, 86–7; upbringing, 88; on Elvira, 108; pets, 109; schooling, 110, 120–21, 131; Brittany holiday, 117; learns to shoot, 119; appendicitis, 122; first trip to Paris, 128; flu, 131; and parents' marriage relations, 133; and father's leaving KW, 141–3, 150; meets father after separation, 150–51; dislikes Newton Road house, 153; juvenile poetry, 157; reads Puffin books, 164; twenty-first birthday, 177; career, 183–5, 200, 239; travels in Far East, 193; relations with father, 194; self-supporting, 200; marriage, 212; recreations and activities, 212; and KW's disabilities, 216; birth of son Daniel, 242; stays with Kate in Hove, 258; life in Spain, 272

Searle, Kate (KW–Ronald Searle's daughter): birth, 73–4; and parents' absences, 86–7; upbringing, 88; as extra on *Belles of St Trinian's* film, 99–100; pets, 109; schooling, 110, 153; Brittany holiday, 117; first trip to Paris, 128; flu, 131; and parents' marriage relations, 133; and father's leaving KW, 141–3, 150;

meets father after separation, 150–51; artistic interests, 157; reads Puffin books, 164; twenty-first birthday, 177; as prop-mistress for *Winterthing* production, 180; accompanies KW to Buckingham Palace, 203; in Canada, 207, 212–14, 230, 232; near-marriage, 212–13, 230; house in Hove, 244, 258; works in props at Covent Garden, 244, 258, 272; stays with mother, 258; and tributes to KW on death, 262–3; maintains relations with father, 272

Searle, Ronald William Fordham: sends cartoons to *Lilliput*, 39; background, 52–3; early drawing, 53–4; as prisoner of war of Japanese, 55–9, 79; corresponds with KW, 60–61; exhibition of PoW drawings (Cambridge 1945), 61; St Trinian's drawings, 61; meets KW at *Lilliput*, 65; works published, 66; illustrations, 67; love affair with KW, 67–8, 73; proposes to KW, 70; KW's mother on, 72; absence from birth of twin children, 74; marriage and family life, 78–9, 95, 106–9, 133, 228, 236; travels to Warsaw, 79–82; paintings, 82; illustrates *John Gilpin*, 84; joint book on Paris with KW, 85–6; in North Africa with KW, 87;

collaborative interviewing with KW on London characters, 89–92; singing, 90; daily routine, 91, 239n; disenchanted with St Trinians's, 91, 126; moves to Newton Road, Bayswater, 91–2; acquires first car, 95; decorates home with drawings, 95–6; earnings, 97; travels in Italy, 98; as *News Chronicle* cartoonist, 103; in Dublin, 104; stage designs and costumes, 105; draws Four-Power Conference in Geneva, 107; commissions and work, 110–11, 118; life membership of Garrick Club, 110; portrait photograph by Baron, 110; peritonitis, 111; visits USA, 117–18, 125, 129, 135; protests at replacement street-lamps in Bayswater, 119; entertains Thurber, 122; meets Monica Stirling on visit to Paris, 122–4; sees life as series of imprisonments, 125; marriage breakdown with KW, 127–8, 139; draws on dusters, 128–9; in Paris for *Punch*, 132; surtax demand on, 132; in Jerusalem for Eichmann trial, 134–5; and KW's mother's death, 140; leaves KW, 141–4, 150; settles abroad, 142; relations with children, 143, 272; illustrates Thurber, 148; illustrates

Willans, 148; meets twins after separation, 150–51; divorce from KW and marriage to Monica, 162–3, 272; retrospective in Bibliothèque Nationale, Paris, 193–4; letter of rebuke from Arthur, 194; TV programme on, 207; KW invites to illustrate Dahl's *Enormous Crocodile*, 219; KW's admiration for, 228; lives in Provence, 239, 269; broadcasts on *Desert Island Discs*, 269–71; honorary degree, 269; ninetieth birthday, 269; influence on later cartoonists, 271; *The Female Approach*, 82; *Forty Drawings*, 67; *Hurrah for St Trinian's*, 76; *Le Nouveau Ballet Anglais*, 66; *Paris Sketchbook* (with KW), 86; *Souls in Torment*, 91; *To the Kwai – And Back*, 57

Searle, William ('Buller'; Ronald's father), 52

Secombe, (Sir) Harry, 168

Segonzac, Comte Adalbert de, 87

Sempé (cartoonist), 95

Sendak, Maurice: *Where the Wild Things Are*, 136

Seven Stories *see* Centre for Children's Books, 265

Severn Sailing Club, near Cheltenham, 171

Seymour, Miranda, 259

Shaver, Buster, 76

Shaw, George Bernard, 38
Shawcross, Hartley (*later* Baron), 84
Shearer, Norma, 117
Sheekman, Arthur, 100, 106
Sheekman, Gloria (*formerly* Stuart), 100, 139, 224, 238–9, 246
Shepard, E. H., 86, 101, 148
Shepherd, Rossiter, 26
Shy, Timothy *see* Wyndham Lewis, D. B.
Sibley, Brian, 41, 244, 253
Sieghart, Mary Ann, 167
Signal (magazine), 181
Signpost Books, 230
Silverbeck (house), Middlesex, 2
Sim, Alistair, 100, 126
Sitwell, (Sir) Osbert, 39
Smallwood, Norah, 186
Smith, Ada, 89
Smith, Dodie, 159
Smith, Emma, 217
Smith, Stevie, 40
Smythe, Pat, 101
Society of Bookmen, London, 186
Something to Do (by 'Septima'), 137
South Africa: KW visits, 209
Speak, Jane, 256
Spender, (Sir) Stephen, 30
Sporting Life, 132
Sprod, George, 57, 101
Sri Lanka: KW visits with Crosse, 239
Stead, W. T.: 'Books for the Bairns', 2
Steadman, Ralph, 271
Steinbeck, John, 126
Stevens, George, 14

Stevenson, Adlai, 96
Stevenson, Robert Louis, 12
Stewart, James, 117
Stirling, Kit (Monica's husband), 123
Stirling, Monica: background, 123; Ronald Searle meets, 123–4, 128; Searle lives with in Paris, 142; meets twins, 151; marriage to Searle, 162; on Searle's working routine, 239n; breast cancer, 269–70; home in Provence, 269
Storr, Catherine, 160, 166, 168
Strand, The (magazine), 82, 127
Streatfeild, Noel: as patron of *Young Elizabethan*, 101; KW publishes, 135; KW negotiates with, 137; qualities, 155; departs for Spain, 155; contributes to 'Birthday Books', 156; watches football on TV, 165; illness in old age, 231; eighty-fifth birthday, 235; death and *Dictionary of National Biography* entry, 244–5; *Ballet Shoes*, 5, 7; *A Vicarage Family*, 155
Stuart, Gloria *see* Sheekman, Gloria
Stwosz, Wit (Veit Stoss), 81
Suez crisis (1956), 110, 113
Summerskill, Edith, 89
Survivor, The (PoW magazine), 56
Sutcliff, Rosemary, 134, 156, 213, 232; death, 252; *Warrior Scarlet*, 8, 250
Suter, Susannah, 18
Swaffer, Hannen, 30

Swann, Donald, 113; *Wild Thyme* (stage musical), 105–6

Symonds, John, 46n, 61

Tangier, 87

Taylor, A. J. P., 81

Taylor, Judy (*later* Hough), 130, 136, 174, 186, 202, 267

Teale, Zoë, 7, 248, 256

teenage readers: and Peacock Books, 154, 216–17, 250

television: effect on children's reading, 220

Tempest, Margaret, 148

Thin, James (Edinburgh bookshop), 215

Thomas, Caitlin, 40, 42

Thomas, Dylan, 40–42

Thompson, Emma, 167

Thompson, Eric, 167

Thurber, James, 122, 156, 218; *The Thirteen Clocks*, 148; *The Wonderful O*, 148

Thwaite, Emily, 166

Times, The: Books for Schools campaign, 266

Today (BBC radio programme), 267

Todd, Barbara Euphan: *Worzel Gummidge*, 3, 236

Tolkien, J. R. R.: Pauline Baynes illustrates, 146, 253; success as Puffin writer, 159; *Farmer Giles of Ham*, 135; *The Hobbit*, 137

Topolski, Feliks, 80–81

Townsend, John Rowe, 148, 199, 218

Townsend, Sue, 250

Toye, Wendy, 93, 98, 106, 124, 141, 144

Travers, P. L., 135, 167; *Mary Poppins*, 159

Trease, Geoffrey, 114; *The Seas of Morning*, 8

Treasure Islands (radio programme), 265

Trewin, Ion, 101

Trewin, J. C., 93, 101, 116, 121–2; *A Sword for a Prince* (play), 101

Trewin, Wendy, 93, 121–2

Trotman, Felicity, 190–92, 197–8, 202, 221, 230, 254

Tucker, Nicholas, 201, 231, 266

Tucker, Nicholas and Kimberley Reynolds: *Children's Book Publishing since 1945*, 158n, 266

Tunisia, 230

Tutin, Dorothy, 105

Unicorn Theatre, 243

United Nations' World Refugee Year (1959), 127

United States of America: Arthur Webb in, 44, 46, 47, 50, 83–4, 96–7; KW visits, 70–73, 117, 131, 135, 196; Ronald Searle visits, 117–18, 125, 129, 135

Unwin, Stanley, 130

Usborne, Richard, 212, 240

Ustinov, (Sir) Peter, 77–8, 93

Uttley, Alison, 148, 156

Vaughan, Keith, 67

Vault, Emmeline E., 235

Verney, John, 105

Vicky (Victor Weisz), 103, 124

Viking imprint (Penguin), 236

Villiers, Linda, 133, 139–40, 145, 154, 176

Voake, Charlotte, 168

Wagner, Erica, 266

Waller, Cliff, 171

Wallingford, Northumberland, 189

Walsh, Jill Paton *see* Paton Walsh, Jill

Warsaw, 79–81

Waterhouse, Keith, 126

Waters, Frank, 87

Watson, Alistair, 255

Watson, Julia, 233, 240

Wayne, John, 117

Webb, Ann (*née* Fahy; *then* Stevens; KW's mother): character and life-style, 13–14; journalism, 13; marriage and family with Arthur Webb, 15; on eating, 21; KW's relations with, 22–4, 72; and Arthur's departure for USA, 45; household management, 46; works for WVS, 46; and death of son John, 49; helps campaign in 1945 election, 59; and KW's trip to USA, 70–71; suffers stroke, 70; on KW's marriage to Searle, 71–2; and KW's pregnancy, 73; looks after KW's twins, 76, 88, 116; celebrates Christmas, 83; health decline, 118, 122, 132, 137–8; death, 138, 140

Webb, Arthur (KW's father): journalistic career, 13–16, 20, 22, 24; letter from Kit Brierley, 34; in USA, 44, 46, 48, 50, 83–4, 96; suggests name for Atlantic Charter, 45; learns of son John's death, 49; posted to Berlin, 50; offers to pay for KW's confinement, 70; sends clothes for KW's children, 87–8; return visit to London, 92–3; lecture tour in Midwest, 107; writes for *Young Elizabethan*, 114; and Ann's decline, 118; returns to UK, 131–2; and Ann's death, 138; holiday in Ischia, 138; settles in Brighton with Ethel, 179; and John Searle's career, 183; letter of rebuke to Ronald Searle, 194; death, 195–6; KW's obituary tribute to, 195; falls out with brother Harold, 251

Webb, Bill (i.e. Louis; KW's half-brother): birth, 14; calls KW 'Kayki', 15; schooling, 17; photography career, 22; works for *Sporting Life*, 27, 132; on KW's marriage to Keith Hunter, 38; discursive wartime letters to KW, 47–8; demobilized from RAF, 59; criticizes Ronald Searle, 72; spends Christmas with Searles, 108; at mother's death, 138; Cyprus holiday with

KW, 193; accompanies KW to
Buckingham Palace, 203;
suffers stroke and death, 224
Webb, Elsie (KW's aunt), 119
Webb, Eva (Bill's wife), 108
Webb, Harold (KW's uncle), 251
Webb, Henry James (KW's great-
grandfather), 12–13
Webb, John (KW's brother), 15, 22,
35, 38, 48; killed in action, 49
Webb, John Patrick (Bill's son;
'Dumps'), 38
Webb, Kaye: succeeds Eleanor
Graham at Puffin, 3; and
burial of Time Capsule, 6–7;
rheumatic fever as child, 11;
relations with parents, 13–15,
22–4; birth, 15; schooling,
15–20; juvenile writing, 18–
19; amateur acting, 20; at
finishing school in Belgium,
21, 23–4; early magazine
journalism, 26–8; romances
and engagements, 28–9;
twenty-first birthday party,
28; marriage to Kit Brierley
and miscarriage, 29; and
Brierley's absence in India,
29, 33–4; works on *Lilliput*
and *Picture Post*, 29–31, 38–40,
43–4, 46–7, 58, 68; divorces
Brierley, 34; marriage to
Keith Hunter, 35–8, 228;
radio broadcasts, 44, 59, 126,
128, 156, 249–51; wartime
voluntary work, 45, 51;
political views and activities,
47, 69; Ronald Searle sends

cartoons to, 54–5;
appendectomy, 59–60; letters
from Searle, 60–61; meets
Searle at *Lilliput* offices, 65;
love affair with Searle, 67–8;
divorce from Keith Hunter,
68–9, 72, 78; pregnancy and
twins by Searle, 68, 70, 73;
courted by Patrick Campbell,
69–70; Searle proposes to,
70–71; visits to USA, 70–73,
117, 131, 135, 196; dismissed
from *Lilliput*, 75; returns to
England from USA, 75; as
show-business editor of
Leader, 76, 83; marriage to
Searle, 78–9; celebrates
Christmas, 83; flat in
Burnham Court, Bayswater,
83; contributes to
Everywoman, 84; joint book
on Paris with Searle, 85–6;
theatre-going with Searle, 85;
in North Africa with Searle,
87; as assistant editor of *Go*
magazine, 88; and twins'
upbringing, 88; collaborative
interviewing with Searle on
London characters, 89–90, 92;
moves to Newton Road,
Bayswater, 91–2; launches
Perpetua Books, 94–5;
acquires first car, 95; family
life and entertaining, 95;
broadcasts on *Woman's Hour*,
98–100, 111, 137, 141, 145, 160,
171, 217, 227, 251; edits *Young
Elizabethan*, 99, 101, 113–15;

Webb, Kaye – *cont.*

visits Rome for *Woman's Hour*, 102; skiing holiday in Austria, 103; in Ireland, 104–5; social life, 104–5, 124; television appearances, 106; name, 107; writes on family life, 107–8; fractures ribs in road accident, 116; gives up *Young Elizabethan*, 119; theatre reviews, 120; persuasiveness, 125–6, 173; marriage breakdown with Searle, 127, 139; appointment and early activities at Puffin Books, 129–37, 147, 148–9; earnings, 129–30, 132–3, 145, 157–8, 209; surtax demand on, 132; life at Newton Road, 133; and mother's decline and death, 137–9; Searle leaves, 141–5, 150; credo at Puffin, 147; selects books for publication, 148–50; selects illustrators, 148–9; crosses to France in Cooksey's boat, 151; compiles 'Birthday Book', 152, 156; Eleanor Farjeon comforts and encourages, 152–3; resumes social life, 153–5; wins Eleanor Farjeon Award, 153, 182, 184; entertains Opies at L'Écu de France, 155–6; visits to Australia and New Zealand, 156–7, 186; attachment to James Mason, 157; promoted to Penguin board, 157; in Israel and Lebanon, 160; divorce from Searle, 162–3, 272; attachment to Jim Cecil, 163; runs Puffin Club, 164–6; and Puffin Club outings, 169–72; buys house in Chiswick, 172–3; requests to friends and acquaintances, 173; and son John's career prospects, 183–5; arthritis, 186–7, 192, 207, 214–15, 230, 236; dresses up for events, 190; staff recruitment, 190–91; takes break in Cyprus, 193; matchmaking, 197; personality and dominance at Penguin, 197; restlessness, 200–201; appointed MBE, 203; moves to flat in Lampard House, 203; autobiography, 204–5; promoted to Editorial Director, Children's Division, 209; visit to South Africa, 209; holiday in Algarve, 212; and effect of social change on children's books, 218–19; proposes strategy for Puffin's future, 219–20; retirement and successor, 221–3, 225–7; sixty-fifth birthday, 221, 224; life and activities in retirement, 228–33, 238; praises Searle, 228, 236; visits Kate in Canada, 230; goes on retreats, 232; film projects, 233–4; attachment to Puffin Club, 237–8; hip

replacements, 238, 243;
collection of drawings
valued, 240–41; seventieth
birthday, 240; homoeopathic
treatment, 241; becomes
grandmother, 242;
hospitalized, 242–5, 248, 261–
2; shoulder operation, 242;
and family history, 251–2;
edits anthologies, 253;
housebound, 253; denied
Damedom, 255; at Puffin's
fiftieth anniversary
celebrations, 256; notes on
early life, 258; broadcasts on
Desert Island Discs, 259–60;
eightieth birthday, 261; death
and obituaries, 262; broadcast
tribute on *Treasure Islands*,
265; papers and archive, 265;
Looking at London and *People
Worth Meeting* (with Ronald
Searle), 97; *Paris Sketchbook*
(with Searle), 86; 'Peace
Comes to Lilliput' (article),
51; *Refugees* (with Searle), 127;
The St Trinian's Story, 126

Webb, Laurence (KW's cousin), 251

Webb, Nick (KW's nephew), 107–8,
193

Webb, William George (KW's
great-great-grandfather), 12

Wells, H. G., 39

Wells House (school), Malvern
Wells, 120–21

West, Dame Rebecca, 116

Westminster School, 131

Whitby, Joy, 201

White, Antonia, 32

Whittington Court, Cotswolds, 189

Whittington Hospital, London,
245

Who's Next? (TV show), 118

Wilder, Laura Ingalls, 220

Wilderspin, Ralph, 187

Wildsmith, Brian: *Mother Goose*,
148

Wilkinson, Lindsay, 255

Willans, Geoffrey, 93, 148; early
death, 111; *Back in the Jug
Agane*, 110; *Down with Skool!*,
103, 110; *How to be Topp*, 110;
Whizz for Atomms, 110

Willard, Barbara, 210

Williams, Bill, 68

Williams, Rowan, Archbishop of
Canterbury, 199n

Williams, Tennessee, 102

Williams, Ursula Moray, 7, 171, 180,
205–6, 221, 226, 230, 262

Wilson, A. E.: *A Penny Plain and
Twopence Coloured*, 12–13 & n

Wilson, Harold (*later* Baron), 148

Winchell, Walter, 162

Wingate, General Orde, 48–9

Wintle, Canon A. O., 96

Wintour, Charles, 53, 124

Wishart, Lorna, 40

Wodehouse, P. G., 218

Woman (magazine), 27

Woman & Home (magazine), 142

Woman's Hour (radio programme),
98–100, 102, 111, 128, 137, 141,
145, 160, 171, 217, 227, 251

women: in publishing, 157–8, 197;
and adversity, 205

Wood, Anne: *Books for Your Children*, 147–8
Wood, Dorothy, 190, 203, 222, 230
Wood, Grace, 252, 261
Wood, Henry, 252, 261
Wood, Victoria, 252, 261, 265
Woodward, Alice B., 251
Woosnam, Barbara (*later* Hunter), 68–9, 74, 79, 242
Wyman, Jane, 117
Wyndham Lewis, D. B.: *The Terror of St Trinian's* (by 'Timothy Shy'), 91

Young Elizabethan (magazine; formerly *Collins Magazine*), 99, 101, 103, 106, 110, 112–15, 117, 119, 164
Young Elizabethans' Club, 114
Young, Loretta, 77

Zindel, Paul, 217

read more ●

JANE ROBINSON

BLUESTOCKINGS

'A gem of a book. Social history of the best kind' *Sunday Times*

Towards the end of the nineteenth century, when the female brain was considered five ounces lighter than the male brain, the first of Britain's women students bravely enrolled at university. From wildly different backgrounds and with only a passion for learning in common, they faced dismissal as mere 'bonnets', and wild rioting when a vote was taken to offer these 'undergraduettes' a recognized degree. But from their teachers and parents they enjoyed unimaginable kindnesses.

Through the inspiring and moving words of the women themselves, Jane Robinson explores the sacrifices they made, the prejudice they met, and the determination, friendship and knowledge they found through their ground-breaking, hard-won educations.

'Inspiring, funny and thoughtful' Rosemary Hill, *Guardian*

'Warm and funny . . . an education to us all' *Independent on Sunday*

'Modern girls need reminding of the long battle, and Jane Robinson's fine book does just that' Libby Purves, *Mail on Sunday*

www.penguin.com

VIRGINIA NICHOLSON

SINGLED OUT

'So powerful and so inspiring … the women Nicholson celebrates changed our culture' *Sunday Times*

Before the First World War a single woman had one aim in life: to get married. But three-quarters of a million British soldiers were killed in that war, leaving not enough men to go round and a generation of so-called 'Surplus Women'. What became of them? And how did they overcome their disappointment?

Singled Out explores the extraordinary lives these women made for themselves. It tells how they challenged conventions – becoming engineers and explorers; how they campaigned to better their lot; how they coped with poverty, childlessness and frustration. Above all, it shows how women proved there is more to life than men and helped change our society.

'Achingly sad, extremely valuable, always riveting' *Spectator*

'Splendid and sympathetic. A celebration of pluckiness, realism, intellectual independence and self-reliance' *New Statesman*

'Ground-breaking, richly nuanced with tidbits of information, insight and understanding. Its tales of endeavour linger on in the mind' *Daily Mail*

He just wanted a decent book to read ...

Not too much to ask, is it? It was in 1935 when Allen Lane, Managing Director of Bodley Head Publishers, stood on a platform at Exeter railway station looking for something good to read on his journey back to London. His choice was limited to popular magazines and poor-quality paperbacks – the same choice faced every day by the vast majority of readers, few of whom could afford hardbacks. Lane's disappointment and subsequent anger at the range of books generally available led him to found a company – and change the world.

'We believed in the existence in this country of a vast reading public for intelligent books at a low price, and staked everything on it'
Sir Allen Lane, 1902–1970, founder of Penguin Books

The quality paperback had arrived – and not just in bookshops. Lane was adamant that his Penguins should appear in chain stores and tobacconists, and should cost no more than a packet of cigarettes.

Reading habits (and cigarette prices) have changed since 1935, but Penguin still believes in publishing the best books for everybody to enjoy. We still believe that good design costs no more than bad design, and we still believe that quality books published passionately and responsibly make the world a better place.

So wherever you see the little bird – whether it's on a piece of prize-winning literary fiction or a celebrity autobiography, political tour de force or historical masterpiece, a serial-killer thriller, reference book, world classic or a piece of pure escapism – you can bet that it represents the very best that the genre has to offer.

Whatever you like to read – trust Penguin.